BURNl
WERE BA

One Fan's Perspe_.ve of
Burnley F.C.'s 1994/95 Campaign

BURNLEY WERE BACK!!

One Fan's Perspective of
Burnley F.C.'s 1994/95 Campaign

Stephen Cummings

JANUS PUBLISHING COMPANY
London, England

First published in Great Britain 1996
by Janus Publishing Company,
Edinburgh House, 19 Nassau Street,
London W1N 7RE

British Library Cataloguing-in-Publication Data.
A catalogue record for this book is available from the British Library.

ISBN 1 85756 252 6

Cover design Harold King

Printed & bound in England by
Antony Rowe Ltd, Chippenham, Wiltshire

INTRODUCTION

Welcome to 'BURNLEY WERE BACK!!'

The book's title derives from the 'BURNLEY ARE BACK!!' logo, which was boldly emblazoned across each and every page of the club programme, during our nine month stay in Division One in the 1994/95 season.

Initially, this was no bad thing. In fact, once we'd found our feet, gone on a ten-match unbeaten run in the league, and seemed to have levelled out at just below halfway up the league table towards the end of November, I must admit to feeling a slight frisson of pride every time I read it.

But just when I'd allowed myself to believe we might survive in the division, disaster struck, and the logo became a grotesque parody of itself.

'Disaster' manifested itself in many ways. There was the abysmal form of some players, in particular the fantastically inept Alan Harper. There were utterly bizarre, often surreal managerial decisions from Jimmy Mullen, including the purchase of a striker who hadn't scored for twenty games in a lower division. There was also a sequence of eight consecutive league defeats, a sequence which equalled a club record that had stood for over a century, and was decisive in our spiral towards relegation. To top it all, the club ended the season with the worst disciplinary record in the history of the Football League. It's fairly safe to say that the season was not vintage Claret.

But putting relegation-Armageddon aside for a moment, (I know it hurts, but be brave), 94/95 was not a complete write-off. I, for one, found there were more than enough moments between

August 13th and May 7th to justify my love for all things claret and blue. I think of the 5-1 obliteration of Southend, the live TV victory, 4-2, over Sheffield United and brilliant wins away from home at Charlton, Luton and most memorably, Millwall.

There were other highlights, not always directly connected with the on-field action. Visits to Molineux and Anfield, Luton's over-the-top devotion to Morecambe and Wise, celebrity spottings of Neil Kinnock at Charlton and Paul Mariner at Barnsley, a weekend spent in Southend, our conversion to the Latter Day Church Of The Banana as we sped towards Watford, and one particularly mad night in Swindon, featuring a soothsayer, Lord Lucan and a seven-foot fluffy robin.

So you see, it wasn't all bad.

Although this book is only written from my perspective, it is my hope that 'BURNLEY WERE BACK!!' will strike chords with yourself and thousands of other members of the Claret and Blue Army who followed the team up and down the country from the optimistic beginning to the bitter and painful end.

It is to the supporters of Burnley Football Club that this book is dedicated.

STEPHEN CUMMINGS – MAY 1995

Saturday 13/8/94
Ayresome Park

MIDDLESBROUGH 2-0 BURNLEY *(Hendrie 28,35)*
League position before and after game: 0 . . . 22nd

Attendance: 23,343

BURNLEY: Beresford, Parkinson, Vinnicombe, Davis, Winstanley, Joyce *(Lancashire 63)*, Harper, Deary, Heath, Robinson, McMinn.
Subs (not used): Wilson, Russell.

MIDDLESBROUGH: Miller, Cox, Fleming, Vickers, Pearson, Blackmore, Robson, Pollock, Wilkinson, Hendrie, Moore.
Subs (not used): Roberts, Whyte, Hignett.

Referee: R. Poulain

Yellow Cards: Fleming (Middlesbrough)
              Heath (Burnley)

Red Cards: None

Somewhat predictably, the morning papers were full of it. Bryan Robson's adoption of the player/manager mantle at Middlesbrough was big news. Indeed, a cursory glance at the tabloids seemed to suggest that the arrival of Captain Marvel on Teeside three months previously was comparable with the arrival of Jesus Christ on Earth 2,000 years earlier. The only difference was that slightly fewer miracles were expected of the latter.

No-one actually expected *us* to win; we were simply making up the numbers. In fact, so intense was the Robbo-hype in the press that one had to trawl through a seemingly endless sea of print in order to discover that we were Middlesbrough's opponents that day. This was, of course, all a huge media conspiracy, specifically designed to undermine the confidence of the good ship Burnley F.C. and all who sailed in her . . . probably.

Still, faint heart never won opening league game of the season. So at 10.45 that morning, a fleet of coaches departed from Turf

3

Moor, brimming with that peculiarly naive beginning-of-season confidence, good humour and 1001 packed lunches.

The journey up to the north-east was excruciating. Long traffic jams, the playing at high volume of the musical *Pandora's Box* that was the 'Burnley F.C.' album, (featuring a particularly rancid version of 'D.I.S.C.O.' by ex-Claret Peter Noble's daughter) and a slow-moving police escort to the ground were all contributory factors.

On entering Ayresome Park two things were immediately noticeable. As the literally brilliant sun shone down, the pitch looked in excellent condition – one of the best this side of Wembley. However, the ground itself was something of a letdown.

Peeling paint, crumbling terraces and a general tattiness lent Ayresome Park an air of dilapidation. It didn't seem a particularly fitting setting for a side seeking a glorious return to the Premiership, under the guidance of one of England's most famous footballing sons.

I expected First Division football to bring many new experiences: bigger grounds, a higher standard of football and better pies. What I didn't expect was an eight-foot cloth lion called Roary to come and throw toffees at us twenty minutes before kick-off.

'I'm sure all the Burnley fans will want to give a big welcome to our mascot, Roary!' shrieked the Ayresome Park Tannoy. I wasn't so sure, and feared for Roary's personal safety as he skipped benignly towards the south-east corner, to be met by torrents of abuse and a chorus of 'Are you Robson in disguise?' I felt for the poor unfortunate inside the costume. They would have to endure this humiliating ritual many more times before the end of the season. Poor Roary.

At around five to three, Bryan Robson and Steve Davis led their respective teams out, to be greeted by a wall of sound that Phil Spector would have been hard-pushed to better. In our new yellow and black pin-striped away kit we at least *looked* fantastic, and judging by the 2,000-strong vocal support, we felt that maybe, just maybe, we could pull off a shock.

BURNLEY WERE BACK!!

After an edgy opening five minutes, we settled down into playing some neat, attractive, and as we grew in confidence, increasingly incisive football. In fact, for the first twenty-five minutes or so, we looked the more likely to score.

McMinn gave their right-back no end of trouble, Heath's deft little touches here and there were beginning to find small but nevertheless discernible cracks in Middlesbrough's defence and Robinson's well-timed runs and tireless chasing of lost causes looked as though they could well pay dividends. Indeed, when Vinnicombe was scythed down following a reckless Blackmore challenge in their area, only to be adjudged to have dived, and Joyce had a header well saved by Miller, it looked to be only a matter of time before their vanguard would collapse.

But luckily for the Boro', Marlon had obviously read all the pre-match guff. He had remembered that this was Robson's big day, not ours. Accordingly, our usually ace keeper, under little pressure, ran to the edge of his area and obligingly thwacked the ball against the legs of the unsuspecting Winstanley who was standing not five yards away.

The rebound fell to the unmarked Hendrie (well it would do, wouldn't it?), who gleefully accepted the opportunity to put Boro's promotion bandwagon on the road, by firing into an empty net.

At this point Burnley's heads dropped, as a Teeside smog cloud of despondency descended on the Clarets. Seven minutes later, Mr Poulain, a poor referee on the day, over-ruled a linesman's decision, and awarded a throw-in to Middlesborough. As our entire back four protested to anyone who was willing to listen (instead of marking up), Blackmore's throw was flicked on by Pollock. The Holgate End roared as one, as Hendrie latched onto the opportunity and shot low and weakly at goal. Marlon, in no mood to play the party-pooper, politely dived over the number ten's shot, allowing Bryan's boys to double their lead.

Two minutes later, and it was tin-hats time, as Moore sent over an inch-perfect cross. Robson, in customary over-dramatic fashion, launched himself a la 'Roy of the Rovers' at the ball. His resultant header crashed against the post and rebounded to Davis, who thankfully hooked the ball to safety.

To cap it all, Boro's supporters began to chant, 'Down with the Mackems, you're going down with the Mackems.' This was quickly followed by the obligatory, 'What's it like to follow shit?' As the referee blew for half-time, a man standing next to me uttered the well-chosen words, 'Welcome to the First Division.' Quite.

In the space of nine minutes we had been taught an invaluable lesson. We could afford to make mistakes against the Chesters and Blackpools of this world, and more often than not get away with it. But give such chances to Middlesbrough, Wolves, Bolton and Derby, and we would probably end up paying the full price . . . three points.

The second half was a relatively timid affair. We had lost any of the inventiveness and flair that we had illustrated in the opening twenty-five minutes, and Robson and Middlesbrough began to wind down, knowing they had got the 'Boy's Own' start to the season that they wanted.

To rub salt into our wounds, Mr Poulain once again over-ruled his linesman after we had been initially awarded a penalty with about ten minutes remaining. But that afternoon was always going to belong to Middlesbrough.

Wending our way out of the ground, the general consensus seemed to be that Middlesbrough had not been not two goals better than us. Perhaps 1-0 may have been a fairer scoreline. However, any football fan anywhere in the country will tell you that a good performance and a fair result are not always bed-fellows.

'If they're the third best team in the division, then I reckon we've a reasonable chance of stopping up' commented one claret-clad comrade. Prophetic words? We all hoped so.

The Radio 5 'Sports Report' theme tune issued forth from the speakers as we boarded the coach. James Alexander-Gordon's warm paternal tones, lost forever in the mythical Home Counties of the 1950's, helped take away a little of the sting of defeat, as he informed us that Blackpool had crashed 4-1 at home to Huddersfield.

Nor did things seem quite so bad when news filtered through from Molineux that fellow new-boys Reading had gone down 1-0 to promotion candidates Wolves. Swindon's 2-0 victory over Port Vale the following day, meant that the three sides promoted from Division Two the previous season hadn't managed a point between them on the opening day.

As the convoy of coaches travelled back down the A1 that evening, there was an air of cautious optimism. We'd gone to Ayresome Park, many of us fearing a four or five-goal stuffing from one of the three teams expected to be there, or thereabouts, come May.

What we'd actually witnessed was an at times spirited performance which had Middlesbrough rocking at one point. We'd been undone by two silly goals and a clutch of bizarre decisions from a referee clearly not in the mood to put the dampers on Captain Marvel's big day. Things could and would get better; hopefully, starting on Tuesday night, with a victory over the previous season's promotion rivals, York City, in the Coca-Cola Cup.

Manchester United beat Blackburn Rovers 2-0 in the Charity Shield.

Fulham manager Ian Branfoot, refers to FIFA's new refereeing directives as 'absolutely bloody ludicrous', as seven are booked and one sent off in his side's opening game against Walsall.

Tuesday 16/8/94
Turf Moor

COCA-COLA CUP. FIRST ROUND, FIRST LEG.

BURNLEY 1-0 YORK CITY (Joyce 73)

Attendance: 6,390

BURNLEY: Beresford, Parkinson, Dowell, Davis, Winstanley, Joyce, Harper, Deary, Heath, Robinson, Lancashire.
Subs (not used): Wilson, Mullin, Russell.

YORK: Kiely, McMillan, Hall, Pepper, Tutill, Barras, McCarthy, Cooper, Barnes, Bushell, Canham.
Subs (not used): Atkin, Naylor, Warrington.

Referee: T. Heilbron

Yellow Cards: Dowell, Joyce (Burnley)
Pepper (York City)

Red Cards: None

The rumour-mill had been in operation all day at work. Ernie came down in the morning and told us that we'd 'signed a player.' By eleven o'clock the player had transformed into a striker. Heads were scratched, memories were jogged. What strikers' names had been bandied about by the papers over the summer months?

At midday we'd signed a Premiership striker. 'Ah,' we collectively thought, 'Lee Chapman.' It made sense. Out of favour and allegedly unhappy at West Ham, the ex-Leeds forward had often been referred to in dispatches the previous pre-season. There had even been rumours that he'd been training with us. Wrong.

Come late afternoon, the mystery was solved. John called down and said we'd got John Gayle on a month's loan from Coventry, with a view to a permanent move. The name rang a very vague bell, but that was all.

Unfortunately, the former Birmingham City and Wimbledon centre-forward had failed to sign a contract prior to the necessary deadline, so we would have to wait until Saturday's game against Stoke City to see what the 6'3" goalscorer could offer us.

Judging by the injuries that we already had at this early stage of the campaign, (the worst at the club for three seasons), Burnley's manager Jimmy Mullen would soon be needing to sign at least another squad's-worth of players. As if our list of casualties wasn't big enough already, both Vinnicombe and McMinn had picked up knocks at Middlesbrough.

It seemed that fate was against us. When Eyres and McMinn, our two wingers, were fit, they were knocking over crosses to Adrian 'Inchy' Heath, possibly the smallest striker ever to play for the Clarets. Now Mullen had attempted to remedy the problem, he had both his widemen side-lined. Such is football . . .

The first half of the York game was perhaps best summed up the following day, by a work colleague who had visited Turf Moor

8

for the first time that evening. When asked for her opinions on the experience, she enthused wildly over two things; not the inventiveness of Inchy, nor the sure-handedness of Beresford, not even the encouraging form of Winstanley. No, she was taken with the high standard of the hot dogs, and the even higher standard of Gary 'Big Boy' Parkinson's legs.

Looking at that first half retrospectively, sampling the Turf Moor cuisine might have been a more enjoyable way to spend that particular forty-five minute period of my life. But the jury is still out on Parky's legs . . .

The match readily lent itself to the cliche 'a game of two halves.' Without wingers, we were sadly lacking in inventiveness, and for sizeable chunks of the first half we looked inferior to York.

Dowell, whose award for 'Man of the Match' caused many a furrowed brow in the ground, looked well out of his depth, and was led a merry dance by whoever chose to pressure him, Harper seemed confused in general, and it appeared that sometime and somewhere between Ayresome Park and Turf Moor, Robinson had lost much of the pace and determination that had threatened to undo the Boro' just days before.

Towards the end of the first half, things started to get a little better, the highlight being a perfect through ball from Heath to Deary, who fired a shot against the York crossbar.

The second half was better; much better. Davis went close with a looping header, Lancashire somehow contrived to miss the target from a quarter of a yard with the keeper on the floor and the goal at his mercy, and Robinson nearly won the hearts of thousands with a shot on the turn which only narrowly missed.

But the undoubted star of the show was Parky. Yes, he of the lovely legs. York seemed happy to settle for the draw, making only a few forays into the Burnley half. This gave Parky the chance to push forward, and push forward he did. For substantial spells of the second forty-five, our number two teased and tormented the Minstermen's back line, firing in some telling crosses that nobody was able to connect with.

Joyce too was impressive. Like at Blackpool and Plymouth the previous season, he looked to be at his best when pushing forward from midfield into the penalty area. Indeed, his goal was very reminiscent of his effort at Plymouth which helped send us to the 1993/94 Play-off final at Wembley. A cross-cum-shot was fired in from the right hand side by Lancashire. Kiely was unable to hold it properly and Joyce pounced on the rebound, forcing it home.

The margin of victory could and should have been greater. Heath missed a one-on-one with the keeper, and with a gaping net only a yard away, Joyce inexplicably opted to shoulder the ball over the crossbar, when a simple nod-down would have done the job.

On paper, the result was disappointing. However, the main thing was that we had a one goal advantage to take to Bootham Crescent seven days later for the return leg. More importantly, we had our first confidence-boosting win of the season under our belts.

Later that evening we were the main feature on 'Soccer Night', Granada Television's mid-week football programme. As Elton Welsby greased and smarmed his way into the homes of thousands, (trying his damnedest to slip in a mention of his beloved Tranmere Rovers), the same old fear began to grip me. It was the same fear that has gripped me every time Burnley have been featured at length in football highlights.

It's an angst that manifests itself by asking questions. 'What will people think of us? What if we look lousy on telly? What if we look *really* lousy on telly, and all those people whom I tell that Inchy is God, McMinn eats full-backs for breakfast etc, etc, are watching? What if . . . ?' And so every time something goes wrong, (someone plays a bad ball, or makes a hash of a clearance, or misses a wide-open goal), I cringe. It's an automatic reaction. If we're bad, it pains me to watch.

Not that I can relax when we play exceedingly well. For example, if Steve Davis has one of his frequent blinders, I will watch in trepidation. What if Roy Evans or Alex Ferguson or Kevin Keegan or anybody else looking for a classy central defender, stumbles in from the pub, flicks on the telly, and sees their dream player?

Ultimately, this is of course, an extremely arrogant attitude. Why should people care about Burnley's gaffes or great moments more than those of any other team?

And so I end up praying for the impossible. I want us to play well enough to justify my frequent and rabid rantings to all and sundry about us being the best team in the world; but I don't want us to play that well that a Premiership manager comes and whisks half the team away from under my nose. Like the meaning of life, it is an insoluble dilemma. Unlike the meaning of life, it keeps me awake at night.

Liverpool table a bid of £3.75 million for Coventry's Phil Babb.

Ken Booth, Rotherham's chairman, puts the club up for sale as 200 fans stage a sit-down protest, following the team's defeat against Shrewsbury.

Joey Beauchamp, reportedly homesick following his summer move from Oxford to West Ham, is transferred to Swindon without having played in a competitive fixture for the Premiership club.

Saturday 20/8/94
Turf Moor

BURNLEY 1-1 STOKE CITY *(Davis 42)* *(Dreyer 93)*
League position before and after game: 22nd . . . 20th

Attendance: 15,331

BURNLEY: Beresford, Parkinson, Vinnicombe, Davis, Winstanley, Joyce, *(Deary 65)*, Harper, Gayle, Heath, Robinson, McMinn.
Subs (not used): Lancashire, Russell.

STOKE CITY: Muggleton, Clark, Sandford, Dreyer, Overson, Orlygsson, *(Butler 44)*, Carruthers, *(Shaw 80)*, Wallace, Biggins, Sturridge, Gleghorn.
Sub (not used): Prudhoe.

Referee: W.A. Flood

Yellow Cards: Harper (Burnley)

Red Cards: None

'I did it to give fans value for money. We have been asked to make up for all time wasted, and that includes expanded substitutions, ceremonial free-kicks and the like. All the time is going to be added on to give supporters better value for their money. It is the thing for the future."

This was the reaction of Mr. W. A. Flood, to those who laid the blame for Burnley's failure to pick up all three points firmly at his door. (Although I must confess to spending many, many hours deep in thought, wondering just what an 'expanded substitution' was, and what form of ritual preceded a 'ceremonial' free-kick.)

In the heat of the moment such accusations are understandable. The referee had, after all, played seven minutes of injury-time, allowing a desperately outclassed Stoke outfit the opportunity to grab an undeserved equaliser.

However, with that most smug of gifts – the benefit of hindsight – events can be given at least a degree of perspective. It would, of course, be easy, too easy in fact, to castigate Mr Flood for adhering to, (or maybe hiding behind?), F.I.F.A. regulations. After all, he could argue that he was merely doing his job.

There were others at fault. Gary Parkinson, lovely legs or no lovely legs, should have done better with his penalty. And quite why Chris Vinnicombe opted to try to walk, rather than whack, the ball out of play, an error which led directly to Stoke's leveller, is a mystery on a par with the Pythonesque signing of Nick Pickering.

Having said all that . . . oh, how this one hurt! For seventy of the ninety minutes, we ran the show – and believe me, at times it really *was* a show. In the last thirty minutes of the first half, we were a different class.

'Big Bad' John Gayle impressed, winning everything in the air, and showing not a little skill on the ground. Considering that he was up against Vince Overson, this was no mean feat. The two of them battled on and off the ball all afternoon, much to the crowd's amusement. Although quite how much Big Bad John laughed when Big Bad Vince landed one of his more spirited slaps across his left jaw, (unnoticed by the officials), is another matter.

Inchy, dropping back into midfield, looked to have been given a new lease of life, ruthlessly exploiting any mistakes made by his former team. Winstanley appeared to be getting better by the minute, and Robinson ran with such pace, frequency and enthusiasm that it would not have surprised me to learn that he and Maradona shared the same drugs supplier.

The goal was scored by Burnley's man of the match, Steve Davis. Following a McMinn corner and an Overson (oops!) flick-on, he soared head and shoulders above the Potters' defence and thundered a header in from about six yards out.

Obviously we went bloody wild. Our first league goal of the campaign, and a belter to boot. But more was to come. Stoke's Sandford started playing basketball inside their area, and we got a penalty – a minute before the interval. Joy upon joy!

In the absence of Eyres, Inchy, who had never missed a penalty for Burnley, picked up the ball. Parkinson, who had never *taken* a penalty for Burnley, clearly had other ideas, and whipped the ball off Heath, placing it firmly on the penalty spot.

I turned to John, and adopting my best prophet of doom voice, opined that perhaps going in 2-0 up at half-time would be too good to be true. I was dead right.

Parky, in charitable mood, opted to gently side-foot the ball straight at the keeper rather than make any genuine attempt to score. Muggleton, taking the piss, pounced on the ball as if Hristo Stoichkov had unleashed a forty yard screamer.

Thus ended the first half. Despite the penalty miss, we were in high spirits. We'd outplayed Stoke by a long chalk, and were a goal to the good, which the majority of the home fans would have settled for three-quarters of an hour earlier. In fact, the only complaint at half-time was from Andy, who was much aggrieved that his meat and potato pie tasted of stale cheese.

The second period was a comparatively drab affair. We shone in patches, and they never seriously looked as though they could do us any damage. And then it happened . . .

Actually, it happened in slow-motion. Three and a half minutes (count 'em) into stoppage time, Vinnicombe umm-ed and ahh-ed over what to do with the ball over on the far side. Butler was having none of this however, and dispossessing our number three, fed Shaw.

The Stoke sub, who had scored twice against us on Stoke's last visit to Turf Moor, was allowed to whip a dangerous ball across our six yard box. There were *three* unmarked Stoke players queuing for the ball. They had enough time to hold a brief debate as to which one of them should score. John Dreyer eventually steered the ball over the line.

Gutted. Believe you me, I have scoured the Thesaurus for a substitute for this cliche, but there really isn't another word in the language which can sum up how I felt there and then. We'd blown it.

As the strains of 'Delilah' rang out from the away enclosure, Justin sat down, head in hands, Mick berated the referee in no uncertain terms, John shook his head, and I just stood and felt numb.

Mr Flood called time a few minutes later, and headed towards the players' tunnel, where he was greeted by a veritable plethora of four-letter insults. But was it really his fault? It was the players who'd made the mistakes. As professionals, they should have been concentrating right up to the final whistle. We'd been taught that we'd be punished for mistakes seven days earlier, but we obviously hadn't learned our lesson.

Still, there had been many encouraging qualities in the overall performance. We'd played some excellent stuff, Gayle had given us another option going forward, and the team was clearly beginning to bond as a unit. For the second time this season though, we needed to beat York, just to give us that bit of extra confidence.

The Premiership kicks off. Liverpool put six past new boys Crystal Palace, Manchester United beat Q.P.R. 2-0, and Jurgen Klinsmann scores on his Spurs debut at Sheffield Wednesday and is then concussed, as Tottenham win 4-3.

'Match of the Day' is 30 years old.

Peter Beardsley fractures his cheekbone in a collision with Leicester's Steve Thompson, who is later to sign for Burnley.

Bryan Robson attempts to sign Gary Lineker from Grampus 8.

Tuesday 23/8/94
Bootham Crescent

COCA-COLA CUP. FIRST ROUND, SECOND LEG.

YORK CITY 2-2 BURNLEY *(Pepper 17, Cooper 71)*
(Robinson 63, Gayle 66)

Attendance: 3,089

BURNLEY: Beresford, Parkinson, Vinnicombe *(Deary 22)*, Davis, Winstanley, Joyce *(Lancashire 79)*, Harper, Gayle, Heath, Robinson, McMinn.
Sub (not used): Russell.

YORK CITY: Kiely, McMillan, Hall, Pepper, Tutill, Barras, McCarthy, Cooper, Barnes, Bushell, Canham.
Subs (not used): Jorden, Naylor, Warrington.

Referee: J. Brandwood

Yellow Cards: Tutill, McCarthy, Cooper (York City)
McMinn (Burnley)

Red Cards: None

This one made me think. And it wasn't for a reason directly connected with the match that evening. As we wandered around York before the game, taking in its genteel tea-shops, its beautiful cathedral and the city's general air of charm and elegance, I became aware that it wasn't meant for me.

When I say 'me', I'm referring to 'me' the football supporter. Strolling around York that night sporting my Burnley top, I, as a football fan, felt strangely de-centred and out of place. Why?

Well, because of the assumed belief that being a football fan and attempting to appreciate culture are two things which are, almost by law, mutually exclusive. For example, it would be inconceivable to many that I, the football fan, could punch the air like a man possessed when John Gayle scored, read some Imagist poetry, *and* listen to a Buffalo Tom album, all of which I did that evening.

15

There are people who don't know better, (and more annoyingly, people who *do* know better), who insist on keeping alive and fuelling the myth of the football fan as a lobotomised lager-swilling lout whose cultural interests begin and end with 'Blind Date' and 'Play Your Cards Right', and who get their kicks from orgies of violence.

Don't get me wrong. I know that there are still small bands of nutters who populate the terraces up and down the country in the same way that I am sure there are large numbers of people the length and breadth of Britain who have wildly inaccurate ideas of what constitutes a football fan. At the other extreme, I don't believe, or even find it desirable, that after a dire 0-0 draw, thousands of supporters should discuss the whys and wherefores of existentialism on the way home.

What I *do* believe however, is that there are thousands like myself, who are heartily sick and tired of the image we have, (or rather, the image we have been given). We can, on occasion, be thinking, sentient individuals. But try telling this to certain sections of the media. It's been said before, and said with a great deal more eloquence, but the media are not, by and large, interested in the truth, just a story.

Which is why it worries me so much when a tiny minority of fans boo during a minute's silence, or a few idiots invade the pitch, for example. It's not just because events such as these are stupid or ignorant, or whatever; it's also because the actions of a few make it that bit easier for the moral guardians of the nation to take a side-swipe at soccer and pigeon-hole its fans as the scum of society.

At the same time, I would hate to see football intellectualised in any way, (which is just as well, because it isn't going to happen). A large part of its appeal lies in its spontaneity and raw excitement. All I am saying is that a football crowd is not composed of cretins and intellectual pygmies.

It would be nice if, just once, the media had a word of praise for supporters, or referred to them as (gasp!) human beings. (If you think I'm exaggerating by the way, then you tell me the last time *you* came across such a piece.) If this proves too hard to do, then I'd sooner they just left us alone. I know I'm asking the impossible.

The game itself was a rum affair and no mistake. The climax

of Tchaikovsky's *1812 Overture* greeted the players as they took to the field. It certainly made a refreshing change from perennial favourites *Simply The Best* or *The Final Countdown*.

Other than the roar that went up when York scored to level the tie, Tchaikovsky's piece, inspired by the Napoleonic invasion of Russia, was the loudest noise to be heard in the first half. Never in all the years that I have been following Burnley, home or away, had I experienced such a paucity of atmosphere. Even the practice sessions that had attempted to hide behind the highly transparent facade of the Marsden Lancashire Cup, just a few weeks beforehand, had generated more noise.

Dreadful passes, appalling distribution, mis-timed tackles, all of which usually invited a barrage of invective from the Turf Moor faithful, were met with deafening indifference. Even Pepper's seventeenth minute goal which levelled the tie was greeted by little more than one or two murmurs of mild discontent by the 800 or so Clarets fans gathered behind Marlon's goal.

It's difficult to explain or defend the apathy that engulfed the Burnley end for the first half that night. My guess is that a combination of our new Division One status, coupled with local media hype, had encouraged a degree of arrogance amongst a section of our support.

Since our Division Two play-off Final at Wembley, we'd been fed on a diet which went largely along the lines of, 'it's goodbye to the grime, and greetings to the glamour.' No more would we visit Hartlepool on a wet and windy Tuesday night. Gone were the days of a 600-mile round trip the day after Boxing Day, to see us struggle in the mud for a point against a determined yet workmanlike Barnet side. Those were the bad old days. Now we were to play football of an infinitely higher quality, in such palatial stadia as Molineux, The New Den, and Kenilworth Road. (Well, some things never change.)

And so the attitude prevailed amongst some that the mighty Burnley F.C., having fought long and hard to escape the evil clutches of the lower leagues, should not be asked to return to the less than glamorous surroundings of Bootham Crescent, to play lowly York City.

This was of course, errant, arrogant nonsense. OK, so York City's ground wasn't the Nou Camp, but it was some way from being the worst I'd ever visited. And as for their team . . . For a start, the Minstermen had finished a place above us in the league not twelve weeks beforehand, and just seven days previously we'd struggled to score against them. In fact, anybody who was at York that evening will tell you that there was only one side in it for the first forty-five.

Not that this was any excuse, and yes, I was as quiet as anybody there, for us not getting behind the team. That having been said, our first half performance plumbed hitherto unchartered depths of banality and ineptitude, and the less said about it the better.

Other than York's goal, the only other first half event worthy of note was the Tannoy announcer's request for the home supporters to refrain from bad language, (yes, *really*), after having greeted McMinn's every touch of the ball with a hearty chorus of 'You fat bastard!'

Jimmy had obviously used some choice words of his own in the fifteen minutes available to him in the interval. The side emerged from their half-time lambasting with a great deal more purpose to their play.

City still came at us, but through a combination of luck, a goalpost, and good defending, (in particular Marlon, who having signed a new contract twenty-four hours earlier, pulled off the cliched 'string of magnificent saves'), we managed to keep the Minstermen at bay.

At the other end, a mis-directed shot from Harper was seized on by an unmarked Robinson, who cracked the ball in from six yards. Three minutes later, Ted 'Tinman' McMinn, beat their right back and crossed to Gayle, who killed the ball dead with his chest, before volleying into the roof of the net from *exactly* the same position from which Robinson had scored.

Having broken his duck, Big Bad John came over to us and did his Ian Wright celebration impersonation: you know, the one where everybody else goes wild and he just stands there, all poise and cool and arrogance.

Steve Cooper grabbed one back for York late on, but it wasn't enough to stop us from winning 3-2 on aggregate, and progressing into the next round.

Of course, we should never have worried. Bootham Crescent had been our lucky ground for some little time. We won the old

Fourth Division Championship there in 91/92, and the previous season it provided us with a thrilling 3-2 F.A. Cup victory, and a nerve-shredding 0-0 draw, which all but guaranteed us a play-off place.

Nevertheless, both the team and its supporters desperately needed to buck their ideas up for the short trip to Oldham on Saturday.

Chris Sutton, at £5 million English football's costliest player, opens his account for Blackburn Rovers in his side's 3-0 victory over Leicester City.

Jurgen Klinsmann scores twice on his home debut against Everton.

Sheffield United manager Dave Bassett and three of his players are sent off in their Anglo-Italian Cup game against Udinese.

Gary Lineker turns down Bryan Robson's offer of a move to Middlesbrough.

Saturday 27/8/94
Boundary Park

OLDHAM ATHLETIC 3-0 BURNLEY.
(Ritchie 50, McCarthy 80 [pen.], 84.)
League position before and after game: 20th . . . 23rd

Attendance: 11,310

BURNLEY: Beresford, Harrison, Parkinson, Davis, Winstanley, Joyce *(Deary 76)*, Harper, Gayle, Heath, Robinson, McMinn *(Russell 18)*.
Sub (not used): Lancashire.

OLDHAM: Gerrard, Halle, Makin, Henry *(Ritchie 32)*, Jobson, Fleming, Richardson, Brennan, Sharp, McCarthy, Holden.

19

Subs (not used): Hallworth, Redmond.

Referee: D.B. Allison

Yellow Cards: Brennan, McCarthy, Richardson
(Oldham Athletic)
Robinson (Burnley)

Red Cards: Beresford (Burnley)

And then there are those matches that you just want to put to the back of your mind as quickly as is humanly possible . . .

'Well, the pies were great', said my dad as we spoke after the game. And whilst he may have had a valid point, I had been hoping to come away from Boundary Park with more than a glowing recommendation of their culinary fare.

This was after all, Oldham; a team relegated from the Premiership the previous season, whose defence allegedly possessed more holes than the average slab of Emmenthal. Not that *our* forward line appeared capable of locating any.

Prior to the game, we'd been in excellent humour. Outside the ground we'd borne witness to a clinically insane programme seller, who bemoaned the presence of a nearby whinnying police horse. 'Christ!' he raged, 'It's no bloody wonder I can't sell any of these with that thing crapping everywhere!'

Two hundred yards down the road, and we encountered the truly wonderful 'Latique', Oldham's hilariously pretentious answer to 'Yves Saint Laurent.' Inside, an American college 'soccer' team were running their eye over the stock. 'Gee, *seven* studs, dude!' enthused one, as he held a boot aloft for all to see, as though he had stumbled across the Holy Grail. Another of their company taunted an Oldham fan about England's less-than-glorious 'two-zero reverse', at the hands of Alexi Lalas et al, just over a year previously. Worse was to come.

Turning the corner, our idle gaze fell upon an horrific sight . . . Oldham's away kit. Obviously designed by somebody who had no interest in either football or fashion, the chief problem with it was an abundance of bright orange. I defy you to name *any* kit, with the exception of Holland '74, that has benefited (aesthetically) from the inclusion of orange in its design. 'That,' said

Chris, 'is bloody provocative.' And on that note, we left to find our seats.

The last (and only) time I'd visited Boundary Park was two seasons previously, in the company of a Newcastle supporter, and an Oldham fan, both of whom I was living with at university. In an exhilarating match, the Latics had lost out 3-2 to a John Barnes-inspired Liverpool. The ground that day looked less than attractive, as it was in the throes of reconstruction, and the playing surface itself was hardly a picture of health.

Two seasons on however, and all that had changed. The ground was now all-seater, and although it wasn't a Wolves or a Millwall, it looked very-tidy-indeed-thank-you. As for the pitch, it was hard to believe the transformation that it had undergone.

Taking their cue from York's apparent devotion to Tchaikovsky, the Latics continued the 'Endsleigh League's Guide To Popular Figures in Classical Music', by having the two teams take the field to the strains of Elgar's 'Pomp and Circumstance'.

As Steve Davis led the rest of the team towards us, those who had been so silent five days earlier at Bootham Crescent found their voices. And they didn't let up for most of the ninety minutes that followed. This was despite an on-the-field performance which at times suggested that soft drugs were freely available in Burnley's dressing-room.

In all fairness, we played reasonably well for the first quarter of an hour. We held our own in midfield without really looking dangerous ourselves, and any attack that Oldham had was snuffed out.

On eighteen minutes McCarthy dinked a ball through for Henry to run onto. Marlon, displaying frightening single-mindedness, came charging a good six yards out of his area. It was clear from his demeanour that 'THOU SHALT NOT PASS' was emblazoned across his line of vision.

As Henry attempted to lob our keeper, Beresford instinctively stuck his hands out and touched the ball away. His inevitable follow through and subsequent collision with Henry produced the kind of facial grimaces in the crowd more normally reserved for motorway pile-ups.

Four minutes later, Marlon had been both stretchered off *and* sent off, Henry *still* didn't know what had hit him, and our substitute goalie, Wayne Russell, had been thrown into the deep end of a local derby which had reached boiling point after less than twenty minutes.

(Which reminds me: I am totally opposed to the law which allows the substitution of an outfield player, in order to bring on a replacement goalie, when the original keeper has been dismissed. One of the greatest sights in football used to be watching an outfield player fumble shots, flap at crosses, and generally provide terrific comic entertainment, due to his marvellous ineptitude between the sticks. Occasionally it worked the other way. I particularly remember Mark Monington putting in one of his best ever performances, in the last game of the 92/93 season at Stoke, pulling off acrobatic save after acrobatic save, following the stretchering-off of Beresford.)

Mullen, displaying marginally less tactical awareness than our cat, substituted McMinn. Why? Apart from being an attacking option, the Tinman had shown at York that he was perfectly capable of running the ball into the opposition corner and keeping it there, thus eating up valuable time.

Still, superbly cheered on by a near 3,000-strong following who outsang a practically inaudible Oldham for the whole game, we reorganised and defended stoutly, Russell in particular looking every inch a trainee Marlon. Inchy even made a few forays goalwards, and Big Bad John was unlucky not to do better with a header that just cleared Oldham's crossbar.

Half-time arrived with the scores still level, and the interval was spent debating our chances of hanging on for a point, whilst simultaneously avoiding large puddles of something that clearly wasn't water, in Oldham's all-new, hi-tech Gents'. All-new that is, apart from any decent plumbing, or so it appeared.

Five minutes into the second half, and a chronic misunderstanding between Parkinson and Russell as to who should deal with a feeble cross resulted in Ritchie nipping in to score with a simple header at our far post.

As the half wore on, Mr Allinson incurred the wrath of the Burnley faithful by making a series of decisions in the home side's favour which quite honestly beggared belief.

Oldham's Lee Richardson, who had almost signed for us pre-season, broke into our area and was presumably blown over by a freak gust of wind; certainly nobody made contact, intentional or otherwise, with his sprawling frame. The resultant penalty was tucked away by McCarthy. Two-nil to Oldham, and the hoped-for point had now well and truly disappeared.

Four minutes later, Oldham were awarded what was a blindingly obvious Burnley throw-in. Blindingly obvious, that is, to all but the man in black. A flick-on from the throw-in found McCarthy in a ridiculous amount of space, and, rounding Russell with consummate ease, he netted his fourth of the season.

Obviously delirious with his effort, the Latics' number ten generously decided to share his joy with the travelling supporters. As he somersaulted and ran over to us, smiling as broadly as a Cheshire cat, I saw grown men in our end being restrained by stewards and police officers. Had said men gained access to the pitch, I very much doubt if the Oldham number ten would ever have somersaulted again.

This is not, of course, excusable behaviour. But then again, how excusable is it for a player to run across to an already wound-up crowd, in order to rub their noses in defeat? The referee considered McCarthy's actions serious enough to report to Joe Royle after the game, which rather begged the question, why was he not sent off, as he had already been booked?

Leaving the ground, our abject misery was compounded still further by Oldham's Tannoy-announcer, who chirpily piped up, 'You Burnley fans will enjoy this one!', before letting us know that our friends from Blackburn had stuffed Coventry 4-0.

The bottom line remained however, that we had taken one point from nine. At this rate we would end up with a grand total of fifteen points at the end of the season. Not nearly enough to survive. The pressure for a win was beginning to grow. This may well have been a hard month, but things had to improve.

Nigerian World Cup star, Daniel Amokachi, signs for Everton for £3 million.

The FA launch an anti-drugs campaign, and announce details of random testing for players.

The FA want to know if England coach Terry Venables is welcome at White Hart Lane, in light of the bad blood between himself and club chairman Alan Sugar. Manager

Ossie Ardiles insists he is, but Sugar accuses the Spurs boss of living 'in cloud cuckoo land.'

Newcastle beat Southampton 5-1.

Liverpool's Robbie Fowler scores a four-and-a-half-minute hat trick against Arsenal.

Tuesday 30/8/94
Turf Moor

BURNLEY 1-1 BRISTOL CITY *(Robinson 40) (Allinson 92)*
League position before and after match: 23rd . . . 20th

Attendance: 11,067

BURNLEY: Beresford, Parkinson, Vinnicombe, Davis, Winstanley, Joyce, Harper, Gayle, Heath, Robinson *(Harrison 73)*, McMinn.
Subs (not used): Lancashire, Russell.

BRISTOL CITY: Welch, Harriot, Scott, Shall, Bryant, Fowler, Loss *(Partridge 80)*, Bent, Baird, Allison, Edwards.
Subs (not used): Kite, Monroe.

Referee: K.A. Lupton

Yellow Cards: Heath (Burnley)
Baird, Scott, Loss (Bristol City)

Red Cards: None

One of my childhood heroes was Dr. Who. (Please, indulge me.) I can still vividly remember one episode, where the good doctor and his assistant were caught in a time warp, wherein the same scenario recurred time and time again. Eventually, our hero, in this instance played by Tom Baker, freed himself from the situation by means of some special Timelord wizardry and the usual time-space continuum was restored.

As I watched Wayne Allison equalise for Bristol City deep into stoppage time, just like John Dreyer had for Stoke nine days previously, how I wished that the inter-galactic time-travelling hero could have visited Turf Moor to work his magic, and break this repetitive sequence of events.

As the ball lodged in the corner of the goal, Marlon punched his fist into his hand and screamed at his defence, Inchy stood on the halfway line, hands on hips, and Steve Davis sat with his head in his hands in the penalty area, facing the Bee Hole End. He was probably thinking of the rollocking which undoubtedly awaited him and the others in the dressing-room, come the eventual final whistle.

Meanwhile, a thousand Robins fans had launched into a joyous chorus of 'Drink up your Cider! Drink up your Cider!' If the scenario hadn't been so frustrating, so gut-wrenchingly awful, so bloody heart-breaking, it might almost have been funny. But it was – and so it wasn't.

The most frustrating aspect of it all was that if, for each of the past two home games, we had just played ninety minutes of football, as opposed to the actual ninety-five which we had played in both, we would have been four points better off, and in the top ten.

In fairness to Bristol, it was no more than they'd deserved. Although whether a team that brazenly sports a hideous luminous lime strip 'deserves' anything other than contempt, is open to conjecture. The warning signs had been clearly visible throughout the first half, unlike Burnley's midfield. City's Rob Edwards had been granted the freedom of . . . well, wherever he chose to roam really, they were a yard quicker to every ball and had twice hit the bar.

There again, we had had our moments too. McMinn in particular was in terrifyingly good form, beating defenders for fun and firing in some sterling centres. Inchy, playing in midfield, was using the ball intelligently and frequently opening up the visitors' defence.

It was in fact Heath who had a hand in setting up our goal. Shaking off the attentions of two Bristol players on the half-way line, he fed a ball out wide to the Tinman. Taking it past a couple of defenders, McMinn whipped over a centre. Robinson, coming in on the far side, managed to get his head to it. Deliberately or otherwise, it didn't really matter, as the ball looped over the hapless Keith Welch in the Robins' goal and nestled in the back of the net. One-nil.

As it happened, Robinson's goal against his former club was his one and only worthwhile contribution to that evening's performance. His substitution midway through the second half was only remarkable in that it hadn't happened sooner. The only plausible reason for this was that Jimmy had been too busy attempting to get in touch with the bank, trying to ascertain whether or not he could recall that £250,000 cheque he had recently posted off to Ashton Gate, by way of payment for Robinson.

Abysmal though his performance was, he had a difficult task in beating off stern competition from the remainder of Burnley's midfield. It was becoming clearer by the game that the area of the team which nearly cost us promotion in the 1993/94 season was looking the most likely to lead us to relegation, come May.

The main problem was their invisibility. When Gayle won headers, there was nobody running onto the knock-downs. At the other end of the pitch, things were no better. Whenever the defence managed to scramble the ball away, there was nobody in midfield to hold the ball up or play it out of harm's way. Consequently, the opposition would regain possession and launch another attack on our goal. The culprits were . . .

Alan Harper, who unfortunately for himself possessed the countenance of a particularly distressed fish. Indeed, his overall physical appearance gave the lie to the widely-held belief that football was 'the beautiful game'. His challenges were lacklustre, his passing was sloppy and he used the ball with all the vision of a partially-sighted Cyclops.

Mullen had brought the ex-Everton player to Turf Moor, on the pretext that his experience would prove invaluable to us at Division One level. Following his showing at the club to date, the supporters were beginning to wonder just what it was that Harper was experienced in. It didn't appear to be anything connected with football.

Joyce was far too inconsistent. A battler one game, but a passenger the next, 'Juicy' was quite clearly suffering from back problems. The rumour was that this was a result of years of playing on the plastic pitch at Preston North End. Whatever the cause, it was evident that he was finding it increasingly difficult to get through ninety minutes. In four of the six games he had started in, he had been subbed. John Deary had always been a whole-hearted midfielder for us; but he had obvious limitations. What made him a regular in the side since arriving at Burnley, was his commendable attitude. Initially a hot-head, he had succeeded in channelling the more aggressive aspects of his character into becoming an excellent competitor and ball-winner. Unfortunately he was not a playmaker, which was exactly what Burnley needed. Adrian Heath could probably have fulfilled this role, but Mullen chose to play him as a striker.

We did have other midfielders. Adrian Randall for one, but he was out of contract. It was also one of Burnley's worst-kept secrets that he and Mullen got on about as well as David and Goliath. There was new boy Gerry Harrison, who had impressed at Oldham, but was only here on trial and had yet to prove himself. Andy 'Mr Utility' Farrell had been a good and loyal servant to the club, but was hardly endowed with the play-making vision which Burnley so urgently required.

From where we stood on the terraces that night, it was obvious that we had problems and it was equally obvious in which area those problems lay. Traipsing off the ground at full time, we just hoped that Jimmy shared our view and was doing something to remedy the situation.

The FA decide to give an edge to the forthcoming England v USA fixture, by offering the Americans a $25,000 incentive to defeat Terry Venables' side.

Liverpool sign Coventry City and Republic of Ireland defender, Phil Babb, for £3.6 million.

After three consecutive league defeats, Leicester City earn their first point in the Premiership, with an 89th minute equaliser against QPR.

The FA sell off the FA Cup to Littlewoods, in a four year deal worth £14 million.

Bournemouth, yet to win a league game this season, appoint Mel Machin as manager.

Saturday 3/9/94
Turf Moor

BURNLEY 0-1 BARNSLEY *(Payton 53)*
League position before and after match: 20th . . . 23rd

Attendance: 11,968

BURNLEY Beresford, Parkinson, Vinnicombe, Davis, Winstanley, Harper *(Joyce 69)*, McMinn, Deary, Gayle *(Heath 58)*, Robinson, Eyres.
Sub (not used): Russell.

BARNSLEY: Watson, Eaden, Fleming, Wilson, Taggart, Davis, O'Connell, Redfearn, Rammell, Payton, Snodin.
Subs (not used): Butler, Jones, Liddell.

REFEREE: J.L. Watson
             (Retired after 20 minutes, replaced by R. Sutton.)

Yellow Cards: None

Red Cards: None

'Come on, Burnley! Score!' As the kid behind me who couldn't have been more than eight years old, implored the Clarets to take the game by the scruff of the neck, I simply didn't have the heart to turn round and tell him that he'd be lucky to see us string two passes together, let alone pose a threat to the Barnsley goal.

At times throughout the game, I wished I could have been that kid. I wished that I too could have been naive enough to have believed that Burnley could have salvaged something, *anything*, from that game.

Unfortunately, I had seen the Clarets in the same mood far too many times down the years to allow such blind optimism to obscure my view. Cynical? Yes. Justified? Yes. Peering through the drizzle as an unmarked Andy Payton headed the ball home from a Danny Wilson free kick, I knew I might as well have gone home there and then.

As the prospect of any entertainment on the pitch seemed to diminish with every passing second, (other than the referee being concussed by a wayward Barnsley clearance – always worth a chuckle), we invented our own game; 'Spot Burnley's Midfield'. Throughout the course of the afternoon, there were many reported sightings. Mick claimed to have seen it just prior to half-time, cowering in the tunnel like a shy, confused child. Andy came back from the Longside pie shop, relating how 'a small dark shape', had momentarily flashed across his line of vision, and my sister insisted she had watched with trepidation, as 'a faint ghostly apparition resembling a midfield, only more transparent', briefly hovered above the half-way line.

Another way of whiling away the minutes until the stewards opened the gates and freed us, was; 'Guess How Long Mullen's Got Left As Manager.' This one, like 'Spot Burnley's Midfield', solicited a variety of ripostes. John said he wouldn't like to say, Justin shrugged his shoulders and I was willing to bet evens on Christmas/New Year. Chris, however, felt that this match, followed by comprehensive thumpings at both Luton and Millwall, a couple of 'unsatisfactory' home performances, and a two-figure aggregate defeat by Liverpool, whom we had drawn in the next round of the Coca-Cola Cup, could see Jimmy picking up his P45 by the end of October. After that afternoon's performance, it was hard to argue.

Flippancy apart, the man who had taken over the managerial reins from Frank Casper really did appear to be losing the plot in no small way. For a start, it was imperative that we beat Barnsley that afternoon. A win against one of the more beatable teams in the division would have made the supporters feel a lot better, whilst simultaneously lifting a good deal of pressure from players and manager alike.

In my opinion, Jimmy got it horribly wrong. Firstly, as a measure of desperation, he recalled to first team action David Eyres, who was quite obviously only seventy per cent fit. So from the off, we were carrying a passenger. That having been said, the previous season's leading scorer never attempted to hide behind his injury, and performed as well as could reasonably have been expected.

Secondly, having opted to play with two wingers, we decided to adopt the 'pump it down the middle to John Gayle, so he can try and get his nut on it' philosophy. This was alright for some of the time, but to employ this tactic without variation? How Big Bad John must have longed to find himself in the box, competing for crosses whipped over from either wing.

Thirdly and most staggeringly, HE DID NOT PLAY ADRIAN HEATH FROM THE START. Those last few words are in capitals, for those who, like myself, had difficulty coming to terms with what I perceived to be a piece of tactical feeble-mindedness.

Since arriving at Turf Moor, Heath had shown time and again why he was so successful for such a long period, at such a high level of the game. His skill and control on the ball were a different class. As far as his reading of the game went, I would have put him approximately two passes ahead of any other player Burnley had on their books since Ron Futcher, a fact which must have thoroughly frustrated Heath at times.

But it didn't stop there. During our time in Division Two, he illustrated that he knew what the game was about at the lower levels, running his socks off game in, game out. His ability, commitment and enthusiasm cannot be overstated. Although I've just had a bloody good go.

'Inchy!', I once shouted at him towards the end of a typically sterling performance, 'I love you!', and I probably meant it. He must have heard me, because when he scored half a minute later, he turned round and blew me a kiss. I didn't stop grinning all weekend.

When Mullen realised the error of his ways, he threw Heath on for the last half hour. Absurdly, he asked him to do the same job that Gayle had been doing for the last hour, the only difference being, that Inchy was a good seven to eight inches shorter than Big Bad John. With these tactics, it was unsurprising, even with Heath on the pitch, that we failed to scare Barnsley's defence once in the last thirty minutes.

The final whistle inevitably arrived, and we all trolled off to a local hostelry to celebrate Chris's birthday. Not that we felt much like celebrating. Two points and two goals from our opening five league games did not for merriment make.

Comparisons with the teams that came up with us from Division Two four months previously, proved equally dispiriting. Reading were sixth, having collected eight points and scored six goals in the process. Port Vale were twelfth, with one point and one goal less. It was about time we got our act together. Luton awaited. As I retired to bed that evening, I wondered if anybody had found our midfield and maybe handed it in at the club shop . . .

Liverpool beef up their defence still further, with the purchase of Wimbledon's John Scales for £3.5 million.

Walsall sack manager Kenny Hibbitt.

Wigan Athletic dismiss Kenny Swain. Their recent gate of 1,231 was their lowest since they entered the Football League in 1978.

Middlesbrough concede their first goal of the season.

Gheorghe Popescu joins Spurs from PSV Eindhoven, for £3 million.

Blackburn Rovers' Alan Shearer scores twice, as England save the FA $25,000, by defeating the USA 2-0 at Wembley.

Joe Jordan leaves Stoke City by 'mutual consent.'

Saturday 10/9/94
Kenilworth Road

LUTON TOWN 0-1 BURNLEY (*Robinson 44*)
League position before and after match: 23rd . . . 20th.

Attendance: 6,911

BURNLEY: Russell, Parkinson, Vinnicombe, Davis, Winstanley, Randall, Harper, Harrison, Heath, Robinson, McMinn.

Subs (not used): Deary, Gayle, Siddall.

LUTON TOWN: Sommer, James, Johnson, Waddock *(Dixon 81)*, Greene *(Thomas 70)*, Peake, Telfer, Marshall, Hartson, Preece, Oakes.
Sub (not used): Barber.

Referee: S. Dunn

Yellow cards: Waddock (Luton)
Harrison, Robinson (Burnley)

Red cards: None

'YEEEEEEES!' As Mr Dunn blew his whistle for the last time that afternoon, the noise made by myself and fifteen hundred other Clarets' fans gathered behind Jurgen Sommer's goal, damn nearly took the roof off. We'd done it! We'd won! Three points!

This was the pay-off for all the torment we'd endured in the opening games of the campaign. The baptism of fire at Ayresome Park, the bitter disappointment against Stoke and Bristol, the previous week's capitulation against Barnsley; it had all been worth it, for that wonderful, unforgettable afternoon.

As a triumphant chorus of 'Burnley Are Back!' rang out from the Oak Road Stand, Inchy ran over to us, hands aloft, a grin from ear to ear. He was followed over by Davis, then Vinnicombe, then . . . well, just about all the team. Even Jimmy briefly turned to us before disappearing down the tunnel. As he raised his arms, a rare smile broke his usually dour expression. Jimmy was king again . . . at least for that afternoon, and we were ecstatic at our first win in Division One for eleven seasons.

Not that we had felt so euphoric as we had boarded our coach early that morning. Following our less than wonderful performance seven days previously, any sense of hope and optimism was subdued, to say the least.

The journey there took around four hours. Plenty of time for those hideous pre-match nerves to build up. Tension was not eased by the choice of videos on the way down. An incongruous triple-feature opened with the bizarrely-entitled film, 'Honey, I Blew Up The Kid', followed by the previous evening's soccer preview

32

from Sky, which included a particularly obsequious report on Alan Shearer, who had scored twice for England against the USA earlier that week. The unholy triumvirate was completed by a documentary on the history of football hooliganism in Britain. This last tape was whipped from the machine quick-smart, as we met up with the police escort which was to take us to the stadium.

Kenilworth Road struck me as a strange ground. Not a bad ground, not a hostile ground, but definitely a strange ground. For a start, the turnstiles for the away supporters attempted to disguise themselves by masquerading as part of the street.

They were cunningly concealed, sandwiched in between two long blocks of terraced housing. I almost got the impression that they didn't want us to find it, a throwback to the days when visiting fans were banned from Luton's terraces.

Entering the ground, I couldn't shake the feeling that I was trespassing on private property. We had to walk underneath somebody's bathroom, (or toilet, or something), to get to our section of the ground. I'm not making this up . . . honestly.

From the back of the Oak Road Stand, which had been allocated to Burnley supporters, we had a wonderful view; not of the pitch, but of the local residents' back yards, which the stand directly adjoined. I was all for encouraging football in the local community, but in people's front rooms . . .?

Having found our allocated seats, (*directly* in line with the crossbar in front of us, which meant that for the majority of the game we were either straining to peer over the offending bar, or through the netting), we were amazed to see that one side of the ground was entirely given over to twenty or so executive boxes, most of which were empty. Luton v Burnley obviously wasn't such a big draw for the local business community and their families.

As the Tannoy crackled into life, the silliness continued. An over-enthusiastic D.J. invited us to turn to page thirty-two of our programmes and join in 'the club song'.

The Burnley end was stunned into a disbelieving silence, as the Morecambe and Wise version of 'Bring Me Sunshine' floated from the speakers. *Nobody* in the ground sang, not even the home crowd. Imagine the scene, 7,000 people all wearing bemused facial expressions – embarrassment for the Luton fans, utter confusion for the travelling Clarets. For those two and a half minutes, Kenilworth Road *was* the Twilight Zone.

Following a well-observed minute's silence for the late Billy Wright, the match kicked off and some sense of normality was resumed, as we struggled to find our feet in defence. Luton would have been three goals to the good in the first fifteen minutes, but for some inept finishing.

After that, we began to settle down and although we looked unenterprising, we limited Luton to just one more chance, a David Greene header, which Vinnicombe comfortably headed off the line.

A minute before the break, Luton's 'keeper, who had briefly appeared as a substitute for the USA earlier in the week, showed all his international class as he raced to the edge of his area, picked up the ball and kindly dropped it at Heath's feet.

Inchy's reactions were razor-sharp. Rounding Sommer, he evaded a defender's challenge, hit the byeline, and pulled the ball back across the area for Robinson, who kept his cool and placed the ball in the back of the net from twelve yards out. Cue scenes of mass euphoria at the Burnley end.

We were still celebrating thirty seconds later, when Heath again broke free, and narrowly missed a one-on-one. Seconds later, the half-time whistle was met with an enormous cheer, fuelled by a mixture of relief and joy.

During the interval, Luton once again tried to psyche us out, as we were revisited by 'Bring Me Sunshine'. It didn't work. In fact, many of us sang along, much to the annoyance of the home fans, although one good sport in the adjacent home end joined in the fun by dancing along to our efforts; mad as a Hatter, indeed.

I was terrified we would make the mistake of shutting up shop and conceding a couple of goals in the second half. I couldn't have been more wrong. Heath and Robinson seemed intent on scaring the living daylights out of Luton's ultra-square back four, and both were unlucky not to score. Heath in particular forced a superb save from Sommer, as he stole a yard on his marker to crack in a volley.

But the real revelation came in midfield. We had one. Credit where it's due, Mullen had recognised the need for a radical rethink in this area and had done something about it. Dropping

34

Deary and the unfit Eyres for the combative Harrison and the attacking Randall, we seemed to have more bite. We were now competing for and winning balls in midfield, instead of defending on the edge of our area.

Harrison in particular impressed, showing well for the ball and running with strength and determination. Even Harper, so dreadful recently, looked solid against his former club, occupying a holding role in the middle of the park.

The last fifteen minutes was end-to-end stuff. They threw on their subs in a determined effort to equalise. But there was no way past Steve Davis and the equally superb Wayne Russell, who was deputising for the suspended Beresford and was outstanding on his full debut for us. At the other end, McMinn decided he fancied playing and sparked into life, repeatedly stretching Luton's defence. Encouragingly, we created several chances and on another day, might have come away with a hatful. That afternoon however, we were more than happy with just the one.

After the game as we sat on the coach, enjoying that feeling that only an away win can bring, one teenage lad was regaling one and all with his tale of how he was nearly arrested for running onto the pitch, as the ref had blown for full time.

'So I says to this copper, 'Don't you understand? Don't you get it? It's our first win. *And* it's away from home. It's our first bloody win!" Maybe the policeman didn't understand, but I did. Millwall, (our next fixture), could wait. All I wanted to do was float on this feeling for a few days . . . and I did.

Hartlepool United and manager John McPhail part company.

Dion Dublin moves to Coventry City from Manchester United, at a cost of £2 million.

Blackburn Rovers suffer a 1-0 defeat at the hands of Swedish part-timers, Trelleborgs, in the first round of the UEFA Cup.

Everton are set to sign Brazilian striker Muller, for around £2.5 million.

Mick Walker is sacked by Notts County.

Wednesday 15/9/94
The New Den

MILLWALL 2-3 BURNLEY *(Savage 46, Rae 73 [pen.])*
(Winstanley 52, 68, Robinson 80)
League position before and after match: 21st . . . 20th

Attendance: 7,375

BURNLEY: Beresford, Parkinson, Vinnicombe, Davis, Winstanley, Deary, Harper, Harrison, Heath, Robinson, McMinn.
Subs (not used): Gayle, Mullin, Russell.

MILLWALL: Keller, Cunningham, Thatcher, Chapman, McCarthy, Roberts, Savage, Rae, Kerr, *(Beard 75)*, Goodman, Kennedy *(Mitchell 65)*.
Sub (not used): Carter.

Referee: M. Bailey

Yellow cards: Thatcher (Millwall)
              Harper, McMinn (Burnley)

Red cards: None

Prior to kick-off I would have sold a vital organ, possibly two, for a draw. After all, Millwall were unbeaten at The New Den in their past twenty-five games there, and four points from two away fixtures would have been a decent enough haul against any teams in the division.

As at Luton, the home side should really have gone in at the interval one or two goals up, but for some inadequate finishing and a top-class defensive display from the ubiquitous Steve

Davis, whose value both as the central component of Burnley's defence and as a club asset, was growing by the game. Towards the end of the half, we did have a go back; Heath, Deary and Robinson, all having half-chances.

There was no shortage of action off the pitch, either. Jimmy had got himself engaged in a frank exchange of views with a small group of Millwall fans to the right of the Burnley dugout. Pointed fingers and contorted facial muscles appeared to be the order of the day, as Mullen slugged it out with East London's finest. This went on for a good few minutes and I can only assume he gave as good as he got, because the second half saw the kind of police presence around our dugout more readily associated with Royal visits.

Nevertheless, half-time arrived, bringing with it a scoreline of 0-0. I *hate* half-time. Unless we are 4-0 up, at home to the bottom team in the league who have been reduced to nine men and who will be playing against the wind in the second half, I find it a physical impossibility to relax in the interval. This half-time did, however, have its comforts. The New Den was one of the very few grounds I'd visited which served alcohol.

Gulping down my pint before the restart, I was also able to watch brief highlights of the first half, on one of the handful of television screens that were installed in the impressive refreshment area. Only the absence of an armchair prevented me from feeling right at home. It also made a pleasant change to see us on the telly, without Elton Welsby proffering his own smugger-than-thou brand of football analysis.

'Dig in', I muttered under my breath, as I climbed the stairs and retook my seat. 'Dig in, and we'll get a point out of this one.' Eighteen seconds in, and Dave Savage unleashed a twenty-yard shot to complement his name. Beresford, back from his one match suspension, never saw it, let alone got near it. One nil, Millwall.

'So much for digging in,' I thought. Meanwhile, insult was added to injury, as the sickening sight that was 6,500 joyous writhing Cockneys, fell across my line of vision.

But spurred on by brilliant vocal support (again), Burnley showed tremendous pluck and within six minutes were level. Robinson's cross picked Winstanley out of a crowded six yard box. At the back of our stand, the travelling support rose as one with our number five, as he thundered his header past Keller. One-all and smiles back on faces. And bloody big smiles at that.

Actually, that's another thing that I can't live with: being on level terms, away from home, with a good half hour remaining. Years of following Burnley away has taught me that no matter how awfully the home side are playing, or indeed how well we are performing, there is an unwritten rule, a cast-iron certainty if you will, that Burnley will eventually concede, but never score, that all important goal. How or when that goal comes is of little import, the thing is that it *will* come. The previous season, we performed this trick against Fulham, Plymouth, Stockport and Swansea, and those are only the games I can remember off the top of my head.

Can you imagine then, my utter, incredulous even, delight, as Winstanley managed to get his head onto a Heath centre and put us in the lead? Two one, Burnley, and I found myself jumping up and down with and hugging a complete stranger, as though he were my long-lost brother of fifteen years. The impossible was happening. This was fairytale stuff for Winstanley. In his ten years at Bolton, he had managed a less-than-prolific six goals. In a ten minute spell with Burnley, he was suddenly our second highest goal-scorer.

All we needed to do now was to hang on for twenty-two minutes. Oh yes. I knew *exactly* how long was left, courtesy of a giant electronic scoreboard away to our left, which seemed to have a spiteful little trick of stretching seconds into minutes, an exquisite torture if ever there was one. On average, I imagine I was glancing across about every thirty seconds.

The referee then had what is perhaps best described as 'a daft ten minutes', re-writing the rules of the game in the most dramatic fashion. Firstly, Steve Davis was struck high on the shoulder by the ball, in our penalty area. This new offence was known as 'shoulder-ball' and was punishable by a penalty. Alex Rae sent Marlon the wrong way; two-all.

Standing there as I began to tense up again, I imagine that my countenance bore the look it always bears when we surrender the lead. The look is one of a dismayed five year old, who has been given a bag of sweets by Grandma, only to have them taken away by Mum, with the words, 'They'll spoil your tea.'

Not content with having let Millwall draw level, Mr. Bailey

attempted to load the dice yet further in the home side's favour, by trying to send off one of our more dangerous players – Ted McMinn. And the Tinman's crime? Happening to be behind the Lions' Mark Kennedy, as he quite simply fell over.

Ted, who had been having a storming second half, comically stood his ground and refused to leave the pitch. The referee was suddenly surrounded by just about every Burnley player, bar Beresford. In the confusion that followed, Alan Harper and John Deary were the most vociferous protesters, all arm gestures and disbelieving expressions.

Enter Clive Middlemass, Burnley's assistant manager, who looked more like a kindly, perhaps dopey uncle, than a man involved at the cutting edge of First Division football. Waddling onto the pitch, he took the referee's arm and gently pulled him to one side, away from the melee. God knows what he said, or bribed him with, but within thirty seconds, Mr Bailey had consulted his linesman and reinstated McMinn. Well done, Uncle Clive!

Of course, even though he had made a mistake in thinking he had already booked the Tinman when he hadn't, the official could not lose face by admitting it. Consequently, Ted was given a stern-looking lecture and a yellow card.

McMinn obviously found the ref's little talk inspirational. He proceeded to tear Millwall's defence to shreds, sending over some Exocet crosses which only narrowly missed their intended targets. It was quite clear that a terrified Kasey Keller had never seen anything quite like this. Believe you me, Millwall's Amercian 'keeper wanted his Mom.

With ten minutes remaining, John Deary swung a foot at the ball on the edge of Millwall's area. The shot looked to be going wide, until it took a deflection off a defender. As the ball hung in the air, (and hung, and hung, and *still* hung), eight hundred Clarets fans held their breath.

Eventually, the ball did re-enter the earth's orbit, but Keller's attempt to palm it away to safety was foiled by Robinson, as he flung himself at the ball and forced it in off the underside of the crossbar.

The pent-up energy that was released following Robinson's goal could probably have run a small nuclear power station for a week or so. 'Um bah bah! Um bah bah!' may look silly when written down, but for the next five minutes, those six words and the naff dance that accompanies it were all you needed to know in our end, as Millwall's North Stand was transformed into an all-singing, all-dancing celebration of claret and blue.

The nine remaining minutes of normal time, plus a couple of minutes 'injury' time, seemed like an eternity . . . to the power of ten. I felt *every one* of those seconds. A couple of close-ish calls later, the referee was eventually forced to concede that not even he could justify any more stoppage time than he had already allowed.

RAPTURE!

This was an incredible result, especially when you consider that Millwall hadn't been beaten at home for a year. In forty-five second half minutes, we had doubled our goal tally, won our second game on the trot on the road, (when was the last time we'd done that?) and, with the notable exception of our play-off Final victory at Wembley, recorded our first win in London for over a decade. What was more, we had done all this by playing some excellent football.

About half past midnight the following morning, still trading inane other-worldly grins with anybody in claret, I found myself sipping the tasteless, tepid fare that passed for coffee at Corley Services. With the rain teeming down outside, a terrible realisation suddenly dawned on me. Here we were, only seven league games into the season, and we could already have experienced its high point.

For Burnley fans, the previous twenty-four hours had given us much to be happy about. The night before, arch-rivals Blackburn Rovers, watched by just over 13,000 (a paltry gathering when you consider that this was the first-ever European game at Ewood), had served up comedy of the highest calibre, going down 1-0 in the UEFA Cup to Trelleborgs, a bunch of Swedish part-timers. One day on, the Clarets had recorded their best result of the season to date, with a highly impressive performance. Just how much better could it get?

40

Archie Gemill and John McGovern take over the reins at Rotherham.

Muller's proposed move to Everton falls through. The Brazilian international wanted the Merseyside club to pay any tax he would have incurred on his wages.

John Layton becomes caretaker boss at Hereford, after Greg Downs leaves, by 'mutual consent'.

Russell Slade is Mick Walker's replacement at Notts County.

Manchester United score a 4-2 victory over IFK Gothenburg in the European Cup.

Saturday 17/9/94
Turf Moor

BURNLEY 0-1 WOLVERHAMPTON WANDERERS *(Bull 59)*
League position before and after match: 20th . . . 21st

Attendance: 17,766

BURNLEY: Beresford, Parkinson, Vinnicombe, Davis, Winstanley, Deary, Harper, Harrison *(Eyres 68)*, Heath, Robinson *(Philliskirk 80)*, McMinn.
Sub (not used): Russell.

WOLVERHAMPTON WANDERERS: Stowell, Smith, Thompson, Emblen, Venus, Shirtliff, Walters, Ferguson, Bull, Kelly, Froggatt.
Subs (not used): Blades, Birch, Jones.

Referee: T. Heilbron

Yellow cards: Robinson, Harrison, Davis, (Burnley)
                  Emblen, Walters, Smith, Bull (Wolves)

Red cards: None

There wasn't an awful lot to say about the game that afternoon. A marvellously entertaining encounter saw us outplay Wolves, and with the chances we created, we really should have won. The only reason we didn't was due to a combination of our poor finishing and benevolent defending. Yet another free header cost us three points.

The visit of Wolverhampton Wanderers, a big club with ambitions to match, made me wonder whether or not there was any chance of the Clarets ever competing with the best in the country again, other than in the occasional Cup fixture and just how 'big' a club Burnley was. One interesting way of addressing the issue was that of comparison.

The obvious and most important comparison, is wealth. In the 92/93 season, Burnley were one of only a few clubs to make a post-tax profit, (to the tune of somewhere around the £300,000 mark). This was an admirable achievement and showed that as a business, the club was financially sound. However, there is a world of difference between financial soundness and wealth.

For example, just look at the value of the two squads that day. Burnley's summer signings; Liam Robinson, Mark Winstanley, Chris Vinnicombe and Alan Harper, cost Burnley £650,000. Pretty expensive, huh? Well, no, actually; not when compared to our opponents that day.

Four players in the Wolves squad were collectively worth more than four times that amount; Neil Emblen, David Kelly, Steve Froggatt and Tony Daley, together cost the lion's share of £3,500,000. And even if Burnley could afford the initial outlay for these players, it could never afford to pay their wages. Wolves obviously could. Now *that*, my friend, is wealth.

What about the stadium? Whilst Turf Moor is a fine ground, better than many in the Premiership even, it pales into insignificance when compared with the grand palatial structure that is Molineux. The Hayward family have ploughed millions of pounds into ground redevelopment, and it shows. Molineux is now an impressive, 28,500 all-seater stadium.

Which brings us onto support. The opening few weeks of the 94/95 season saw Wolves pull in regular crowds of somewhere around the 27,500 mark. In the corresponding period, Burnley's average gate was in the region of 12,000. Which begs the question, how much more support could Burnley attract? Between 1973 and 1976, the last time the Clarets were regulars in the top flight, the average gate was not much over the 19,000 mark.

Don't get me wrong. I'm not knocking the quality of Burnley's support (in fact, surveys have shown the Clarets to be the best-supported club, per head of population, in the country). Neither am I taking a pot-shot at Burnley's ground. I am utterly in love with Turf Moor, and have been since my dad first took me there. What I *am* trying to do, is introduce a little perspective.

So, where are we now? The progress that Burnley Football Club have made in the eight seasons since 'the Orient game', is phenomenal. ('The Orient Game', for the benefit of non-Burnley fans, took place on 09/5/87, and was the most cruel, embarrassing, nerve-shredding, emotionally-charged game in the history of the club. It was a game Burnley *had* to win. Had they lost that day, they would have dropped out of the Football League and probably out of existence. Both victory and league status were secured, and it is now widely regarded as a major turning point in the fortunes and history of the club. And I still get a genuine lump in my throat every time I watch the footage.)

Both on and off the pitch, the club has undergone a major transition, and is much healthier than it has been for many a season. In many ways, we are in a position that many clubs envy. We are stable in all the important areas: we have financial security, a fine ground, and wonderful support for a town this size. But we are not, and probably never will be, a Wolves. Burnley are an average-sized club, which could certainly survive in the Premiership in terms of attendances, but would never win the title.

Ultimately, unless a Jack Walker figure moves in at Turf Moor, Burnley's potential will remain just that. The best we could possibly hope for is to do an Oldham; get into the Premiership, fight like hell to stay there, and hope for a good run in one of the Cups.

The abolition of the maximum wage and the then inevitable arrival of big money into the game, ended an era in which

Burnley was a major player in English football. We missed the party, but wouldn't it be wonderful if we could gatecrash it, even if it was only for a little while?

David Sullivan, chairman of Birmingham City, gives manager Barry Fry until November to get the team into the top three in Division Two.

Sheffield Wednesday boss, Trevor Francis, vows to hunt out the mole, who fed a Sunday newspaper the story that there was discontent in the Owls' dressing-room.

Chris Nicholl is installed as manager at Walsall.

The Football League want the FA to consider the idea of 'shrinking' teams, as an alternative to the penalty shoot-out method of settling drawn cup ties.

Wednesday 21/9/94
Anfield

COCA-COLA CUP. SECOND ROUND, FIRST LEG.

LIVERPOOL 2-0 BURNLEY (*Scales 42, Fowler 84*)

Attendance: 23,359

BURNLEY: Beresford, Parkinson, Vinnicombe, Davis, Winstanley, Eyres, Harper, Harrison (*Deary 77*), Heath, Robinson (*Philliskirk 84*), McMinn.
Sub (not used): Russell.

LIVERPOOL: James, Jones, Bjornebye, Scales, Ruddock, Molby, Barnes, Redknapp, Rush, Fowler, McManaman.
Subs (not used): Babb, Clough, Stensgaard.

Referee: R. Dilkes

Yellow cards: Molby (Liverpool)
Parkinson, Winstanley (Burnley)

Red cards: None

The signs were ominous. An immense and intense-looking blood-red sun hung over the city as we made our way towards Anfield. (I *swear* it had 'Carlsberg' written across its centre.) 'ENTER AT YOUR PERIL,' it seemed to say, as our car, one of many from Burnley that evening, threaded through the streets of Walton, like so many lambs to the slaughter.

Actually, I was beginning to wonder if we would have the chance to enter Anfield at all. We'd hit a huge traffic jam, not a million miles from the ground, (we could see the stadium), but certainly far enough away to cause me acute anxiety that we might miss the kick-off.

As the car clock ticked ever closer to quarter-to-eight, I could feel myself beginning to tense up. This was Liverpool. One of the biggest games we'd play all season – and we were going to be late for it.

Eventually, we made it to the head of the bottle-neck. Here we were met by a policeman, but not just any policeman. He had been given a specific brief. His mission was to let traffic flow from every junction except ours, so as to make us, just us and no-one else *but* us you understand, late for the start of the game. Looking back, this might not have been *strictly* true, but that's exactly how it felt at the time.

We eventually abandoned the car in a side-street and cursing Liverpool's traffic police, sprinted to the stadium in a time which Linford Christie would have done well to equal. We made it to our seats with literally seconds to spare.

This was my first visit to Anfield, and I was suitably overawed. Away to my left loomed the massive two-tiered Centenary Stand. It looked to be eight miles high, give or take a couple of inches, and could probably have accommodated the population of a small European country.

To my right was situated the Main Stand. Less lofty, but no less impressive, this could probably only have housed the population of London. And maybe one or two other provincial cities.

It was then ironic, that the Kop, (*the* wall of sound, *the* terrace that had helped carry the mighty Reds to many a famous victory, the legendary, mythical Kop), was in the throes of being rebuilt, and consequently looked as if it had arrived on loan from Rotherham, not half an hour ago.

However, castrated Kop aside, this was easily the most impressive and intimidating football arena, (but by no means in an unpleasant or violent way), that I had ever visited. Anfield seemed to say, 'Win – if you dare.' And that was just the terraces.

Reading the team line-ups on the back of the programme, Barnes, Rush, Fowler, McManaman, (Clough and Babb on the bench, for Christ's sake), I took a deep breath and prayed they'd be gentle with us. Say, 5-0 at half-time.

Any misgivings I had about playing Liverpool on their patch were clearly not shared by the players. Right from the off, we went straight for the Scouse jugular.

Inspired by Inchy, Burnley threatened to make Roy Evans eat his patronising programme notes, (We will . . . pay Burnley the same respect as any other visiting team.' [2] Yeah, sure, Roy), by terrifying the ridiculously over-priced Ruddock and Scales.

Harrison and Robinson were both unlucky with headers which narrowly missed the target, and Heath's volley forced a super-lative save from James in the Liverpool goal. Ruddock and Scales were exchanging one or two nervous glances.

But the best chance of the half fell to Gerry Harrison. A speculative McMinn ball into the box fell to the Burnley number eight, who turned 'Razor' Ruddock with ease. The ex-Tottenham man was still trying to work out where Gerry had gone, five minutes later. Finding himself in more space and time than he knew what to do with, he snatched at the opportunity and the ball rolled safely into the palms of a visibly relieved David James.

The home side had their chances, too. Marlon performed a slightly more impressive miracle than raising Lazarus from the dead, by somehow getting across to a deflected twenty-five yard screamer from Jan Molby (whose misfortune it is to be referred to as 'The Great Dane' in any article ever written about him).

Impressive though we undoubtedly were in the first half, there was something almost inevitable about the moment when John Scales headed his side in front. This was, after all, Liverpool. What was disappointing was the manner of the goal and its timing: a free header, just three minutes before the break. That having been said, 1-0 down at half-time fell some way short of the drubbing I had gloomily predicted. There was still all to play for.

Roy Evans had clearly 'had words' at half-time and Liverpool began to turn it on. Barnes threatened to split the defence every time he got the ball and McManaman toyed with Parkinson, in a way that at times bordered on cruelty.

However, try as they might, the Reds could not make any headway against a defence which played the offside trap with such precision that you might have thought they had invented it. Rush and Fowler (the ugliest strike force in the Premiership?) were made to look incredibly naive, as time after time they went charging through, only to have Roger Dilkes call them back like a pair of errant schoolboys.

Other than stout defending, (what exactly does that mean?), Burnley had little to offer in the second period. Then, with twenty minutes to go, it started. Just as it had started at Derby, at Sheffield United, at Spurs.

A low but nevertheless audible and persistent chant had started somewhere away to our left. It had been going on for a couple of minutes and had remained constant, as other, more sporadic singing had come and gone: 'Jimmy Mullen's Claret and Blue Army.'

Another couple of minutes passed, and the chant had got a little louder and a little closer: 'Jimmy Mullen's Claret and Blue Army.'

Ten minutes left, and we were still holding our own. The entire left side of the stand behind Marlon's goal gradually joined in the chorus, its volume and intensity growing by the second: 'Jimmy Mullen's Claret and Blue Army.'

Bjornebye crossed from the bye-line. Fowler took the ball on his chest. With about one square inch of goal to aim at, the heir to Rush's throne poked the ball past an unsighted Beresford. Two-nil to Liverpool. Surely that would change the mood of the travelling support. It did. With three sides of the ground rising in unison to celebrate Fowler's strike, the chant continued twice as loud, twice as strong, as the rest of the Anfield Road Stand got to their feet and joined in: 'Jimmy Mullen's Claret and Blue Army.'

This was incredible. That second goal had practically killed the tie off, we now had little chance of progressing any further. To carry on singing was almost perverse. But that wasn't the point. We were Burnley Football Club. We were at Anfield. We were letting them know – in style: 'Jimmy Mullen's Claret and Blue Army.'

As the final whistle blew and players and officials left the field, over 4,500 Burnley fans had taken up the incantation. Had you been walking past the ground, you could have been forgiven for thinking that not only had we trounced the Scallies, but we had also brutally murdered the home team and were now indulging in some bizarre pagan dance, on the sacred Anfield turf: 'JIMMY MULLEN'S CLARET AND BLUE ARMY!'

This was a superb demonstration of support. The chant, by now having taken on a mantra-like quality, continued for a good fifteen minutes after the final whistle. As Phil Babb warmed down at the opposite end of the pitch, (Christ knows what *he* must have thought), it hit home just how special and unique, nights and crowds such as these were.

I find it difficult to articulate how I, and I suspect many others, felt that night, as we sang ourselves hoarse, at an empty football ground in the middle of Liverpool.

Maybe I find myself at a loss for words, because there is no precedent. This kind of football support is rarely written about. There *was* no orgy of destruction, there *was* no rampaging through the city centre, there *was* no post-match brawl. Consequently there *was* no 'story'; not for the media at any rate.

It didn't matter that we'd lost 2-0. Who cared that we hadn't scored in almost 200 minutes of football? We were fourth bottom in the league with a difficult month of fixtures ahead; so what?

There was no room that night for gloom, doom and despondency. It was a celebration. A celebration of being a supporter of Burnley Football Club. There was a genuine sense of community on the terraces that evening, as the best part of 5,000 travelling supporters pledged their allegiance to all things Claret and Blue.

That was the wonderful, special thing about the crowd that night. You could forget who or what who you were. The job, skin colour, sex, religion, class and politics of 5,000 *people*, were of no concern. They were all irrelevances. Burnley Football Club – the common bond.

And to the inevitable, sneering cynic; a question. Name me one other area of life, of society, where the kind of scenario I have described manifests itself.

If you were there, you'll know what I mean, when I say I was proud to be a Claret.

Some shocks in the Coca-Cola Cup, as Everton go down 3-2 to Portsmouth, West Ham are knocked out by Walsall, whilst Crystal Palace and Manchester City are both defeated 1-0, by Lincoln and Barnet respectively.

Manchester United are to appear before a Football League Commission, to defend their team selection, after they field six reserve team players, (five in their teens), in their Coca-Cola Cup game at Port Vale.

Saturday 24/9/94
The Hawthorns

WEST BROMWICH ALBION 1-0 BURNLEY *(Taylor 71)*
League position before and after game: 21st . . . 22nd

Attendance: 13,539

BURNLEY: Beresford, Parkinson, Vinnicombe, Davis, Winstanley, Harper, Harrison *(Deary 75)*, McMinn *(Philliskirk 76)*, Heath, Eyres, Robinson.
Sub (not used): Russell.

WEST BROMWICH ALBION: Naylor, Parsley, Darton, Phelan, Strodder, Herbert, Hunt *(McNally 70)*, Ashcroft *(Lilwall 85)*, Taylor, Boere, Donovan.
Sub (not used): Lange.

Referee: T. West

Yellow cards: Donovan (West Bromwich Albion)
                McMinn, Davis, Deary, Vinnicombe (Burnley)

Red cards: None

49

OK, quiz time. Who spoke the following words the Monday after the West Brom game? 'I must admit, I felt pretty guilty when they scored. After all, I was the nearest marker.'

Chris Vinnicombe? Wrong. Mark Winstanley? Try again. Alan 'Mooncat' Harper, maybe? Nah, 'fraid not. These were in fact the words of my mate Chris, who was stood next to me on the small, corner section of terracing we had been allocated, about twenty-five yards away from our penalty area.

As Bob Taylor wheeled away to celebrate his second half winner, in front of thousands of howling Baggies, I was made to reflect on a comment Inchy had made in the programme notes: 'We all know Bob Taylor's a big threat and we'll have to watch him.' [3]

The grim irony was that 'watching' Bob Taylor was *exactly* what we did; no challenge, no attempt to clear our lines, we just 'watched' and admired almost, as Taylor gleefully accepted his free header. The West Brom number nine had enough room to swing not just *one* cat, but a whole litter.

It was bad enough conceding a goal, but this was another one of 'those' goals. The number of teams who had scored free headers from set pieces on our left-hand side was getting ridiculous. We weren't so much asleep, as positively comatose.

In 22 days, Barnsley, Wolves, Liverpool and now West Brom had all benefited from our ineptitude in dealing with these situations. You might have thought we would have learned by now.

If we continued leaking goals such as these, I would soon be able to mint a set of silver coins, similar to those 'World Cup' ones you could acquire from Esso petrol stations in the Seventies. 'Calamity in Claret' I would call the collection. One side would depict a scene, highlighting our inability to mark from set pieces in our eighteen yard box. The other side of the coin would give the name of the team and the scorer and a comment on the goal from Jimmy, or one of the players: 'disappointing', 'frustrating' etc.

Besides anything else, it was humiliating to have lost to an Albion team who, up until our visit, had not managed a single victory, home or away, that season. What was more, they were firmly rooted to the foot of the table.

Like, I suspect, many football fans, I have a deep-seated fear of playing the bottom side in the division. It is far easier to go away from home and play the top of the table team, who have bagged fifteen goals and conceded none, in their last three outings. At least that way, the burden of expectation is lifted. When you get thumped, nobody laughs at you. But to lose to the *bottom* of the division?

West Brom were hardly high quality opposition. Actually, they were bloody lousy. In fact so utterly rank were they, that the only time they even remotely looked like posing a threat to our goal in the first half, was when Lovely Legs Parkinson sold Marlon murderously short with a woefully inadequate back-pass.

Fortunately for us, Jeroen Boere, having done the hard work of intercepting the ball and rounding Beresford, somehow missed an open goal from a matter of inches. I could only assume that having trained with us for a week pre-season, Burnley held fond memories for him, and he simply didn't want to hurt us. Either that or he was crap.

As the half wore on, we began to get a grip. Heath put the Tinman clean through, only for him to pea-roll his 'shot', not that it could *truly* be termed as such, into Stuart Naylor's welcoming arms. Robinson forced a good save from their keeper with a twenty-yard rasper and Eyres shot narrowly wide from a tight angle.

Then with less than ten minutes to go to the break, an Alan Harper through-ball was chased into the area by Inchy and Gary Strodder. In the ensuing tussle for the ball, Strodder palmed it away. 'Penalty!', screamed 1,000 goal-hungry Clarets fans. And a penalty it was.

Normally when we are awarded a spot-kick, I am gripped by the kind of tension which normally visits sixteen year-olds, waiting for the results of their GCSEs. But for some reason, that afternoon just felt different. Any degree of fear and therefore sanity, deserted me. I still can't work out why, but I was one hundred per cent certain that Eyres would score – no bother.

But then I hadn't banked on fate, a goalpost and the talismanic qualities of Stuart Naylor's nose conspiring against us. The penalty kick itself was fine: hard and low and towards the right-hand corner. It was going in.

In the momentary pregnant silence that enshrouded the ground, you could hear the sickening sound of the ball thudding solidly against the inside of the post. This was instantly followed by 12,500 home fans yelling their heads off, for the first time that afternoon.

Another day, and the rebound might have fallen to Eyres. But this wasn't another day. Instead, the ball smacked into Naylor's not unsizeable hooter and crossed the line for a corner. 'Bollocks!' yelled someone behind me. And what the knee-jerk reaction might have lacked in subtlety and eloquence, it more than made up for in pithiness and accuracy of sentiment.

'Baggy baggy boing boing!' screamed the West Brom fans, bouncing up and down as if some invisible puppet-master were controlling them.

Half-time arrived, and with it the news that Blackburn were beating Aston Villa 1-0. Whilst this provoked an hysterical reaction amongst the home fans, it only served to plunge the rest of us further into the slough of despond.

'We're going to lose 1-0', announced Chris, as the teams came out for the second half. 'Nah', I replied, forever the optimist, 'We'll get a point out of this, three maybe.' Would I *ever* learn?

Other than a Davis header which was cleared off the line and that awful, awful goal, Burnley bored me in the second half. I just wanted to go home. As we pumped aimless ball after aimless ball in the very vague direction of the West Brom goal, (eventually we even abandoned that idea, settling instead for running round in circles in our own half), Eyres' penalty miss began to haunt me.

It was still haunting me as I watched 'Match of the Day' that night. Its spectre stuck with me all weekend, and throughout the following seven days. It replayed itself over and over again in my memory: in slow-motion, from a different angle, with commentary. At home, at work, talking to friends in the pub, lying in bed at night, it didn't matter where I was. There was no escape from the memory of a West Brom upright and Stuart Naylor's nose.

Ipswich score a surprise 3-2 victory over Premiership Champions, Manchester United.

Blackburn Rovers are knocked out of the UEFA Cup, as they can only manage a 2-2 draw against the part-timers of

Trelleborgs and exit the competition 3-2 on aggregate. 'TWIN TOWN TRELLEBORGS' placards are tied onto Burnley's town boundary sign.

Newcastle sail comfortably through to the second round of the UEFA Cup, as they knock out Royal Antwerp 10-2 on aggregate.

Manchester United grind out a 0-0 draw, on their return to Galatasary in the European Cup.

Aston Villa proceed to the second round of the UEFA Cup, following a dramatic penalty shoot-out against Inter Milan.

Chelsea and Arsenal are both in the hat for the second round of the Cup-Winners Cup.

Lou Macari is appointed manager at Stoke City.

Tottenham's Steve Perryman dismisses speculation that Ossie Ardiles is facing the sack.

Saturday 1/10/94
Turf Moor

BURNLEY 1-1 TRANMERE ROVERS (*Eyres 70* [pen.])
(*Aldridge 25*)
League position before and after game: 22nd . . . 22nd.

Attendance: 12,427

BURNLEY: Beresford, Parkinson, Vinnicombe, Davis, Winstanley, Harper, McMinn, Harrison (*Philliskirk 67*), Heath, Robinson, Eyres.
Subs (not used): Deary, Russell.

TRANMERE ROVERS: Nixon, Stevens, Mungall, McGreal, Garnett, O'Brien, Morrisey, Aldridge, Malkin, Brannan, Nevin.

Subs (not used): Kenworthy, Edwards, Coyne.

Referee: K. Lynch

Yellow Cards: Philliskirk, Davis (Burnley)

Red Card: Davis (Burnley)

So far as professional fouls go, it was an absolute corker. Four minutes into injury time and Ged Brennan had only Beresford to beat to secure Tranmere's first away win of the season. Steve Davis, however, had GBH on his mind.

As the Rovers' number ten shaped to shoot from the edge of the area, Davis turned terminator, pulled back his right leg, and *absolutely clattered* Brannan. Poor old Ged was catapulted a good couple of feet into the air and (eventually) landed somewhere on a level with the penalty spot.

As the Tranmere physio sprinted across the pitch to help Brannan locate his missing limb, the referee gave a penalty, and, turning to Davis, reached for his breast pocket.

My heart missed a beat. Just two minutes earlier, our skipper had been booked for dissent. There was only one colour card that was going to emerge from Mr Lynch's pocket.

Davis knew this too. Casually tossing his captain's armband over his shoulder, he wiped his nose on his arm (is it only me who remembers the minutiae of incidents such as these?), and headed for the player's tunnel.

Had someone asked me before the match which scenario I would have hoped to have avoided most of all in this particular game, it is quite likely that my reply would have contained the phrases 'scores level', 'injury time spot-kick to Tranmere' and 'John "Mr Penalty" Aldridge'. All of these phrases featured in the situation which confronted us now.

(By the way – why is it that whenever we get a penalty, I *know* we will miss it, but whenever the opposition get one, I feel that I could quite safely put everything I own on them scoring?)

And so I went through the bizarre little ritual that I go through every time the ball is placed on that small white spot twelve yards in front of our goal. I try and psyche out their penalty-taker.

Now, because the opposition spot-kicker rarely makes eye-contact with me (he obviously knows who and where I am, and is avoiding my deadly gaze), I have to do this by attempting to engage with and then disrupt, his id, or his ego, or whichever part of his psychological make-up he employs when taking penalties. I look at his head, concentrate *really* hard and say 'Miss it', three times. (To myself, of course. I don't want people thinking I'm mad.)

Yes, really; I honestly do this; and perhaps more worryingly, I must believe it works, because I've been doing it since I was seven. I'm now twenty-seven. This represents two decades of fantastical self-delusion.

Aldo placed the ball on the spot. 'Miss it.' My mouth went dry. 'Miss it.' He turned to face the goal and began his run-up. 'Miss it.'

Mr Penalty hit it hard and away to the right. Marlon flung himself at the ball and pushed it onto the post. The cheers went up, but it still wasn't safe. The ball came back off the upright, bounced off Beresford's head, and flew up in the air.

Marlon got to his feet and looked around. He found himself in the truly unique position of being the only person out of the 12,500 people gathered inside Turf Moor who didn't know where the ball was. This was becoming less and less a penalty and more and more a farce.

With Nevin and Malkin rushing in for the rebound, he caught sight of the ball in the nick of time and tickled it off Nevin's boots. It *still* wasn't clear. Recovering himself, he launched into one last super-human effort and, pouncing on the ball, smothered it, making it his eighth penalty save out of thirteen since joining the club, shortly before disappearing underneath a heap of Burnley players. Mr Lynch, illustrating a fine understanding of dramatic climax, blew the final whistle. After the penalty incident at the Hawthorns seven days earlier, this was an unbelievable irony.

Unlike thousands, I didn't cheer and join in the two-minute chants of 'Ooh Aah Beresford!' Marlon had saved the day, no doubt about it, and I was as relieved as anybody; but the Davis sending-off, the penalty kick, the desperate, but oh so beautiful save and the massive outpouring of emotion when the ref blew for time, (all in the space of sixty seconds or so) left me feeling a nervous wreck. I felt like I'*d* just played a full ninety minutes. It

55

required an effort of near-Herculean proportions for me to drag myself to the exit.

The general consensus of the post-match committee meeting was that it would have been unfair, had Burnley lost the game. I wasn't convinced. Sure, if you go on chances created, possession and goals scored, (although for one heart-stopping moment, I was *sure* Eyres had blasted his penalty against the crossbar), then yes, in a way it would have been unfair not to have come away with at least a point.

On the other hand, since when has 'fair' had anything to do with football? Never, there's your answer. 'Fair' assumes a level playing field, where truth and justice will always triumph over the vagaries of fate and the often strange decisions of those men in black.

Try telling anybody who attends football matches on a regular basis that whatever happens, the outcome after ninety minutes will be 'fair', and they will laugh long and hard in your face.

Football and football history is littered with unfairness. Was it, for example, fair that England were knocked out of the 1986 World Cup Finals because a referee and a linesman failed to see Maradona cheat and punch the ball into the net? In the 1980 FA Cup Final, West Ham's Paul Allen was upended by Arsenal's Willie Young, thirty yards away from goal, with just the keeper to beat. His only reward was a free-kick which came to nothing. Was that fair? And what about . . .

There's another problem with this 'fair' thing. It isn't really a concept us fans find desirable, unless it works in our favour. (And yes, I include myself in this bracket. I whinge and whine as much as the next fan, if the ref dares to show so much as the merest *hint* of bias towards the opposition.) Look at penalties, for example.

I invite you to think back to the last time your team were awarded a spot-kick, after your centre-forward threw himself to the ground, with no-one within five yards of him. As the referee pointed to the spot, did you greet his decision with howls of derision and begin a spontaneous chant of 'The referee's a wanker!'? I bet you didn't.

Conversely, when the opposing team scored a perfectly legitimate goal, only for the ref to disallow it, did you scream blue murder at the man in black, or write a letter to the FA, asking for him to be removed from their refereeing list? Of course not. And why? Because in both instances you wanted your team to win – by hook or by crook.

Earlier in the season, Bristol had done enough to earn a point against us when they scored deep into stoppage time. I defy any Burnley fan to tell me it didn't hurt like hell when that equaliser went in. But think about it; on the balance of play, it was fair. What we actually wanted from that game was unfair. We wanted three points, when one was our just desserts.

We only want fair, when fair ensures us a league victory, or a passage to the next round of a Cup competition. And desire for that victory will always override any (at the best of times spurious) notion of fairness, because the fan always has a vested interest.

So, the next time somebody tells you that it was unfair that their side lost to a goal that was a mile offside, by all means sympathise, but bear in mind that time when they told you how they laughed themselves silly when their team won with an injury time penalty that should never have been given in a million years . . .

Hartlepool United appoint ex-Manchester United and Northern Ireland midfielder David McCreery as player-manager.

Manchester United announce a 156% rise in profits, to £10.8 million.

Chester City record their first win of the season as they beat Division Two leaders Oxford at home.

Duncan Ferguson joins Everton on a three month loan.

Wednesday 5/10/94
Turf Moor

COCA-COLA CUP. SECOND ROUND, SECOND LEG.

BURNLEY 1-4 LIVERPOOL *(Robinson 83)*
(Redknapp 15, 67, Fowler 50, Clough, 75)

Attendance: 19,032

BURNLEY: Beresford, Parkinson, Vinnicombe, Davis, Winstanley, Harper *(Harrison 45)*, McMinn *(Gayle 67)*, Philliskirk, Heath, Robinson, Eyres.
Subs (not used): Russell.

LIVERPOOL: James, Jones, Bjornebye, Nicol, Babb, Ruddock, McManaman *(Jones 71)*, Clough, Redknapp, Fowler, Molby *(Thomas 67)*.
Sub (not used): Stensgaard.

Referee: J. Worrall

Yellow cards: None

Red cards: None

There wasn't a huge amount to say about that evening. We were outplayed, outclassed and out of the competition.

With a good twenty minutes to go, with Liverpool 3-0 up and playing superbly, my mind turned to the young lad I'd seen, naively enthusing us to score against Barnsley. Once again, I wished I was him. At least when you're eight years old and the game is depressing you, you can whinge and whine, (cry even), at your dad to take you home.

But I was twenty-seven years old. Having reached adulthood, I was expected to stand on the terraces and take on the chin the full abject horror and humiliation of being torn apart by one of the best teams in the country.

There was one other curious moment in this match. With seven minutes remaining and 6-0 down on aggregate, Liam Robinson leathered a stunning volley past James into the top corner of Liverpool's goal. The home support loved it. Why?

It didn't alter the result of the tie. It was probably the most 'nothing' goal we would score all season. (I certainly hoped so.)

58

So why did the vast majority of fans, myself included, greet it with an almighty roar?

The reason was that it was a goal. Simple as that. Any goal scored by your side provokes a knee-jerk reaction. You've managed to pierce the armour of the opposition. So, any notion of 'reason' deserts you. It isn't something you can control, this colossal tidal wave of adrenalin, which makes you jump and shout and scream and hug the person standing next to you. Well, that's how it affects me, anyway.

There are of course some goals which solicit a more ecstatic response than others. Experience has taught me that it is the context in which the goal is scored, rather than how spectacular it is, that determines the level of abandon with which it is received.

For instance, a last minute winner scrambled over the line in a local derby match, is infinitely more gratifying than a thirty yard piledriver in a drab end-of-season 'nothing' game. Similarly, although a twenty yard screamer into the top right-hand corner, when you're 4-0 down with two minutes left, may be more aesthetically pleasing, it just doesn't have the same emotional impact (and that's what counts) as a mis-hit cross, which somehow ends up in the back of their net and wins you a Cup-tie in injury-time.

Of course, the ideal scenario, the ultimate goal if you will, would necessitate the involvement of a number of factors. For example, my ideal goal would be a thirty-five yard free-kick, which should never have been given in the first place, curled around a six-man wall, preferably by Inchy, with the last kick of the game in injury time of the FA Cup Semi-Final against Blackburn Rovers. (Every football fan knows it's more heartbreaking to lose a semi-final than a final.)

It doesn't worry me that there is little chance of this happening in the foreseeable future. Fantasies are often better left unrealised. That way, reality can't impinge and ruin things, like it did that night.

In the Coca-Cola Cup, Leeds, Everton and Leicester make early exits at the hands of Mansfield, Portsmouth and Brighton, as Matthew Le Tissier scores all four second-leg goals at the Dell, in Southampton's 5-0 aggregate demolition of Huddersfield.

John Fashanu is charged with misconduct by the FA, after he refers to Eric Cantona as 'a dirty, nasty bastard' in his 'Sun' column.

Tranmere are also in the FA's bad books, after their programme notes for the visit of Sheffield United suggest the Yorkshire team's board are as helpful as 'a piggy bank without a hole.'

Pressure mounts on Mike Walker to resign, following Everton's disastrous start to the season. Walker says he 'will treat the speculation with the contempt it deserves.'

Saturday 8/10/94
Turf Moor

BURNLEY 2-2 BOLTON WANDERERS (*Davis 67, Deary 73*)
(*McGinlay 5, Coleman 82*)
League position before and after game: 22nd . . . 22nd.

Attendance: 16,687

BURNLEY: Beresford, Parkinson (*Harrison 46*), Vinnicombe, Davis, Winstanley, Randall, McMinn (*Gayle 46*), Philliskirk, Deary, Robinson, Eyres.
Subs (not used): Russell.

BOLTON WANDERERS: Branagan, Lydiate, Phillips, McAteer, Thompson, (*De Freitas 55*), Spooner, Coleman, Sneekes, Paatelainen, McGinlay, Lee (*Fisher 75*).
Sub (not used): Davison.

Referee: P. Harrison

60

Yellow Cards: Winstanley, Gayle, Beresford, Eyres (Burnley)
Thompson, Lydiate (Bolton)

Red Cards: Lydiate (Bolton)

The local radio phone-in was virtually wall-to-wall Burnley fans that evening. And they weren't happy. Irate caller after irate caller branded Bolton, and in particular John McGinlay, 'cheats', 'disgraceful', and 'unsportsmanlike', for an incident earlier that afternoon which many believed had robbed us of our first home win of the season.

So what had happened to solicit such a torrent of Claret invective? With eight minutes remaining, Bolton sub Fabian de Freitas (who with such a fabulous name, might have been better employed carving out a career for himself in Hollywood, rather than spending his Saturday afternoons sitting on the Trotters' subs bench) had gone down injured, following a clash of heads.

Vinnicombe had put the ball out of play, so De Freitas could receive treatment. Instead of throwing the ball back to us, the done thing in such situations, McGinlay threw the ball to McAteer who forced a corner, from which Bolton equalised.

True, it wasn't within the spirit of the game and it was a pretty lousy thing to do, but it would have been interesting to have heard the same callers' reactions, had *we* pulled a similar stunt. I would imagine the general, considered response would have been, 'Well, that's football, innit? No point whingeing. You just get on with it.'

And anyway, we might have helped ourselves by defending the corner. There were no less than four Burnley players, marking no-one but each other in the six yard box, as Coleman blasted the ball home from about twelve yards out.

As the ball crashed into the back of the net, they all looked at each other with *that* expression: the one that says, 'But I thought *you* were marking him . . .'

Aside from that incident, we should have won anyway. Things hadn't started too well, with McGinlay contributing another goal to the 'Calamity in Claret' collection, after just five minutes. Exactly what our defence thought it was doing in allowing Philliskirk to mark their leading scorer, remains a mystery to this day.

The goal had the effect of knocking the stuffing out of us, and try as we might, we couldn't get an equaliser. Half-time arrived, and not for the first time in the season, we found ourselves chasing a game, having conceded a soft goal.

However, as the second half wore on, we pressured more and more; and they didn't like it. The enigma that was Adrian Randall, (Robert Lee one game, Sunday League player the next five), was central to our attack. Jason Lydiate was well aware of this and thought the best way of stopping our Adey was to disembowel him with his studs. Mr Harrison, obviously not a fan of Martial Arts, dismissed the Bolton number two, making him the first opposition player to receive his marching orders that season.

I don't know about you, but I believe that an opposition player getting sent off can be almost as entertaining as a goal. Like a goal, the ideal dismissal requires three or four factors to come into play.

Firstly, the dismissee must be wholly innocent. There are surely few funnier sights on a football field than seeing your injury-free player roll around on the turf, clutching some imaginary wound, whilst their big number five gets a severe talking-to. Secondly, he must remonstrate long and hard with the official, preferably squaring up to him face to face, as he attempts to protest his innocence. Thirdly, the referee must produce the red card with an almost theatrical flourish and finally, (but perhaps most importantly), the innocent victim has to walk past *your* stretch of terracing, to get to the dressing-room.

Anyway, as I mentioned a couple of paragraphs ago, they were starting to crack. One of Vinnicombe's enterprising runs was brought to a crude halt by McAteer. From the resultant free-kick, Eyres touched the ball off to Davis, whose shot was so ferocious that Branagan thought better of getting in its way and dived in the opposite direction. One-all.

Now with only ten men, they looked twice as vulnerable and were hanging on for dear life. An Eyres shot was cleared off the line, but it fell to Deary, who let rip with an almighty shot from just outside the area. We were yelling with delight before it had reached the back of the net. Two-one! We were going to do it!

Three minutes later and having used both their substitutes, Bolton were reduced to nine men. Spooner had been stretchered off with a broken leg, after being naive enough to believe he could go for a 50/50 ball with Big Bad John and come out of it unscathed. Surely we were going to win now?

But no, that combination of bad sportsmanship and more annoyingly, our by now legendary inability to get rid of anything that came into our box from a set piece on the left-hand side, undid us.

And yet again, our finishing was our Achilles' heel, proving to be less accurate than a blindfolded, one-armed sniper. Deary's goal was the first in open play since that memorable night at Millwall, and that was almost a month ago.

In the first half, Phyllis and Robinson both had half-chances and the Tinman, whose form was deserting him more rapidly than rats desert sinking ships, capped a terrible personal performance by toe-poking an effort at the corner flag from ten yards out, when judging by the crowd's reaction, the wide-open goal may have proved a more popular choice.

'Miss of the Match' however, fell to Phyllis. Seven minutes into second half injury time, (much longer and 'Granada Goals Extra' could have been televised live from Turf Moor), with the scores level, the ball came to him, unmarked at the far post. All he needed to do was bring it down on his chest and tap it home. But oh no, not Phyllis. Rather than do the simple thing, i.e. score, he attempted the kind of flash scissor-kick finish, more normally practised by yer flashy continental types. In doing so, he ballooned his effort so far over the bar that I was surprised to see it return to earth without any snow on top.

In fairness to Philliskirk, he hadn't had such a bad game. He competed well, and in the process created opportunities for others. Which was half the problem, really. All the strikers at the club were too busy creating chances, instead of scoring goals. Inchy, Robinson, Gayle, take your pick. Each one was more than capable of working openings – a defence-splitting pass from Heath, a knock-down from Gayle or Phyllis, or a bit of pace from Robinson – but when it came to scoring . . .

It was obvious that something needed to be done. And whilst all the transfer speculation centred around strikers, I couldn't help feeling that it was a creative midfielder we needed, to drag us out of the mire. Such a player would create chances for our centre-forwards, thus taking the pressure off them to do so. In

63

turn, this would free the front men to get in where it hurts and start converting some chances.

There were, I thought, two players at the club who could perhaps fulfil that role. One was Randall, but he was always going to be far too inconsistent. The other was Inchy, but after playing him as a forward for more or less two years, it was unlikely that Jimmy would change his game plan at this stage. We would have to wait and see. But something had to change . . . and quickly.

Dennis Wise is accused of assaulting a taxi driver and causing damage to his cab.

Everton remain the only side in the Premiership not to have won, as they crash 2-0 at Southampton.

Lou Macari launches a court action against Celtic, claiming more than £400,000 for wrongful dismissal.

Gordon Strachan announces his decision to retire at the end of the season.

In response to rumours concerning the safety of Ossie Ardiles' managerial position at Spurs, Alan Sugar backs him, saying 'Nobody is going anywhere.'

A Robert Lee goal gives England a 1-1 draw with Romania.

Saturday 15/10/94
Roker Park

SUNDERLAND 0-0 BURNLEY
League position before and after match: 22nd . . . 22nd.

Attendance: 17,700

BURNLEY: Beresford, Parkinson, Vinnicombe, Hoyland,

Winstanley, Randall, Harper, Philliskirk *(Gayle 70)*, Deary, Robinson *(Heath 58)*, Eyres.
Subs (not used): Russell.

SUNDERLAND: Chamberlain, Kubicki, Ord, Ball, Melville, Smith, Martin Gray *(Howey 77)*, Russell, Phil Gray, Goodman, Snodin.
Subs (not used): Michael Gray, Musgrave.

Referee: K. Breen

Yellow Cards: Vinnicombe, (Burnley)
Phil Gray (Sunderland)

Red Cards: None

A grey day, a grey performance and a grey result. As if to emphasise the point, Sunderland had three players bearing that surname on their team sheet that afternoon. Back home, the local papers wrote the game up as a display of heroic stoicism, but to myself and almost everybody else I spoke to who had been at Roker Park that dreary day, the game was less than inspiring.

Other than the impressive debut performance of loan signing Jamie Hoyland, filling in at centre back for the suspended Steve Davis, it was one of those matches where I wondered just why I'd bothered to not only part with over twenty pounds, but also travel the best part of 400 miles in one day, in order to witness the depressing exhibition of mediocrity that was on display that dull afternoon.

As the icy drizzle blew off the North Sea and into my face, and yet another attack broke down as hopelessly and inevitably as all the others had, something deep inside told me that there were better, more fruitful and more rewarding ways, of spending my time on earth. Stopping in bed, or hacking off a limb, for example.

So it may sound strange, when I say that I wouldn't have missed it for the world. A substantial part of me actually enjoyed *every* minute of the whole, lugubrious experience. Which I suppose made me some kind of pervert. What made it acceptable and made *me* feel a whole lot better was that there were 2,000 other perverts standing there with me, all loving and hating it just as much.

It's true what they say about strength in numbers. I knew I wasn't alone, physically, spiritually or emotionally that afternoon. So when Winstanley 'distributed' the ball in that otherworldly fashion of his, as though he were wearing boots with triangular points, or Philliskirk fell over it on the edge of their area with no-one near him, it was somehow reassuring to know that I wasn't mad to have invested all that time and money to be there watching it all. Or at least if I was, then there were many others around me who shared my peculiar brand of insanity.

As soon as we attempted to enter the ground, it became evident that it was going to be one of those days. They were charging us nine pounds to stand on a terrace which was both crumbling and roof-less. (that's 'roof-less' as opposed to 'ruthless', which was an apt description of Sunderland's pricing policy that day), with the wind and rain blowing into our faces. That the turnstile operators managed to take our money whilst at the same time keeping a straight face, was truly amazing.

Underneath our stand before the game, large groups of Clarets huddled together for warmth. Given the inclement conditions, none of us fancied taking up our stations on the ground until we felt it absolutely necessary, ie two minutes to three.

Then suddenly and without warning, the DJ began playing Steel Band music; and not just one song, but a whole LP's worth. Memories of Kenilworth Road and 'Bring Me Sunshine' flooded my mind. Were they trying to out-weird Luton? There was something deliciously incongruous about hearing sunny, Jamaican calypso rhythms in a city whose average annual rainfall was probably on a par with that of an Amazonian rain forest.

After three or four tunes, most notably a pertinent re-working of 'Listen to the Rhythm of the Falling Rain', we decided that we could no longer stand this particularly surreal style of aural bombardment, and with a good twenty minutes to kick-off, decided instead to brave the elements and venture forth onto the terraces.

My first glimpse of Roker Park through a thin grey mist, left me feeling slightly disappointed. This was partially my own fault. For some reason I'd expected a field of dreams, a stadium fit for kings (despite the best efforts of a Geordie friend to convince me otherwise). What I actually saw put me very much in mind of Ayresome Park, just down the road. Neither of them were particularly bad grounds, they simply fell some way short of what I had envisaged.

Other than the stand to our right, the ground seemed irretrievably lost in a mid-seventies time-warp. I was half-expecting the strains of Slade and T Rex to explode from the Tannoy, but they didn't manifest themselves.

Neither did the much-lauded Roker roar. Maybe it was something to do with the wind conditions, or the place in which I was standing, but rarely did I hear anything approaching a mumble throughout the game, never mind anything so fear-inducing as a roar.

Maybe they were jaded. It was understandable. With Newcastle playing like world-beaters and Middlesborough looking fair set for promotion, Sunderland's status as the 'forgotten' club of the North-East, coupled with an impending season of mid-table obscurity, couldn't have done much for the morale of the Rokerites.

With fifteen minutes to the start, the teams were announced. It took just four, small words to ruin the afternoon for many. 'Number seven,' – pause for effect – 'Alan Harper.' Some closed their eyes and sighed. Others put their heads in their hands. Most just swore; lots. 'Mooncat', a nickname given to him by Everton supporters during his time at Goodison, was not the most loved player ever to have donned the famous claret and blue shirt. That much was obvious from the reaction he had received during previous matches.

What was different about the Sunderland game, was that it marked a new nadir in Harper's popularity on the terraces. Although not yet as universally loathed as Gerry 'Master of Incompetence' Gow ever was, huge chunks of the travelling support, certainly where I stood, were quite clearly unimpressed with what he had to offer, and were not slow in letting him know.

The method that lay in the madness of playing Harper seemed sound enough. Mullen wanted him to occupy a holding role, somewhere between defence and midfield. The idea seemed to be that Harper should fill gaps: either in the back four when Davis or Vinnicombe ventured forward, or in the middle of the park, when one of the midfielders pushed up into attack.

67

But however good the idea might have seemed in theory, the fact was that it had rarely come off in practice. Never had this been more obvious than at Roker Park.

Straight from the kick-off, it was clear that the gods had chosen to visit a thunderbolt on Alan that day. With his first touch he gave the ball away, resulting in a two-minute spell of pressure, from which Martin Smith almost headed Sunderland in front. 'BLOODY HELL, HARPER!', came the cry from a rotund gentleman just in front of me, who was not at all impressed with Alan's early touch. It was a comment aired with alarming frequency throughout the game; and not just by him.

But the unhappy knack he had of gifting the ball to the opposition was not the only act of footballing impropriety he committed that incited the Turf Moor faithful to threaten acts of violence upon his person.

For example, Mooncat was not possessed of much speed of thought. Time and again he would destroy a promising move, by putting his foot on the ball and 'having a look' around. (I swear I could hear the rusty cogs of his mind turning round and round and round and round and . . .) Sometimes, this was no bad thing; but generally speaking, when you are crowded out by three players, and your only option is an easy pass to a team-mate who is yelling for the ball and haring down your right-hand side into acres of space, then unless you are a player of great genius, which unfortunately for Alan he fell some way short of, then *that* is the ball you play, without hesitation.

Mooncat, however, weighed up *every* option, two, often three times, before deciding to either play the ball, in which instance it was invariably three to five seconds too late, or relinquish possession in some embarrassingly simple fashion. Alan Harper was perhaps the only footballer on the face of the planet who was able to transform a two yard square ball into a philosophical crisis.

For seventy of the ninety minutes I looked on in bewilderment, as the malaise known as 'Harper's Disease' spread through the side. A general sloppiness was apparent in the performance, as I watched us mis-pass, mis-time and mis-hit our way through the majority of the match.

With twenty minutes remaining, the introduction of Heath for Robinson and Gayle for Philliskirk, who had played with all the enthusiasm and ability of a three day old corpse, added a bit of life to the proceedings. Indeed, the period of pressure we had in the last ten minutes would have yielded a goal for many teams.

Not so for Burnley however, who seemed to be sticking by the new club motto, 'Thou shalt not score from open play'. Inchy and Parky both had efforts which went narrowly wide, and Big Bad John might have had more joy, had he aimed his shot in the direction of goal, instead of at the legs of a Sunderland defender standing only a yard in front of him.

Sporadic applause in the Burnley end and a mixture of boos and jeers from the home fans greeted Mr. Breen's final whistle. If you wanted to look at things in a positive light, we'd gone to Sunderland, grabbed a point and not conceded a goal.

Being a naturally miserable sod however, (a condition for which I held Burnley Football Club and the twenty years I had spent watching them, at least sixty per cent responsible), I found myself unable to get worked up over what I had considered to be a stale and insipid contest.

There was one winner that day: me. On the coach journey up to the North-East, I succeeded in buying the winning ticket in the raffle. The prize was a Supporters Club sweatshirt. Its colour? You might have guessed . . . predominantly grey.

Everton's slump continues, as they lose 2-0 to Coventry.

Keith Burkinshaw is sacked as manager of West Bromwich Albion, as they languish at the foot of the table. John Trewick is placed in temporary charge.

Sheffield Wednesday's Des Walker is reported to the FA for violent conduct, for butting Ipswich's Simon Milton, moments after the final whistle.

Manchester United top the Champions' League, despite being held 2-2 at Old Trafford by Barcelona.

Rumours circulate that Rod Stewart is to take over ailing Leyton Orient.

Saturday 22/10/94
The Valley

CHARLTON ATHLETIC 1-2 BURNLEY *(Whyte 81)*
(Davis 52, Robinson 61)
League position before and after match: 22nd . . . 21st.

Attendance: 9,436

BURNLEY: Beresford, Parkinson, Vinnicombe, Davis, Winstanley, Randall, Harper, Hoyland, Deary, Robinson, Eyres.
Subs (not used): Heath, Philliskirk, Russell.

CHARLTON ATHLETIC: Petterson, Brown, Sturgess, Jones, Chapple, Balmer, Bowyer *(McGleish 71)*, Grant, Walsh, Whyte, Robson.
Subs (not used): McLeary, Ammann.

Referee: M. Bailey

Yellow Cards: Brown, Balmer, Sturgess (Charlton Athletic)
                  Hoyland (Burnley)

Red Card: Hoyland (Burnley)

'I'm sorry about the plastic glasses, love', said the cockney landlady, shrugging apologetically as she handed me two pints of bitter. 'The police have told us not to let you lot have real glasses.'

By 'you lot', she was of course referring to football fans, who as everybody knows should not, repeat *not*, be entrusted with sharp objects, or indeed anything that could be used as a potential weapon to maim or disfigure. And really, who could blame the police for adopting this attitude? After all, it's a well-known fact that at least ninety-five per cent of all football supporters like nothing better than to kick seven bells out of each other, prior to the match.

As Chris and myself sat chatting and drinking with a couple of Charlton fans, it was obvious that *really*, we were itching to leap

70

over the table and grind the jagged edges of broken pint glasses into each other's faces. We couldn't possibly have been acting as normal people, talking about how our respective teams had been playing and how the game might go that afternoon. Football fans don't behave like that, do they? Just ask Charlton police.

Anyway, over-the-top policing policies aside, we bade farewell to our red-and-white-clad drinking partners and set off to the Valley, buoyed up with the kind of ridiculous pre-match confidence that is usually engendered by the consumption of alcohol half an hour prior to kick-off.

And believe me, we needed confidence, whatever its source. The previous season they'd hammered us 3-0 in the FA Cup and before our visit this term, the Reds had lost just once at home and were the division's joint leading scorers.

Having successfully negotiated the labyrinthine complexity of the sidestreets which led to the Valley and survived as intensive a body-search as one can undergo whilst fully clothed from a far too over-enthusiastic steward, we took our seats behind the goal in the South Stand.

The sun and the rain, who had spent the past couple of hours slugging it out for meteorological supremacy, called off their duel and produced not one, but two rainbows over the Valley as the teams took to the field of play, having emerged from a highly unlikely Portakabin.

Equally unlikely was the fact that Inchy was on the bench again and Mooncat, despite his execrable performance at Sunderland seven days previously, had somehow managed to cling on to a first team place.

We started sprightly, with Eyres and Robinson (who Andy believed suggested a plumper, quiffless version of Freddie Starr) making inroads behind their back four. In fact, after six minutes, Eyresie had the ball in the back of the net. 'Yes!' I shouted, bouncing up and down ecstatically, 'Get in!'

'He's not given it', said a woman next to me. 'Yeah, superb wasn't it?' I yelled, the inane grin on my face testimony to the fact that I had neither taken in what she had just told me, nor seen the linesman's flag raised on the far side. Once I realised he'd disallowed it, I stuffed my hands deep into my coat pockets and bit my lip, as thousands of Charlton fans laughed at us and gave us the wanker sign.

'It's OK' I thought, 'We're on top here. We're bound to get one in a minute.' The alcohol was obviously still swilling around in my system.

Five minutes later, Charlton were all over us, particularly down our right-hand side, where Mark Robson was tying Parky's lovely legs in the most unseemly knots. As our number two lay on the ground untangling his limbs, Robson crossed to Whyte who, instead of scoring, snatched at the opportunity, cracking it against the post. I breathed out again.

Burnley fought back, and within five minutes a hard low corner from Deary pinballed around in their six-yard box, before being scrambled over the line. Once again I was in vertical-take off mode, punching the air and screaming as Eyres ran towards us, kissing his shirt in an attempt to dispel all the midweek rumours that he wanted to leave Burnley.

'Sod off!', spat someone behind me. I didn't agree. I thought it was a great goal and carried on celebrating. Then, looking to my right, I realised why the voice behind me was so full of venom. Once again, the linesman's red flag fluttered in the light mid-afternoon breeze and the ref was indicating a free-kick on their six-yard line. Which was the cue for yet further laughter and wanker signals from three sides of the ground.

'It's that bastard that tried to send McMinn off at Millwall!' yelled the woman next to me. A quick glance at the programme confirmed that Mr Bailey had indeed made the short journey across from the New Den to have a second attempt at scuppering Burnley's hopes of surviving in this division. He was doing fine so far.

Undeterred, we pressed forward. Parky and Robinson fired wide, a Davis free-kick was deflected for a corner and a twenty-yarder from Vinnicombe grazed the top of the crossbar. It was fair to say that Charlton were more than a little worried.

A couple of minutes before the break, Eyres was sent sprawling on the edge of their area. Davis thundered the resultant free-kick goalwards and Petterson being only human, was unable to hold the ball. Robinson was quickest to react, and slid the ball over the line. One-nil. At last we'd scored. He couldn't disallow this one, because there was bugger all wrong with it! But he did. The contest, and a particularly one-sided one at that, was now descending into the realm of sheer pantomime.

The Charlton fans, who must have been unable to believe their luck, provided us with yet more raucous laughter and a fresh batch of wanker signs (how original), accompanied this time by a jaunty rendering of 'You're going down with the Millwall!' Thanks, ref.

Jimmy was clearly unimpressed with the man in black. No sooner had the half-time whistle been blown, than he was off his bench and over to him, as though he'd been fired from a cannon. One particularly brave steward stopped a potential fist-fight by diving between the two, as opinions were exchanged on the veracity of Mr Bailey's decisions. I don't know exactly what was said, but I'm sure you can have a stab. (Which I feel sure Mullen would have done, given half the chance and a sharp implement.)

Off for a half-time wander, I chanced to bump into a friend I hadn't seen for some time. 'We've lost this, you know,' he said, doing nothing to raise my spirits. 'Three goals disallowed. *Three* bloody goals. There's nowt for us here.' How could I argue?

'Have you seen who's over there?,' asked Chris as I retook my seat for the second half. Fifteen feet in front of me and to my left, sat Neil Kinnock. Flanked by Alistair 'I support Burnley but I don't like to talk about it' Campbell, (Tony Blair's personal secretary), the ex-Labour leader was engaged in an extended bout of hand-shaking, with roughly half the South Stand.

The sighting of the most famous living Welshman was undoubtedly a good thing. Having brought us good luck with his attendance in the Wembley play-off Final, he was welcome at any Burnley fixture, particularly one where an eccentric referee was officiating.

The celebrity sighting proved a turning point in our fortunes. Seven minutes into the second half, and an unmarked Davis got on the end of a Deary corner, side-footing us into the lead. This time, not even Mr Bailey could find fault with the goal, and began his run back to the half-way line.

It was perhaps the most satisfying goal we had scored so far that season. As the South Stand rejoiced, (good style), the home fans went remarkably quiet. No guffaws of laughter, no dubious hand gestures and definitely no singing.

Ten minutes on, and things got even better. From just inside his own half, Davis knocked a speculative ball towards Charlton's penalty area. Liam Robinson, accompanied by Phil Chapple,

73

gave chase and with the keeper standing on his six yard line rather than coming to claim a ball that should have been his, Robinson stuck out a foot and just got enough on it to poke it home.

'Down with the Millwall! You're going down with the Millwall!' sang the thousand-strong claret choir. This was the business. Two-nil up, away from home, playing like champions, (playing so well in fact that even Harper looked the part), *and* singing their own songs back at them.

Although Robinson's strike had sent us into the throes of ecstasy, it had the unpleasant side-effect of stinging the home side into life. Robson started picking on Parky again, Whyte was just beaten to a loose ball in our six-yard box by Winstanley, and Vinnicombe had to produce a top-drawer tackle to get in the way of Jones and a certain goal.

With ten minutes remaining, the ball broke kindly for Whyte, who advanced into the area and drilled his effort into the bottom corner.

As the ball hit the back of the net, I got that horrible sinking feeling in the pit of my stomach. Two-one up, away from home, Charlton piling on the pressure and a good ten minutes left. Any feeling of smugness had just gone out of the window. Now, it was purely and simply about hanging on.

Hard, low crosses fizzed across our goalmouth, (hanging on), Deary cleared a Whyte volley off the line, (still hanging on) and Marlon had to save twice at the feet of Charlton forwards to deny them an equaliser (*still* hanging on). This was agonising.

Two minutes into injury time, and Mr Bailey started playing silly buggers again. This time Jamie Hoyland was sent off . . . for saying the word, 'that'. Apparently the ref had mis-heard, thinking Hoyland had sworn at him, using an expletive that rhymed with 'that', but is more often used to describe a referee who makes crackpot decisions. I very much doubt wether he could have mis-heard the chant directed towards him from the South Stand that greeted the on-loan star's dismissal.

The cheers that coincided with the final whistle owed as much to relief as they did to joy. It was a good job we weren't playing until the following Saturday. My nerves, which at that point were thoroughly shredded, simply couldn't have coped with a midweek fixture.

Ambling back to the coach, it struck me that the contrast in the season's form to date, and that of the previous season, could hardly have been starker. The entire 93/94 campaign had seen us win only four games away from home, yet lose just twice at Turf Moor. Out of seven away games played in the league in 94/95, we already boasted superb victories at Millwall, Luton and now Charlton. It seemed not a little perverse then, that we had yet to record a home win.

The following Saturday would see Notts County visit the Turf. Lying at the foot of the table, with just one win all season and possessed of the leakiest defence in the division, we would surely never have a better opportunity to rectify the situation.

Blackburn Rovers lose 4-2 to Manchester United at Ewood Park. Many believe the turning point to have been a dubious penalty award in United's favour, when Blackburn were leading 1-0. As a consequence, Henning Berg, who conceded the penalty, is sent off. Rovers' boss Kenny Dalglish comments, 'You prefer to lose because of the ability of your opponents, not the inability of the referee.'

Manchester City scores five to Tottenham's two, in one of the Premiership's games of the season.

Everton lose *again*, 1-0 to Crystal Palace.

The third round of the Coca-Cola Cup produces just one shock: Notts County 3-0 Tottenham. The pressure on Ardiles mounts.

Gillingham are fighting for survival. The club, losing £250,000 a year, is put up for sale at around £200,000. Chairman Bernard Baker offers to stump up £1 million to help save them.

Saturday 29/10/94
Turf Moor

BURNLEY 2-1 NOTTS COUNTY (*Eyres 7* [pen.], *Hoyland 52*)
(*Davis 51* [og])
League position before and after match: 21st . . . 18th.

Attendance: 12,976

BURNLEY: Beresford, Parkinson, Vinnicombe, Davis, Winstanley, Randall (*Heath 82*), Harper, Hoyland, Deary, Robinson, Eyres.
Subs (not used): Philliskirk, Russell.

NOTTS COUNTY: Reece, Gallagher, Walker, Turner, Yates, Daniel, Devlin, Butler, Legg (*Williams 74*), McSwegan, Agana.
Subs (not used): Murphy, Cherry.

Referee: J.W. Lloyd

Yellow Cards: None

Red Cards: None

And so it came to pass, that after seven attempts, we eventually managed to take maximum points from a home game. There was to be no late equaliser for the opposition, no addition to the 'Calamity in Claret' collection and no bad sportsmanship from Scottish internationals.

The first win at Turf Moor for six months, was not however, the incandescent display of white-hot, footballing brilliance that I had hoped it might be. 'It was a bit boring at times. I kept looking around to see if I recognised anybody,' said somebody at work the following Monday who had made the pilgrimage to the hallowed Turf for the first time.

I knew how she felt. This was a game where the Clarets huffed and puffed, rather than dazzled and thrilled. For the last half-hour in particular, I wished the ref had had a watch which could have turned minutes into seconds.

But to be honest, it wasn't entirely unexpected. With Notts County looking for a win to lift them off the bottom of the table and ourselves desperate for a first home victory of the season, it was, in the words of many a football pundit, 'never going to be a classic'; and it wasn't.

Other than scoring the winner, the hitherto excellent Jamie Hoyland was invisible, Winstanley's already pitiful distribution, in stark contrast to his excellent defensive play, took another step down the road signposted, 'irredeemable', Eyresie had the post to thank for his penalty going in, and at times Marlon's coronary-inducing antics suggested that beneath that usually cool goal-keeping exterior lay a burning desire to become a circus clown.

That afternoon, Marlon decided he fancied being a left back, as he deserted his goal and attempted to 'skin' County's speedy winger, Tony Agana, a good ten yards outside his area. (An episode which saw Marlon inevitably lose the ball and very nearly gift the visitors an opener.)

No, the best way, the only way to look at that game, was as three points gained, three points that lifted us out of the bottom four, three points that made our survival in this division (undoubtedly our priority) that much more likely.

Actually, that's wrong. There was another way of looking at that game and others like it, and that was to view them as small investments. In order to experience the massive adrenalin rush induced by an away victory, and certainly if you wish to have that buzz amplified, it is necessary to attend those other fixtures, where you wonder if there isn't something far less painful to do on a Saturday afternoon.

For every breathtaking victory at Luton, Millwall or Charlton, the football fan has to endure the mind-numbing tedium of a 0-0 draw at Sunderland, the crushing mediocrity of a 1-0 home defeat by Barnsley, and the utter humiliation of a 3-0 panning away at Oldham. In other words you have to put in to get out. And so having put in plenty that afternoon, I looked forward to a substantial return on my investments, in the next home game against Watford, that coming Tuesday evening.

Twelve league games have now elapsed without Everton taking a single point.

The BBC screen a documentary which questions the legitimacy of certain of Terry Venables' business deals.

Four days after Newcastle knock a relatively inexperienced Manchester United team out of the Coca-Cola Cup, the Reds exact revenge with a 2-0 league victory.

Tuesday 1/11/94
Turf Moor

BURNLEY 1-1 WATFORD (*Eyres 72* [pen.]) (*Nogan 39*)
League position before and after game: 18th . . . 17th

Attendance: 11,739

BURNLEY: Beresford, Parkinson, Vinnicombe, Davis, Winstanley, Randall, Harper (*Heath 70*), Hoyland, Deary (*Philliskirk 60*), Robinson, Eyres.
Sub (not used): Russell.

WATFORD: Miller, Lavin, Johnson, Holdsworth, Millen, Ramage, Hessenthaler, Nogan (*Beadle 84*), Moralee, Porter, Mooney (*Bazeley 79*).
Sub (not used): Digweed.

Referee: J. Winter

Yellow Cards: Eyres (Burnley)
　　　　　　　Johnson (Watford)

Red Cards:　None

The hoped-for return on my investments did not materialise during the course of this match. Indeed, this was by quite some margin, the most atrocious display of 'football' I had borne witness to in a long time. I use inverted commas, simply because I cannot bring myself to employ such a wonderful word to describe the on-the-field debacle that occurred that evening.

The first indications that the contest would be found wanting in terms of entertainment came with the announcement of the teams. Much to my chagrin, neither Perry Digweed nor the equally amusingly-monikered Perry Suckling (not so much names, as good hands at scrabble), had made the first eleven. In a game where Mooncat was roundly, richly and deservedly booed from the field, after seventy minutes of a performance so abysmal it could not be described using existing vocabulary, it was the kind of game where a five yard pass that reached its intended target was regarded as being something quite special.

It was then little wonder, that the superlative and wholly professional performance put in by Steve Davis that evening, elevated him some way above the rest of the stragglers assembled on the pitch. What *was* amazing, was that he was producing this kind of classy display game in, game out.

With Adrian Heath getting fewer and fewer starts, the Hexham-born Davis was putting in a serious challenge for the mantle of 'Official Club God'. I remained convinced that his own goal against Notts County was merely an attempt to persuade all those watching that he was only human after all. I begged to differ.

Signed for what now seemed a paltry £60,000 from Southampton in 1991, the Burnley number four had been a highly influential member of the squad in our rise from the old Fourth Division. The 94/95 season had seen Davis given the additional responsibility of the captain's armband, and far from being a burden, it had spurred him on into playing the best football of his career.

If you were looking to construct the perfect centre-back, he was possessed of many of the qualities you would look for. A cool head, strong in the tackle, great distribution – many a diagonal, pin-point, cross-field pass to Eyres had taken my breath away – a desire to play the ball out of defence, (not just an ability, a *desire*; there's a world of difference), and a happy knack of chipping in with some vital goals – seven in the 93/94 season, and three already in the 94/95 campaign – were all evident in his game.

It seemed only a matter of time before a Premiership club, many of whom had had Davis watched, would come and steal him away. There was no doubt whatsoever in the minds of anybody who had seen him perform that our skipper would be capable of coping with life at the very top. In fact, with every passing game, the £2,000,000 price tag slapped on Davis by Jimmy to ward off Chelsea seemed less and less ridiculous.

But by far the most thrilling (and I choose that word very carefully) aspect of Davis' game was his ability to scare the pants off the opposition, simply by running at them. Picking the ball up on the edge of his area and seeing no options open to him, Davis would run at players and beat them with the kind of skill and ease usually associated with silky wingers.

The fact that these runs were fairly infrequent was on the one hand disappointing. There again, it was their very infrequency which added a certain piquancy to those occasions when they did occur.

A classic example of this is to be found on the video of our play-off triumph at Wembley. With ten minutes left, our hero picks up the ball deep inside his own half. He skips over one challenge, skips over a second, cuts inside a third and unfortunately screws his shot way wide. Watching it in ultra-slow-motion, I personally and genuinely believe it is probably as graceful as anything Rudolf Nureyev ever achieved, and roughly one million times more exciting.

It is forever to the cameraman's credit that he manages to capture all this in close-up, as it must rank as one of the *truly* seminal moments I have experienced in twenty years of watching Burnley.

Ladies and gentlemen, boys and girls; I give you a captain, a hero, a God. I give you Steve Davis.

Both Newcastle United and Aston Villa are knocked out of the UEFA Cup on away goals, by Athletic Bilbao and Trabzonspor respectively.

Brighter news at Goodison, where Everton record their first win of the season, 1-0 over West Ham.

Gary Lineker announces his retirement from football.

Ossie Ardiles is sacked as Spurs' manager. 'At the end of the day,' he says, 'I did it my way.'

Confusion at QPR, as Gerry Francis walks out after the board hold talks behind his back with Rodney Marsh.

Manchester United are on the receiving end of a 4-0 hammering by Barcelona, as 115,000 look on in the Nou Camp.

David Pleat is approached by Spurs, as a replacement for Ardiles.

Both Chelsea and Arsenal progress into the next round of the Cup-Winners Cup, with victories over Austria Vienna and Brondby.

Saturday 5/11/94
Elm Park

READING 0-0 BURNLEY
League position before and after match: 17th . . . 21st

Attendance: 8,115

BURNLEY: Beresford, Parkinson, Vinnicombe (*Francis 80*), Davis, Winstanley, Randall, Harper, Heath, Deary, Robinson (*Gayle 65*), Eyres.
Sub (not used): Russell.

READING: Hislop, Bernal, Kerr, Wdowczyk (*McPherson 35*), Hopkins, Parkinson, Gilkes, Gooding, Taylor, Jones, Osborne.
Subs (not used): Carey, Sheppard.

Referee: P. Foakes

Yellow Cards: Parkinson, Bernal (Reading)

Red Card: Bernal (Reading)

And so to Reading, a club whose crest, based loosely on the BBC Test Transmission Card except not *nearly* as interesting, could lay a very strong claim to be the naffest in all the Football League.

Arriving outside the ground at half-past-one, our first priority was to find a pub. This, gentle reader, should not be perceived as myself attempting to establish some kind of 'laddish' scenario; it was less the desire for a drink, and more the fact that alcohol had played a major role in our three victories away from Turf Moor that season, that drove us on in our search for liquor.

A pre-match tipple at Luton, a half-time pint at Millwall and a visit to The McDonnells Arms in Charlton, had secured an impressive nine-point haul. And as football fans like myself are prone to clinging onto these superstitions like some sort of security blanket, it was imperative that a public house was sought out within the hour.

However, our quest was in vain. It seemed that every pub within a two mile radius of the ground had either locked its doors for the afternoon, or wasn't too keen on being invaded by large platoons of the 1,500-strong claret and blue army. They made sure we got the message, by employing doormen of unlikely proportions and even more unlikely ugliness.

Desperation forced us to take refuge in a can of cheap beer-flavoured water, purchased from a local off-licence. Skulking around the rainy back streets of Reading, (in order to avoid the police), furtively sipping from our cans, we felt a vague sense of guilt; it was as though we were back at school, hiding behind the Art Block and hoping that our form tutor wouldn't catch us in possession of a can of Shandy Bass.

With the sky growing greyer and the rain becoming more intense by the minute, we opted for the covered seats, (reasonably priced at £9.00), rather than risk a Sunderlandesque dowsing by standing on the open end behind the goal.

Sitting in the back row, ('No kissing', the turnstile operator had grinningly advised us), we had a splendid view . . . apart from a bloody huge pillar which cut a five yard swathe from our line of vision. For the benefit of those who watch their football on television, five yards cut from your line of vision may not sound like a lot, but the effect is somewhat akin to listening to your favourite record, with a vital five seconds randomly removed.

As the players warmed up, Inchy came over to sign autographs for the fans. I yelled down and asked him if he would be playing. 'Yeah,' came his reply, coupled with a thumbs-up gesture and a grin. Well, it isn't like you get to chat with a bona fide God every day of the week, is it?

Reading was the first time we'd come across one of the two teams that had been promoted with us the previous season, the other being Port Vale. Having gone up as Champions, they had found their feet considerably quicker than the Clarets. Fourth in the league and having conceded a miserly two goals at home prior to our visit, we would have been quite happy with a point that afternoon.

After a shaky start, which saw Reading go close on a couple of occasions, (the pick of which was a wildly hilarious incident, wherein Scott Taylor received the ball in the area and raised his arms aloft in celebration of his 'goal', shortly before horrendously scything it over the bar), we began to impose ourselves on the game. Inchy had a header cleared off the line, Robinson's turn and shot went just wide, and Harper – who beggared belief by not putting a foot wrong all game – forced Hislop into a good save, with a volley from the edge of the area.

Half-time brought a sighting of David Armstrong, ex-Southampton star, who had become Reading's 'Football in the Community' Officer', in one of the executive boxes just behind our seats. One of these boxes contained a television set, on which flashed the half-time scores. As the boxes were situated above head height, the only way we could actually see the telly was by bouncing up and down.

Thus, half-time became a feast of entertainment, as Steve pogoed up and down to relay the vital information, to whoever was prepared to listen. 'Wolves nil, Luton two.' BOING! 'Swindon one, Millwall nil.' BOING! 'Watford one, West Brom nil.' BOING! Unfortunately, Steve's Jack-in-the-box impersonation meant that his ankle joints had completely given out by the time the BBC got around to putting up the Division Three half-times. Consequently we never got to know if Preston were adding to their run of seven consecutive defeats.

The interval also brought with it that most cruel of ritual humiliations that takes place at football grounds the length and breadth of Britain every Saturday. I am, of course, referring to the exercise in public embarrassment, more commonly known as the kids' penalty competition. These events are the product of a particularly twisted mind.

My heart goes out in particular to those unfortunates cast in the role of goalkeeper. The poor kid, having been lured to the ground on the pretext that they will be treading the same hallowed turf as their heroes, is, at the towering height of three feet nothing, asked to defend a target roughly eight feet by twenty four, as another group of six-year-olds smash penalty after penalty past him, quite literally right, left, and centre. When you bear in mind that this torturous session takes place in front of friends, family and thousands of strangers, the description 'cruel' smacks of chronic understatement.

In a second half in which Burnley might have laid claim to all three points, had both Deary and Eyres not panicked at the crucial moment and blasted their respective one-on-one chances straight at Hislop, one event overshadowed all others.

With eleven minutes remaining, Marlon punted his kick out towards the halfway line on the left wing. As the ball dropped, Vinnicombe kept his eye on it, and appeared to be blissfully unaware of Andy Bernal, who was haring towards him like a greyhound on speed. Both players jumped.

From hereon in, there were two versions of what led to Vinnicombe's jaw being broken in three places and the Reading number two's dismissal. Bernal, Reading manager Mark McGhee and some sections of the press claimed that the aerial collision between the two was a total accident, that it was Bernal's momentum rather than malice which accounted for Vinnicombe's grisly injury.

However, there were those who maintained that the scenario had a decidedly more sinister air to it. Personally, I found it impossible to tell whether or not there was any malicious intent. As I saw it, both players went up; Vinnicombe from more or less directly beneath the ball, Bernal from a good six or seven yards away.

As the two met in mid-air, I distinctly remember hearing a faint, yet truly sickening, cracking sound, followed by the altogether more solid 'thud', of Vinnicombe hitting the deck. It was clear that something was horribly wrong. He wasn't moving.

Then all hell broke loose. All around me, Burnley fans were up in arms, shouting the odds, baying for blood and paying little heed to the 'No Swearing' notices displayed around the ground. Mullen was on the pitch, leaning over Vinnicombe and barking out instructions to Eyres. Davis was pushing Winstanley and Parkinson away, as they threatened to turn vigilante. The ref was calling Bernal over. Our physio was on. Bernal was off. Vinnicombe would be out for four months.

It was a tragic way for our left back to leave the field. An unsung hero, the £200,000 buy from Rangers had proved value for money. Determined in the tackle, quick on the overlap and able to deliver a good cross, he would be very badly missed.

The game fizzled out after that, other than a pitch invasion by two Reading fans who were obviously so incensed by the ref's decision, that they made it clear to Mr Foakes that he would be more than welcome atop their bonfire that evening. The stewards dragged them away, the ref blew the whistle, and we all went home.

Travelling back that evening, it was difficult to know how to feel. On the plus side, we'd gone to Reading and got a good point, we might even have grabbed three. Having been twice outclassed by the Royals the previous season, this was a good indication of the progress we had made. On top of that, we were seven league games unbeaten, not having lost since back in September at West Brom, and defensively we were looking pretty solid.

On the other hand, we'd only won two of those seven games, scored just eight goals, and remained fourth bottom. And I for one believed our defence would seem a lot shakier without our first choice left back.

Doug Ellis, Aston Villa's chairman, estimates the club's exit from European competition will cost them £1 million. Shortly after this, he dismisses Ron Atkinson.

David Pleat turns down the chance to manage Spurs.

Mike Walker is dismissed by Everton.

Southend United chairman, Vic Jobson, voices concern about the possible formation of a Premiership Second

Division. The FA deny that there is any truth in the rumours.

Allegations are made against Bruce Grobbelaar that he took money to throw matches from a Far East gambling syndicate. Grobbelaar denies the charges.

Joe Royle is appointed manager of Everton.

Humiliation for Manchester City, as a Cantona-inspired Manchester United destroy them 5-0.

Saturday 12/11/94
Turf Moor

FA CUP SPONSORED BY LITTLEWOODS POOLS. FIRST ROUND.

BURNLEY 2-1 SHREWSBURY TOWN *(Heath 28, Deary 46)* *(Spink 36)*

Attendance: 9,269

BURNLEY: Beresford, Parkinson, Dowell, Davis, Winstanley, Randall, Harper, Heath, Deary, Robinson *(Francis 72)*, Eyres. Subs (not used): Gayle, Russell.

SHREWSBURY TOWN: Edwards, Hockaday, Withe, Taylor, Williams, Patterson, Wooods, Hughes, Spink, Summerfield, Stevens. Subs (not used): Clarke, Seabury, Evans.

Referee: J. Worrall

Yellow Cards: None

Red Cards: None

At least partially prompted by England's heartbreaking failure to qualify for USA '94, (and thereby deprived of the massive revenue such qualification would have generated), the FA had finally, pathetically, inevitably succumbed and sold off the jewel in English football's crown. 'The FA Cup in Association with Littlewoods.' Not very catchy, is it? Not easy to swallow, either. In fact, I found the more I said it, the more it stuck in my throat. It wasn't just the fact that they'd sold the damn thing. What was of equal concern, was who they'd sold it to, and at what price.

The FA could hardly have picked a more parasitic financial backer. Writing in 'When Saturday Comes', Ed Horton made the following observation about Graham Kelly and Co's choice of sponsor. 'No company in history can have made more money out of football than Littlewoods have done. They have made the most enormous profits out of football – not by organising a single match for the entertainment of the public, but by relieving the public of their money for the benefit of Littlewoods Pools.' [4] In other words, the sponsors were getting maximum returns from minimum investments.

No matter how desperately the suits at Lancaster Gate dressed things up and tried to justify their decision, there was no escaping the fact. The game's domestic governing body had committed a shocking and extraordinarily cheap act of prostitution. That the FA obviously didn't think the average football fan capable of seeing through this, only served to make them look even more stupid than many already believed them to be.

Littlewoods didn't give a damn about the FA Cup, (or at least, not in the same way as a football supporter did). What they *did* give a damn about was raising their public profile. The best way to do this was through advertising, and what better vehicle for advertising was there, than the most famous, prestigious domestic Cup competition in the world? Think FA Cup and you think: romance, prestige, tradition, drama, glamour, high standards, winner etc. It is small wonder that Littlewoods wished to project a public image, which associated them with such qualities.

You might say it was an expensive advert at around £15,000,000, but was it really? I don't think so. For a start, they would never have invested the money in the first place, if they thought there was even the faintest chance of it being a flop. Aside from that, just think of the size of audience they reached.

The First Round saw somewhere in the region of thirty-five ties played. You can bet your life Littlewoods had at least three advertising hoardings at every one of those grounds. Every match programme sold on the afternoon of the first round proper, (not to mention the midweek replays), bore their logo. Every time the results were read out on local and national radio and television, (and indeed every time the competition was mentioned), the sponsor would receive a name check. And don't forget, this lasted from early November when the draw was made, right up to the Final in mid-May. So Littlewoods would receive national advertising, for the ridiculously small sum of £15,000,000. The duration of the sponsorship? Four years. Yet another winner from Lancaster Gate . . .

The game? Ah yes, the game. Thankfully, from Burnley's point of view, none of the particularly lame cliches which are religiously dragged out of the cupboard and dusted down on FA Cup First Round day, were applicable. No form books were seen flying from windows, Shrewsbury didn't rise to the occasion and consequently there was no David and Goliath-style giant-killing act.

Which is something that I for one was particularly relieved about. Being one of only two First Division sides to have to take part at this stage of the competition, we were, albeit temporarily, giants. Call me a cynic if you will, but I am not a believer in all this 'romance of the Cup' tosh. Like 'fairness', the concept of being given the runaround either by a side from a lower division, or an assembled group of estate agents, plumbers and garage mechanics, has limited appeal. It is only enjoyable when it is happening to some league side other than our own. Bearing that in mind, a large part of me was quite glad, when Bristol, Crewe and Birmingham thumped non-league opposition and a little saddened to see Cardiff and Brighton make an early exit, at the hands of part-timers.

We never looked like losing this one. Inchy, having been given a rare start, had an absolute blinder. Playing a more withdrawn role, just behind the front two, he produced his performance of the season to date, and along with John Deary, made sure we never lost control of the midfield.

It was in fact Heath who opened the scoring. Receiving the ball from Robinson just outside their box, Inchy *placed* (whereas lesser mortals may have elected to thump) the ball into the right-hand corner. The net billowed. The crowd roared. We were on our way.

Unlike myself, Marlon clearly *was* a sucker for the romance of the Cup and was well up for giving Shrewsbury a fair crack of the whip. So much so in fact, that he gifted them an equaliser. Having claimed a corner, Beresford somehow contrived to clatter into Parky and drop the ball at the feet of Dean Spink. Still laughing at this piece of unscriptable comedy, the Shrewsbury number nine lashed the ball into the top corner, as Burnley's answer to Laurel and Hardy lay poleaxed and shamefaced on the deck.

One-all at half-time was hardly the ideal score. Nevertheless, I steadfastly refused to panic, knowing deep down that there was no way we could lose to a side who boasted somebody named Hockaday in their first eleven, and who played their home fixtures at a place called Gay Meadow.

Andy visited us at half-time, and he wasn't happy. He'd been queuing for a pie when Inchy was giving his master-class in finishing and had missed the goal. He also expressed his disgust at the first-half performance of Adrian Randall, who had, in Andy's words, 'dug a bloody hole and hidden in it', for the preceding forty-five minutes.

I knew what he meant. In my opinion Randall, was vastly overrated; an unaffordable luxury. His workrate was exceedingly low, he lacked pace and invention, and worst of all, had a pair of sticky-out ears which knocked Mr Spock into a cocked hat, and no mistake. Given that the majority of games are won or lost in midfield, it was at best risky and at worst irresponsible, to include such a player in the side.

It was also worth remembering that just two months previously, Mullen had been so convinced of Randall's ability to cope with life in Division One, that he all but sold him to Cardiff. That Jimmy cajoled him into signing a two-year deal just one month later tended to suggest that either we had a schizophrenic in charge, or that one of the manager's hands wasn't entirely au fait with what the other one was doing.

In Adey's defence, it might have been argued that there were fewer exciting sights to be had at Turf Moor than Randall in full flight, running at defenders and causing havoc in the opposition box. The problem was, this happened with less frequency than a solar eclipse. Turning it on for twenty minutes every fifth game was simply not enough. However, to voice an opinion along these lines was as good as treason to an alarmingly high number of supporters who regarded Adey as the living definition of genius, or as I heard one fan say, 'the answer'. Personally, I felt that if Adrian Randall was the answer, then it must have been a bloody stupid question in the first place.

True to form, Randall gave yet another supreme exhibition of ball-watching, in a second half which began in fine style. John was still engrossed in his programme, when after just twenty-four seconds, Inchy skipped around three Shrewsbury players with almost obscene nonchalance and fed a perfect through ball to Deary. The sheer strength of the Burnley number nine carried him past two defenders, as he took aim and drilled a hard, low shot past Edwards in the visitors goal. That was it. There was no way they were coming back from that.

The rest of the match was a formality. Or at least it looked that way from where I stood. (However, there was one nervous moment, when Stevens was clumsily but clearly fouled by Winstanley on the edge of our area, only for Joe Worrall to wave play on.) Eyres twice hit the crossbar, Davis thundered a thirty-yarder straight at their keeper, and both Deary and Heath had chances to kill the game off. But intuition told me that we could miss all we wanted; Shrewsbury were going out. At ten to five we were through and through comfortably, without any assistance at all from Littlewoods.

QPR accept Gerry Francis' resignation, after board and manager fail to reach an agreement over his position at the club. Soon after, he is appointed boss at Spurs, and Ray Wilkins assumes Francis' post as QPR manager.

Dennis Wise appears in court, accused of damaging a London taxi.

FA Cup First Round day sees Brighton, Oxford and Cardiff lose out to non-league opposition, in the shape of Kingstonian, Marlow and Enfield.

A Mike Conroy goal gives Preston victory in their FA Cup First Round tie over local rivals Blackpool.

Russell Osman is dismissed as Bristol City manager.

The FA charge Bruce Grobbelaar with bringing the game into disrepute, and 'acceptance of consideration with a view to influencing the result of the match.'

Joe Jordan takes over the managerial hot-seat at Bristol City.
A David Platt goal gives England a 1-0 victory over Nigeria.

Graeme Sharp is appointed as Oldham's first new manager in twelve years, following Joe Royle's appointment as Everton boss.

Aston Villa show an interest in Brian Little as Ron Atkinson's successor; Leicester say they would want £1.5 million compensation.

Sunday 20/11/94
Turf Moor

BURNLEY 4-2 SHEFFIELD UNITED
(*Robinson 23, Hoyland 54, Gayle 71, Davis 78*)
(*Winstanley 45* [og], *Scott 84*)
League position before and after match: 21st . . . 15th

Attendance: 11,475

BURNLEY: Beresford, Parkinson, Dowell, Davis, Winstanley, Randall, Harper (*Gayle 65*), Heath, Hoyland, Robinson, Eyres. Subs (not used): Francis, Russell.

SHEFFIELD UNITED: Kelly, Gage, Nilson, Hartfield, Gayle, Marshall, Rogers, Veart (*Scott 69*), Starbuck, Flo (*Hodges 60*), Whitehouse.

Sub (not used): Mercer.

Referee: P. Vanes

Yellow Cards: Hodges (Sheffield United)

Red Cards: None

One of those days when life actually worked.

Nothing could have ruined that afternoon. Not the monsoon-like conditions we had to endure walking to the ground, not Sheffield's dull predictable style of play, not even the presence of the truly odious Elton Welsby in the ground, could take the shine off a game where everything finally clicked for the Clarets.

Perhaps the most thrilling aspect of the game, was that thousands of people were watching it live on the box, and were seeing US, seeing BURNLEY FC, playing the most vibrant, intoxicating football of our season to date. I imagined thousands of armchair football fans, who would have put the telly on simply because it was 'a game', sitting up and taking notice of the skills of Inchy, Big Bad John and Steve Davis and being highly impressed with what they saw.

As I took up my usual position on the Longside, I casually glanced to my left and was considerably more than alarmed to see that two large Portakabins had grown on top of the Bee Hole End since the Shrewsbury game. This, it transpired, was to house the commentary teams of both Yorkshire and Granada television for the afternoon. A vicious rumour was doing the rounds that our existing gantry would have sufficed, had it not been for the megalithic proportions of Mr Welsby's ego.

Having kept us waiting till five past three, Granada television and their various advertisers very kindly allowed us to kick off. The opening twenty minutes saw Sheffield United effectively disrupt any flowing moves we attempted to construct. However, sticking to our passing and moving game and refusing to fall into the obvious trap of punting the ball long, eventually paid dividends.

Receiving the ball in midfield, Inchy ghosted past one, left a second for dead, sold Brian Gayle such an audacious dummy that it might have been illegal, hit the bye-line and pulled back a superb cross for Robinson, who powered home a header from six yards. After a moment's hesitation as to whether or not the ball had crossed the line, Mr. Vanes pointed to the centre-circle, much to the joy of the home supporters.

Lou Macari and Jim Beglin, Granada's 'expert' summarisers, were not so sure however, believing Kelly had clawed it off the line. 'He's made a wrong decision. Unless there's something wrong with our eyes, Jim,'[5] whined Macari, in a tone so cocksure that it made it doubly funny when Granada's camera in the Bee Hole End goal showed beyond any doubt that the ball had travelled a good six inches over the line. 'Oh yes,' bleated Beglin pathetically when confronted with the video evidence, 'it probably was over.'[6] Probably? Yeah, sure – in the same way that you could 'probably' persuade someone who was dying of thirst to have a drink of water.

It was pretty much honours even for the remainder of the half. Eyres saw his exquisite eighteen yard chip force Kelly into a contender for 'Save of the Season', Robinson should at least have hit the target from ten yards out, instead of achieving the improbable feat of blasting the ball higher than his hair-line, and Parky's centre was inches away from connecting with Eyres' boot.

At the other end, United had pumped some dangerous-looking balls into our area, but Marlon, having learnt how to catch the ball cleanly since what had become known as 'The Shrewsbury Affair,' had little trouble dealing with them.

But then, in first half injury time, Dowell, who was in for the injured Vinnicombe and who had had an OK game up to that point, allowed Kevin Gage to fire in a hard, low cross. Poor Winstanley and his triangular boots had no chance as he made a lunge for the ball which had 'desperate' written all over it, and steered the ball home. 'He can't quite believe it!'[7] said commentator Rob Palmer of United's Kevin Gage. Neither could Marlon, who sat on the floor with his head in his hands . . . probably cursing Winstanley and his angular footwear.

Half-time saw Rob 'The Cat' McCaffrey, Granada's touchline reporter, in earnest discussion with Jimmy as to how Burnley might go about restoring their lead. 'I'm sure that if we continue to do the same in the second half,' announced Jim, fixing the touchline reporter with the steely gaze of the master tactician, 'we'll do the same.' [8] This was a blinding piece of insight and amply illustrated the genius that inhabited the mind of Jimmy Mullen . . .

Nine minutes into the second half, Randall swung in a corner which Davis knocked down. The ball fell to Jamie Hoyland, who volleyed it into the United net with such ferocity that I would have been only mildly surprised to have seen the ball tunnel its way through the Endsleigh Stand and out onto the car park at its rear. That one definitely crossed the line.

The following Monday, the 'Lancashire Evening Telegraph' published a fantastic picture of Hoyland, taken the instant after he had netted his goal. His face is the definition of ecstasy and you can see just what it meant to him to score against the club he had been with a month or so earlier. 'Thank you very much for Jamie Hoyland!' sang the Longside. Amen to that.

The sixty-fifth minute saw the introduction of one John Gayle to the proceedings, to rapturous applause. 'He looks like he'd give Lennox Lewis a fight,' [9] quipped the commentator. And therein lay a large part of Big Bad John's appeal.

Six foot four and built like a tank, (and a very hard-looking tank at that), the £75,000 signing from Coventry cut an intimidating figure. Every time he went up for a challenge, there was a delicious murmur of anticipation, as to what physical damage might be inflicted on anybody who dared to compete with him. The irony was that although he could undoubtedly mix it if needed, he wasn't essentially a dirty player and was more often fouled by opponents than vice versa.

It was, in a way, a shame that his physical presence overshadowed the more unsung side of his game. Apart from being someone who was never afraid to get into the thick of the action, he also possessed a subtle touch, often laying the ball off and making intelligent runs into the opposition's danger zones.

The cameras and the commentators clearly loved him, (particularly Lou Macari, who was rumoured to be about to put in an offer for the man he referred to as 'a pussycat', [10] a name which I would wager Macari never called Gayle to his face) and were eager to get his face on screen whenever possible.

They had all the more reason to love him, when he made it 3-1 to Burnley. Randall fed Robinson on the right hand side, and he knocked over an inch-perfect cross. As Gayle rose menacingly

94

(and he *was* menacing) at the far post, it became frighteningly clear that Big Bad John was going to smash *something* into the back of the net, be it an Irish international keeper, Brian Gayle, the ball, or all three.

As it was, the ball ended up there and was followed by the biggest roar to have greeted a goal that season, since Steve Davis' effort against Stoke in the opening home game of the campaign. Everybody: players, fans and TV cameras alike, was highly delighted. Mullen, in particular, was beside himself with joy.

With twelve minutes remaining, Davis sealed the three points with a beautifully placed side-foot past a crowd of players in the area, making sure that he maintained his position as Burnley's second highest scorer of the season. This was party time.

In light of this, I found United's second goal distasteful. It seemed churlish, impudent almost, for Andy Scott to try and tarnish our best performance of the season to date, merely for his personal satisfaction. We were, despite Kevin Gage's laughable post-match contention, at least two goals better than the Blades.

However, we had to look at what had been achieved that afternoon. We'd played fabulous flowing football in front of an audience of thousands. We'd beaten a team who were competing at the very highest level just six months ago. We'd climbed to fifteenth in the league, ('Go any higher and we might get a nose bleed,' said John) and perhaps most importantly, we'd given the watching public more entertainment in our first ever live league game on television, than old Elton's Tranmere had done in two or three seasons. Not bad for ninety minutes work. As Burnley now had four consecutive fixtures away from home, the next time the Clarets would play at the Turf was December 18th against Middlesbrough. This game too was to be shown live on television. In the meantime, cue the adverts . . .

Joe Royle's career as Everton boss gets off to the best possible start. His first game in charge is the Merseyside derby, which Everton win 2-0.

John Gorman is sacked as Swindon boss . . . twenty-four hours before Burnley are due to visit.

In stark contrast to Manchester United, Manchester City report a record club deficit of £5.5 million.

Wednesday 23/11/94
The County Ground

SWINDON TOWN 1-1 BURNLEY *(Scott 17) (Gayle 68)*
League position before and after match: 15th . . . 15th

Attendance: 7,654

BURNLEY: Beresford, Parkinson, Dowell *(Gayle 62)*, Davis, Winstanley, Randall, Harper, Heath, Hoyland, Robinson, Eyres. Subs (not used): Francis, Russell.

SWINDON TOWN: Digby, Robinson, Bodin, MacLaren *(Horlock 52)*, Thomson, Tiler, O'Sullivan, Beauchamp, Fjortoft, Mutch, Scott.
Subs (not used): Hamon, Hammond.

Referee: K. Lynch

Yellow Cards: Davis, Dowell, Hoyland (Burnley)

Red Cards: None

I shamefacedly admit that I had far too much to drink before this game; five or six pints in fact, which over the course of an evening may be neither here nor there, yet in the space of ninety minutes and on an empty stomach, is practically inviting trouble.

Not that it was entirely my fault. Burnley's game against Swindon afforded me an opportunity to meet up with a friend whom I hadn't seen for quite some time. As there were a good couple of hours to kill before kick-off, and we had plenty to catch up on, we retired to a nearby pub.

I shall never forget the Tap and Barrel in Swindon. It was populated almost entirely by the kind of stereotypical yokel figures usually found lurking twixt the pages of Thomas Hardy novels. One clearly deranged local was, for a reason known only to himself, standing by the darts scoreboard whilst muttering to himself and chalking up Swindon's worst results of their previous season in the Premiership.

When one travelling Claret asked him how Burnley would do against the Robins, he walked over to the window, gazed out for a moment, (as though in consultation with some greater force) and, cackling to himself, predicted a 7-0 drubbing for the Clarets. 'Then again,' he whispered, and altered his previous prediction, to 3-1 in our favour. Surreal wasn't in it.

Leaving the sage of Swindon and making for the ground, I hoped he was right. Encouragingly, Swindon hadn't won in seven league matches prior to our visit. Less encouraging, was that just two days previously, they'd sacked their manager, John Gorman, after a 3-2 defeat at Bristol City. Teams who have just parted company with their manager quite often have a nasty habit of winning the game that follows; which in this instance was us. Well, it would be, wouldn't it?

The vacation of the mangerial position at Swindon was the main talking point on Radio Wiltshire's sports programme that evening. I knew this not because I was listening to local radio, (I hadn't had *that* much to drink), but because I was interviewed by their roving reporter outside the ground, who bore more than a passing resemblance to Lord Lucan.

'Ah! A *Burnley* fan!' shrieked Lucan, obviously delighted with his discovery. 'Who do you think should take over the reins at Swindon?' Frankly, I couldn't have cared less, but humoured him anyway. 'Ardiles'll get it,' I replied in an assured tone, dazzling him with my insider knowledge of the football world. 'No way!' yelled the missing Lord, with such venom that you might have thought I had just hurled a particularly offensive insult at his mother. 'What's the score going to be tonight?' he asked, taking up a different line of questioning. '5-0 Burnley, 10-0 at full time,' I grinned, just before I was hit by the awful realisation that I had made a bloody fool of myself on the radio . . .

On entering the ground, it became apparent that we had been given the Building Site End. Half of it was closed off for a reason beyond my ken and the rows of disturbingly bright red seats looked as though they had been bolted onto the terracing not half an hour before our arrival.

The pitch, however, looked immaculate, as you might have

expected from a side who had a reputation for playing attractive football. As we were committed to playing in the same style, this had the makings of a good game. So I sat back, or at least would have done, had there been a 'back' attached to the lump of plastic on which I sat, and waited for the game to start.

Following the inane ramblings of the Swindon soothsayer and Lord Lucan's cameo as a local radio presenter, I perhaps shouldn't have been surprised, (but was), when ten minutes before kick-off, a gargantuan fluffy robin and a troupe of ten-year-old majorettes emerged from the players' tunnel and began cavorting around the County Ground to the strains of The Jackson Five's 'Rockin' Robin'.

As the oversized bird and its pre-pubescent cohorts jigged awkwardly towards the Building Site End, I couldn't help wondering, 'Why?' After all, who was benefiting from this sorry spectacle? The fans? Get away. The club? How? The person inside the robin? Well, maybe; at least they were getting paid for it. But they would have had to be in receipt of one hell of a handsome wage, to put themselves through this ritual humiliation thirty or so times a season.

'Piss off, Harper!' screamed someone behind me, as Rockin' Robin waved a wobbly wing in our vague direction. The comment was met with uproarious laughter from the terraces.

What *wasn't* met with uproarious laughter was the first half performance of either side. This was amongst Burnley's worst displays so far this season. Mooncat, having played reasonably well in his past two outings, reverted to type and sprayed his passes around with all the vision of Stevie Wonder. Randall, doing a fair impersonation of a scarecrow, looked as though he couldn't be bothered, and for all the use Hoyland was, he might as well have been sitting on the Building Site End with the other 1,000 Clarets who had made the trip.

For a contest which had promised so much, it had delivered very little, and although Swindon went into the interval one sloppy goal to the good, they were booed as roundly as the Clarets.

Part of Burnley's problem lay in the formation. Ever since the Sunderland game, the philosophy of out-and-out wing-play, a philosophy which had helped win us two promotions in three seasons, had suddenly been jettisoned in favour of a diamond-shaped formation in midfield. Or so we had been asked to believe.

Personally, I didn't believe this formation existed. It was a fancy way of saying that we had drawn our wingers closer to the centre of the field. The phrase 'diamond shape' flattered to deceive. Whatever the formation was, it sometimes worked: Charlton, Notts County, Shrewsbury and Sheffield United being examples, (although anybody who witnessed the Notts County and Shrewsbury games would have testified that they were hardly glorious demonstrations of quality football). Other times it didn't work: Sunderland, Watford and Swindon. It simply cancelled out the opposition midfield and produced the kind of tedious, bogged-down battle in the middle of the park that cried out for that bit of space and width, which wingers could have supplied. Whatever your opinion, we were undefeated since the system's inception. Although that record seemed as though it might be coming to an end. Still, there was always the second half.

'Who the bloody hell is *that?*' asked the friend who'd come along to the game with me, a slight tremor detectable in his voice. He was looking over towards our bench, where the unmistakable figure of John Gayle was stripping for action. 'That,' I said, 'is Big Bad John. He'll mix it up a bit.' He had half an hour to do the business.

As it was, he didn't need half an hour. Within six minutes Harper drifted in from the right and fired a shot goalwards. Fraser Digby, who, blessed with such a name, should surely have been a gentleman's outfitter rather than a goalkeeper, could only parry the shot. Gayle, sharp as a tack, slid in to slot home the rebound.

'I see what you mean!' shouted my suitably impressed friend, as the Building Site End launched into a hearty chorus of 'Big Bad John.' For the second game running, Gayle had scored within six minutes of appearing as a substitute. Cult status was assured.

As the wind blew stronger and the effects of the alcohol were replaced by a thumping headache, I longed for it all to end. So, I think, did poor old Marlon, who was bearing the brunt of wave after wave of a Fjortoft-inspired Swindon forward line. The Scandinavian striker did everything but score. He shot wide, hit the bar, had a penalty claim turned down and forced Beresford into two magnificent saves.

Come the final whistle, the celebratory tones of 'Jimmy

Mullen's Claret and Blue Army' were in stark contrast with the chants of 'Sack the Board' and 'Where's the Money Gone?' from the clearly disgruntled Swindon fans away to our left – chants which, incidentally, the travelling supporters took great delight in joining in with, as a means of rubbing yet further salt into the Swindon supporters' wounds.

The unbeaten league run was now stretched to nine games, we'd consolidated our highest league position for over a decade and Big Bad John had come up with the goods once again. These were good times.

The point we won that evening also meant that in four days, we had taken four out of six points from two sides who had been playing in the Premiership the previous season. There was no doubt that we had found our feet. And so we bade farewell to the soothsayer, Lord Lucan and Rockin' Robin, and headed home to prepare for the weekend's visit, to sixth-placed Grimsby.

Brian Little quits Leicester City, claiming he hasn't been approached by Villa, he's just not enjoying the job any more.

In the FA Cup First round replays, Hereford and Barnet fall to Hitchin and Woking, Fulham need extra time to see off Ashford Town and Bury squeeze through against Bishop Auckland on penalties.

Manchester United's hopes of progressing any further in the European Cup are dealt an almighty blow as they crumble 3-1 against IFK Gothenburg.

Saturday 26/11/94
Blundell Park

GRIMSBY TOWN 2-2 BURNLEY (*Woods 43, Gilbert 67*)
(*Davis 58, Parkinson 90*)
League position before and after match: 15th . . . 15th

Attendance: 7,084

100

BURNLEY: Beresford, Parkinson, Dowell *(Gayle 57)*, Davis, Winstanley, Randall, Harper, Heath, Hoyland, Robinson *(Francis 74)*, Eyres.
Sub (not used): Russell.

GRIMSBY TOWN: Crichton, Croft, Jobling, Handyside, Lever, Groves, Childs, Dobbin, Livingstone, Woods, Gilbert.
Subs (not used): Shakespeare, McDermott, Pearcey.

Referee: R. Poulain

Yellow Cards: Jobling, Dobbin (Grimsby)

Red Cards: None

Contrary to what some people might say, football is *not* the most important thing in life. There are many other areas of existence which take precedence over it. The death of a close friend or relative, the birth of a child, falling in love and completing your first Panini football-sticker album all have a greater impact on people's lives than the beautiful game. That having been said, football is undoubtedly much more than just a game, and produces more than its fair share of moments which transcend the everyday, and are, without question, life-enhancing.

For example, picture the scene: you're 2-1 down, away from home, (Grimsby to be precise), you haven't touched the ball for what seems like the last ten minutes and with fifteen seconds to go, it looks like you're going home empty-handed, your unbeaten run finally at an end.

But then, with the home fans screaming for the final whistle, Randall picks up a ball on the right hand side. He passes to Hoyland. Hoyland sidefoots the ball to Parky, out on the right. The whistles get louder. The Grimsby midfield, who have been so well marshalled for the last eighty-nine minutes, inexplicably allow Lovely Legs to run forty yards, without putting a challenge in. Suddenly Parky's on the edge of the area. Although the goal is practically obscured by a wall of Grimsby defenders, he finds a chink somewhere, pulls back his right leg, and smashes a twenty-yarder into the bottom right hand corner of their net.

At which point the 3,000 other Burnley fans around you go

completely berserk. And I mean, *berserk*. You're hugging strangers, bouncing up and down like a crazed Jack-in-the-box, punching the air with both fists, shouting 'YES! YES! YES!' over and over again, and you've got *the* biggest smile on your face. Moments such as these are absolutely priceless and give what Nick Hornby in 'Fever Pitch' describes as, 'this powerful sensation of being exactly in the right place at the right time.' [11] Football; I love it.

A statement, issued by arbitrators, rules that Tottenham's ban from the FA Cup was unlawful. Spurs' lawyers now look at the possibility of overturning the six point penalty and the £1.5 million fine, imposed by the FA.

On his forty-first birthday, Brian Little is appointed as Aston Villa manager.

Leicester take a dim view, saying they had a written agreement with Little that he would not be Villa's next manager. They are to sue him for personal damages and breach of contract.

Arsenal's Paul Merson breaks down in tears at a press conference, as he tells the media of his recent, successful struggle to beat his addiction to cocaine and alcohol.

Blackburn Rovers top the Premiership, easing past QPR 4-0.

In his first game in charge, Brian Little's Aston Villa draw 1-1 with Sheffield wednesday.

Steve McMahon takes over as Swindon player-manager.

Eddie May is sacked after Cardiff's FA Cup humiliation at the hands of Enfield. He is replaced by Mike Aizlewood.

Ex-Claret Mick Docherty takes over the reins at Rochdale, following Dave Sutton's resignation.

Rumours abound of financial irregularities in Arsenal's signings of John Jensen and Pal Lyderson. Rene Hauge, who acted as agent in the deals, also comes under close scrutiny.

Troubled Exeter have a fortnight to organise a rescue package for the club.

Another former Burnley player moves into management, as Brian Laws becomes Grimsby's new boss.

In the Fourth Round of the Coca-Cola Cup, Bolton claim another Premiership scalp, disposing of West Ham 3-1. Nottingham Forest are the other Premiership club to take a tumble, as they go down 2-0 to Millwall.

Paul Merson announces he is to undergo a rehabilitation programme and simultaneously announces his addiction to gambling.

Gary Peters takes over as manager of Preston North End, following John Beck's resignation earlier in the week.

Sunday 4/12/94
Deva Stadium

FA CUP SPONSORED BY LITTLEWOODS POOLS. SECOND ROUND.

CHESTER CITY 1-2 BURNLEY (Milner 76)
(Eyres 49 [pen.], Heath 85)

Attendance: 4,231

BURNLEY: Beresford, Parkinson, Dowell (Gayle 57), Davis, Winstanley, Randall, Harper, Heath, Hoyland, Robinson, Eyres.

Subs (not used): Francis, Russell.

CHESTER CITY: Felgate, Jenkins, Lightfoot, Alsford, Jackson, Shelton, Flitcroft, Bishop *(Milner 62)*, Preece, Page, Hackett. Subs (not used): Burnham, Newland.

Referee: A. Wilkie

Yellow Cards: Lightfoot, Bishop, Jenkins (Chester City)
Winstanley, Hoyland (Burnley)

Red Cards: None

I'd been worrying about this one ever since the draw had been made the previous month. The seven days leading up to the game had been a nervy affair, my mind cluttered with so many 'what if . . . ' scenarios, that my capacity for rational thought had been even more seriously diminished than usual. Perhaps that was what people meant when they spoke about 'Cup Fever'.

The tie was perfectly set up for us to make an early exit. With Port Vale having gone out twenty-four hours previously, we had the dubious privilege of being the highest-placed club in the FA Cup that afternoon.

Chester, on the other hand, were second bottom in the division below us, they had garnered a mere twelve points from seventeen games, were holders of the unenviable record of being Division Two's joint lowest scorers, and had just been thumped 6-0 at home by Crewe five days prior to our visit. Oh, and the game was live on 'Sky', making the potential for humiliation absolutely massive. It was then with not a little apprehension that we took up our positions inside the ground, that chilly Sunday afternoon.

Unlike some Burnley fans whom I overheard making less than complimentary remarks about Chester's ground, (another attack of 'the mighty Burnley shouldn't have to play here' syndrome, as witnessed at York), I actually liked the Deva Stadium. In no way could it compete with Turf Moor, but it was neat, compact and was also one of the few grounds I had visited where you didn't need supersonic hearing in order to make sense of what came out of the PA system.

Not that the state of Chester's ground mattered, of course. The name of the game that afternoon was getting through to the next round of the Cup, which the Clarets did, but not without yet further eroding my already ravaged nerves.

The misgivings I had about this game were clearly shared by Jamie Hoyland, who in the second minute of the game underhit a backpass to such a degree that Marlon would have had to have arms twelve feet long in order to retrieve the situation. Fortunately for both Hoyland and Burnley, Don Page overhit his centre, and the ball was cleared.

A few minutes later, and Hoyland was lucky to be on the field at all. A Chester punt fell to Don Page who hared down the right hand side. Jamie, back-pedalling, lost his footing, tumbled to the ground in classic silent comedy style, and stopped the Blues number ten, via the time-honoured method of practically ripping his kit off. Luckily, the ref only deemed the offence worthy of a yellow card. Glancing round at the faces in the crowd, it was obvious that I wasn't alone in thinking this wasn't going to be our day.

It was left largely to Lovely Legs, the last-minute hero at Grimsby, to provide Burnley's most attacking moves of the half. As well as his surging runs down the right hand side, his two efforts on goal, which both narrowly missed the target, were the closest we came to scoring in the first period, especially as Robinson and Eyres had seemingly taken a pre-match vow not to go anywhere within ten yards of white rounded objects.

There are times when the lot of the football supporter can be described as being substantially less than happy. Half-time during this game was a case in point. A bitterly cold Sunday afternoon, away from home, your heroes playing as if they'd been introduced to each other five minutes before kick-off, and to top it all the DJ started playing us Elton bloody John records, which was proof that having a swanky PA system did have its down side.

The second half started worryingly enough, with Gary Hackett defying the existing laws of physics, by somehow missing the simplest of headers from just under three millimetres out. From thereon in though, we started to get our act together and threatened Chester like we should have done an hour earlier.

Inchy was brought down in the box, just as he was about to score, and instead of being covered in glory, had to make do with being plastered with mud. Amazingly the ref waved play on. Eyresie was the victim of Iain Jenkins' murderous sliding tackle, which only just left his legs attached to his torso. From that free-kick we got a corner.

'Oh well,' I thought, as Chester cleared their lines, 'at least we're looking like we might score.' And then for no apparent reason, Mr Wilkie gave a loud, shrill blast on his whistle and pointed to Chester's penalty spot. A subsequent scrutiny of the 'Sky' footage showed Davis was clearly impeded, but I didn't know that at the time, and set about celebrating what I assumed to be an act of capricious whim on Mr Wilkie's part with much gusto. A minute later, I had more cause to celebrate, as Eyresie smacked the ball high and handsome past the hapless Felgate.

As the game wore on, we imposed ourselves more and more on Chester, who were visibly beginning to tire. This was thanks in no small part to Adey Randall, who, having decided that this was the one game in five he would shine for, ran the midfield and ran the Blues ragged. Every penetrating pass, every little jink or shuffle, every little bit of something special seemed to emanate from our number six. 'Christ,' I remember thinking to myself at the time, 'if he'd been doing this all season we'd be top of the league by now.'

With twenty minutes left, we were well on top. Harper, whose hair over the past few games had slowly but strangely been taking on the appearance of a neurotic haystack, forced a fine save from Felgate, Randall shot just wide and Gayle was unlucky not to double our lead, after Davis had played a superb through-ball to the big man. 'We're cruising here!' I shouted to Andy, a grin from ear to ear, 'Cruising, I tell you!'

We were 'cruising' for about ten more seconds, when Andy Milner popped up and, following an extended bout of pinball in our six yard box, slammed home the equaliser. The proverbial deathly hush fell over the Burnley supporters, as Chester's fans went insane with delight at the opposite end of the pitch.

'That's buggered it somewhat.' came a disembodied voice to my rear. The voice was right. And I couldn't help the feeling that it was *my* fault that Chester had equalised. If only I'd kept my bloody mouth shut, Andy bloody Milner wouldn't have scored and we'd be a quarter of an hour away from the Third bloody Round. But oh no, I had to open my trap and start shouting the odds, didn't I? I felt I should be apologising to all those Burnley fans who'd given up their sumptuous Sunday lunches to watch the Clarets, only for myself and my almighty gob to ruin it all for them. I was still castigating myself and making mental plans for an inevitable stress-inducing replay, when with six minutes to go, Eyresie drifted what I thought looked a fairly innocuous ball, over the top of Chester's midfield to the edge of their area. In one graceful movement, Inchy simultaneously brought it down and pulled it inside the defender, to make more space for himself. Looking up just once, to pick his spot, he somehow rifled *and* placed the ball, over the diving Felgate's outstretched fingertips, to make it 2-1 to Burnley. As goals go, it was positively Godlike.

It would take something ultra-special to prevent *that* beauty from getting Goal of the Season come mid-May, and that included Parky's incredible effort at Grimsby the week before. As Inchy ran off in the direction of the centre-circle, arms aloft, I mentally thanked him for relieving me from the massive yoke of guilt I would have borne, had the scores stayed level. This time, I made damned sure I kept absolutely mum until full time.

Come the final whistle, I could feel the tension of the last seven days drain from my body, as Big Bad John came over to applaud us all. 'Thank God that's over,' I thought out loud. And what was our reward to be for surviving this living hell? A chance to do it all again in the Third Round, with what many pundits might have referred to as 'a tricky away trip', to Cambridge United, third bottom of the Second Division. Leaving the ground, I could feel the nerves starting to build up already.

Now manager of Aston Villa, Brian Little returns to Leicester as the two clubs clash in a 1-1 draw in the Premiership. The Leicester fans aren't happy with Little, who greet his return to Filbert Street with chants of: 'There's only one lying bastard!'

John Lyall resigns as manager of Ipswich, after four and a half years at the helm. Paul Goddard is put in temporary charge.

Following his dismissal from Everton, Mike Walker sues the club for £400,000.

Manchester United beat Galatasary 4-0 in the Champions' League, yet fail to qualify for the next phase, as IFK Gothenburg can only draw in Barcelona.

The FA announce that Green Flag, owners of National Breakdown, are to become official sponsors of the England team.

Saturday 10/12/94
The Victoria Ground

STOKE CITY 2-0 BURNLEY *(Orlygsson 68 [pen.], 83)*
League position before and after match: 17th . . . 18th

Attendance: 13,040

BURNLEY: Beresford, Parkinson, Hoyland, Davis, Winstanley *(Philliskirk 85)*, Randall *(Mullin 80)*, Harper, Heath, Gayle, Robinson, Eyres.
Sub (not used): Russell.

STOKE CITY: Muggleton, Clarkson, Sandford, Cranson, Overson, Orlygsson, Shaw *(Biggins 66)*, Beeston, Carruthers *(Siggurdsson 84)*, Peschisolido, Gleghorn.
Sub (not used): Sinclair.

Referee: C. Wilkes

Yellow Cards: Beeston, Shaw, Clarkson (Stoke)
Davis (Burnley)

Red Card: Eyres (Burnley)

Little-known facts, number twelve: In Stoke, it is illegal for five people to stand together on a street corner and hold a conversation.

Let me explain. Arriving in Stoke at half-past-one, we decided that the best way to kill the time before kick-off was to have a quiet wander around the streets that adjoined the ground. If we were lucky, we might even find a pub. As we stood on a corner outside the Victoria Ground, debating which way to go, we were approached by four police officers.

'Who are you waiting for, lads?' asked one of them, his tone less than welcoming. 'No-one. We were just going for a wander,' I told him. This however proved to be the incorrect response, as we were strongly advised to 'Just go into the ground lads, OK?' Frankly it wasn't 'OK'. I for one, certainly didn't fancy being stuck inside a football ground for ninety minutes before the game started. So I tried again. 'We were only going to go for a walk, though.' This was another wrong thing to say and it provoked a threat from the officer. 'Well if you *don't* go inside the ground now, then I'm afraid that we're going to have to start picking one or two of you out.'

His facial expression left us in no doubt that being 'picked out' would not be the most pleasant of experiences. So as the prospect of appearing at Stoke Magistrates' Court on Monday morning didn't hold much thrall for us, we grudgingly followed his advice and made for the terraces.

Not that things were any better there. This time, it was the stewards who were having a pop: at fanzine sellers, who are, as everyone knows, a group of people who will stop at nothing in their pursuit of mindless, bloody violence. As a young lad – no more than thirteen, I'd say – walked up and down the visitors' end, flogging copies of 'Marlon's Gloves', he was accosted by somebody on the other side of the fence, sporting a fluorescent orange jacket.

'Oi!' yelled the steward, shaking his head furiously. 'You can't sell them in 'ere, son!' and called the hapless teenager over to the fence. The gist of the subsequent conversation was that the young lad had his fanzines confiscated until after the match, on the grounds that selling them would 'affect sales of Stoke's match day programme.' At that exact moment a large pig was spotted flying over the ground.

One poor chap selling copies of another Burnley fanzine, 'No, Nay, Never' wasn't quite so lucky. Apparently, he had all his copies confiscated and was ejected from the ground. Well, you can understand it, can't you? You don't want that kind of literature on the terraces. It's just propaganda. It puts silly ideas in your head. You can't believe half of what you read in there. Not like your official programme, the very forum of open debate about your football club.

There were many other infuriating examples of oppression, (and it was oppression, let's be perfectly clear on that score), from both the police and stewards that afternoon. Fans were told to take their flags down off the hoardings, or to get down off fences, because they would obscure the crowd's view; this before a ball had been kicked. What did the stewards think we were all doing – watching the grass grow on the pitch? For the duration of the game, small yet intimidating pockets of policemen hovered menacingly in the Burnley end, occasionally and randomly fishing out the odd away fan, just – in footballing parlance – to let us know they were there.

This hostile and wholly unnecessary treatment of travelling fans both upsets and infuriates me. When I travel to away games, I'm worried that I'll get trouble. Not from the thousands of home supporters, but from the small handful of police and stewards – the very people who are supposed to be engendering an air of security.

I fully appreciate that these people have a difficult job to do. But what is their job? Harassing innocent football supporters and enforcing petty rules which cause more problems than they resolve, or being there to ensure that fans are safe and acting as a deterrent to the thankfully very tiny minority of idiots, for whom football still holds an attraction? Sure, go ahead, *please* go ahead and arrest the handful of drunkards, trouble-makers and racist cretins who occasionally appear on the terraces, but the overwhelming majority of us know how to conduct ourselves in public and are not about to set about the opposition fans with knuckle dusters and other spikey objects.

It is insulting, ignorant on behalf of the relevant bodies, but above all sad, that the authorities concerned feel that the best way to encourage football fans to 'behave', (not that 95 per cent of us *need* any such encouragement), is to intimidate us into co-operation. There are thugs on the terraces. It's just that they're not always who you might think they are.

We had a point to prove against Stoke. Like I suspect many of

the Clarets who had made the trip to the Potteries that afternoon, I was still smarting from the memory of City's undeserved
injury-time equaliser, when we'd played them at Turf Moor in
August. From a fan's point of view, this wasn't so much a football
match as a revenge mission.

A highly entertaining first half was as much a contrast in styles
as anything else. Stoke constantly looked to hit us on the break,
with Peschisolido and in particular, Orlygsson, running the show.
Burnley were more patient, playing the possession game, and
were by some distance the better team. Gayle, on from the start,
was particularly impressive. In fact, I have *never* seen a defence as
worried as Stoke's back four were, whenever the big man cast his
towering shadow in and around their eighteen yard box. Lou
Macari, Stoke's boss, had obviously played them a videotape of
Big Bad John's performance against Sheffield United.

Being by far the better team was all well and good, but what
we needed was a goal. We nearly got a hatful. Parkinson, enjoying his best form of the season, shot narrowly over the crossbar
from eighteen yards. A hard low cross from Eyres got a deflection
and sped teasingly across Stoke's six yard box, with no Burnley
player able to get that all-important touch. Inchy leathered a
thirty-yarder that went narrowly wide after colliding with
Overson's hindquarters. But the miss of the half went to Gayle.

Randall swung a cross in from the right. Heath met the ball
and nodded it down past the defender, leaving Big bad John six
yards out with just the keeper to beat. I was sure he would score,
but instead, he hammered the ball straight at Muggleton, instead
of aiming for the more obvious option of the gaping expanses of
net either side of him. The Stoke keeper was more than grateful
for the opportunity to claw the ball away to safety.

Three minutes later, Marlon, whose defence had momentarily
entered their own personal Bermuda Triangle, had to perform
considerable heroics by getting in the way of a Carl Beeston
effort which wasn't so much a shot as a heat-seeking missile. How
Beresford's hands remained connected to his wrists remained an
insoluble mystery, as did how half-time was reached with a 0-0
scoreline.

Burnley's big mistake in the second half was trying to play
Stoke at their own game. It might have worked, had we possessed
the kind of players necessary to hit them on the break. In order

to counter-attack, we could have done with a mid-fielder with good vision and all-round awareness, and a pacey striker. We were then doubly unfortunate, in that we were trying to play this system with Harper and Eyres.

Harper's inability to think with anything approaching pace, has already been well documented in this book, (cf Sunderland), and all that needs to be said on that score is that that afternoon's game only reinforced my already concrete belief. Eyres, on the other hand, was beginning to irritate me to the point where I wanted to run onto the pitch and shake him furiously – just to check whether or not he was really alive. There was precious little evidence to suggest that he was.

Everywhere we had gone on our travels this season, the programme writers had picked out Eyres as the man most likely to wreak havoc amongst opposition defences. Whoever compiled these notes had clearly not seen our number eleven in 'action' in the 94/95 campaign. That having been said, Clarets fans themselves had hardly witnessed the man they called 'Budgie' set the division alight.

The truth was that he was having a lousy season. Including that afternoon's outing, the man Mullen had brought to Burnley from Blackpool for £90,000, had yet to score from anywhere but the penalty spot, in sixteen appearances. This made grim reading, especially when you reckoned that he scored nigh on thirty goals the previous season.

There were reasons for this dramatic dip in his performance, not least of which was the fact that Eyres had always had a tendency to drift in and out of the game. However, whereas he was able to get away with that in a lower league, this division demanded that you got involved for ninety minutes. This clearly didn't suit Budgie, who spent more time spectating than making inroads into defences. Consequently, the team spent a lot of time carrying him.

It was then not a little ironic that the very man who was invisible for sizeable chunks of the proceedings was at the heart of the game's turning point.

On sixty-eight minutes, Toddy Orlygsson broke from midfield, just like he'd been threatening to do all afternoon, hared into the box and thumped his effort into Marlon's midriff. Eyres, who had been chasing Orlygsson back, made contact with the Icelandic international's heel, just (as far as I could see, and I was directly in line with the incident, behind the goal) *after* he had shot. Mr Wilkes didn't see it that way, and gave Stoke a penalty. This decision proved only slightly less popular with Burnley fans than an invitation to a John Bond party. (For the benefit of any non-Burnley fans who may be reading, John Bond took over as Burnley manager in June 1983, having just taken Manchester City down to the Second Division, a failure which resulted in his sacking. On arriving at Turf Moor, he said he believed Burnley to be a club full of potential.

Bond was obviously keen to exploit this potential, but only in a financial way, selling such rising stars as Lee Dixon, Trevor Steven and Brian Laws, and also ridding the club of established favourites, including Tommy Cassidy and the then Clarets' God, Martin Dobson. Over a decade after his departure, he is still loathed by Burnley fans, so much so in fact, that when Burnley played Shrewsbury in the FA Cup in the 92/93 season, he didn't attend the game at Turf Moor on police advice, and disguised himself for the replay at Gay Meadow.)

The referee's decision provoked pandemonium in the Burnley enclosure. Things were no better on the pitch, where the man in black was surrounded by a crowd of Burnley players, all wanting to know what the bloody hell he thought he was playing at. Harper in particular was absolutely livid, his already ruddy complexion taking on a frighteningly scarlety/purple hue, as though his entire head was about to explode.

Mooncat must have said something right, as Mr Wilkes trotted across to consult his linesman. This was agony. Would the ref change his mind? What *was* the linesman saying to him? When would Harper get his hair cut? The whole episode could only have taken three or four seconds, yet the wait seemed like an eternity; my stomach did impossible somersaults, as the two officials played God with our ten-match unbeaten run.

An almighty roar went up from the Stoke fans above us, as Mr Wilkes pointed to the spot for the second time that afternoon and red-carded Eyres for the first time in his career. Orlygsson made no mistake with the penalty, lashing it straight down the middle.

We were up against it now, and no mistake. Jimmy responded by throwing John Mullin on for Randall. If you were super-stitious, (and believe me, when you're 1-0 down away from home and reduced to ten men, you'll cling tenaciously to the most tenuous of hopes), this was a good sign. The last time Mullin had come on as a sub, was also in the Potteries, against Port Vale, where he scored a dramatic late equaliser.

And indeed Mullin was involved in a goal, but not in the way the travelling support would have liked. With seven minutes left, the nineteen-year-old reserve team striker gifted the ball to Peschisolido in midfield, who released Orlygsson. Mullin gave chase, but was never going to catch him. He obviously realised this, because he stopped pursuing the Stoke number six a good thirty yards from goal. Orlygsson smashed the ball past an advancing Beresford, and that was pretty much that.

Jimmy finally capitulated, by substituting Winstanley for Philliskirk, a signal universally acknowledged in football, as meaning, 'We surrender!' His impact on the side was instant. Although down to ten men, Phyllis somehow made it seem as though we only had nine, possibly eight, men on the pitch.

The ref signalled full time. The Stoke supporters sang 'Delilah', and our ten-match unbeaten league run was at an end. To be undefeated in the league since that dismal afternoon at West Brom was no mean feat. We'd played some good sides: Bolton, Sheffield United and Grimsby, for example. However, the fact that the run contained just three wins out of ten, (sixteen points out of a possible thirty) and left us a mere three points above the relegation zone, amply and frighteningly illustrated that such a sequence of results counted for very little. We needed to win a few. Middlesbrough, at home the following Saturday, would be the first opportunity.

Spurs are officially allowed back into the FA Cup. They also have their six point penalty quashed, after an arbitration tribunal rule that the FA acted outside its jurisdiction in punishing those currently at the club for their predecessors' misdemeanours.

Le Tissier scores the goal of the season at Ewood Park, dancing round two Rovers' players, before floating a 40-yard chip over a despairing Tim Flowers.

George Graham denies accepting a 'bung' in the John Jensen deal, as he prepares to face a Premier League Commission. His side of the story is that he received the £285,000 as a gift for his part in the transfer.

Duncan Ferguson makes his loan move from Rangers to Everton a permanent one. It costs the Toffeemen a club record £4 million.

Billy Ayre resigns as manager of Scarborough.

Ipswich begin interviewing for the manager's job.

Mark McGhee leaves Reading to become manager at Leicester City, and kicks off his reign with a 0-0 draw against Blackburn Rovers.

Manchester United relinquish the only unbeaten home record in the Premiership or the Football League, as they go down 2-1 to Nottingham Forest.

Sunday 18/12/94
Turf Moor

BURNLEY 0-3 MIDDLESBROUGH (*Hendrie 15, 63, 90*)
League position before and after match: 20th . . . 20th

Attendance: 12,049

BURNLEY: Beresford, Parkinson, Dowell, Davis, Winstanley, Randall, Harper (*Gayle 55*), Heath, Hoyland, Robinson (*Mullin 67*), Eyres.
Sub (not used): Russell.

MIDDLESBROUGH: Miller, Cox, Fleming, Vickers, Whyte, Pearson, Robson, Mustoe, Wilkinson, Hendrie, Moore.
Subs (not used): Kavanagh, Blackmore, Roberts.

Referee: P. Wright

115

Yellow Cards: Dowell (Burnley)
Robson, Pearson (Middlesbrough)

Red Card: Dowell (Burnley)

Crap. Absolute crap. If you were to take the worst aspects of the worst performances we'd put in, in previous fixtures this season (against Barnsley, West Brom, Swindon and Watford), and then multiply them by one hundred, you would still be a million miles away from even beginning to imagine how utterly, utterly abysmal this display actually was. This was something else. It was also live on Granada and Tyne Tees television. Oh, the shame of it all.

It wasn't so much the fact that we lost that bothered me, (although that in itself was enough to send me spiralling into despair, especially when I thought of the fiver I had bet my 'Boro-supporting work colleague that we would turn them over), but more the manner in which we relinquished the points. We approached the task of defeating the league leaders with all the application and enthusiasm of a condemned man who has just been told he must spend his final hours on earth cleaning toilets, using a tooth brush, with only Michael Bolton's back catalogue for company. There was no passion. There was no spirit. There was no desire. Consequently there was no victory, only a thoroughly humiliating defeat.

A huge part of the blame for the way we lost that afternoon had to go to Jimmy Mullen. After the match he argued long, hard and with passion, that the referee was the most inconsistent he had seen in his twenty-five years in the game, following an incident in which an already-booked Bryan Robson got away with clattering Adrian Heath, after Wayne Dowell had been dismissed for an almost identical offence a few minutes previously. Whilst he might have had a fair point, the issue was really a secondary one, and was used as a smokescreen by Jimmy, to avoid talking about the real, more worrying issues the game threw up, of which there were several.

Tactics, for example, were conspicuous by their absence. No-one (manager, player or fans) seemed to have a bloody clue what was going on any more. Nowhere was this more apparent than in midfield, where it was alleged that we were operating a diamond

116

formation, although if it *was* a diamond, then it was one hell of a strange shape. It was then a pity that nobody had bothered to tell the team this. Randall, Harper, Heath and Hoyland looked less and less like points of any jewel, and more and more like decapitated chickens, with every passing game.

The desperate need for a decent left back was also a major cause for concern. It had never been more glaringly obvious that we required somebody of maturity, skill and experience in that position, than that afternoon. Putting in a youth teamer, with only four league games to his name, against a speedy, physical and vastly experienced Middlesbrough outfit, was practically inviting trouble. And we got it. Boro's winger Alan Moore started on the left side, but after seeing the less pacey Robbie Mustoe run Wayne Dowell ragged, he soon switched wings and began to torment the life out of our nineteen-year-old.

Lacking pace and experience, it soon became apparent to young Wayne that the only way he was likely to stop Moore repeatedly racing past him, was to attempt to scythe boot-sized chunks out of the Boro' number eleven's legs. This he did twice. Both times he received a yellow card for his attentions, with the result that Mr. Wright requested that he take an early bath, two minutes after the restart.

The sending-off could have been avoided by Mullen. He should have seen the lad was well out of his depth and substituted him at half-time for John Gayle, which he was probably going to do after an hour or so anyway. This would have meant rearranging the defence, but it was a tactic that had been successfully employed already that season. Instead, he gave our number three a little bit more rope with which to hang himself.

It had been over six weeks since Vinnicombe had had his jaw fractured at Reading, and Mullen *still* hadn't replaced him. I simply didn't believe that in the month and a half that had elapsed since that early November afternoon, Jimmy hadn't been able to find an adequate replacement, or get someone on loan, or sign a right back and move Parky to left back. The options were there, they just weren't being exploited. Why?

But by far the most obvious and depressing problem that afternoon was one which had been with us for the entire season to date: namely, there was no-one who looked even remotely capable of putting the ball in the back of the opposition's net.

117

Not that we exactly helped ourselves against Middlesbrough, by lobbing high balls into their area for our two five-foot-nothing strikers to compete with their three six-foot-something central defenders.

It was a disturbing, but very real truth, that there were less quality strikers at Burnley Football Club than there were Blackburn fans who could remember the pre-Jack Walker days. This sorry state of affairs started me thinking about the strikers we had on our books at that time.

Robinson had deceived me . . . big time. Judging by his glossy and over-inflated £250,000 price tag, it seemed he had deceived Jimmy in a similar fashion. Whilst his endless chasing of lost causes and his tremendous 'engine' (just for the record, I hate that phrase, but it describes perfectly one of the chief aspects of Robinson's game), were both admirable qualities, I would gladly have traded them both for some of those good old-fashioned goals that I always associated strikers with.

Five league goals in twenty-one starts could hardly be read as Robbo 'paying back a huge slice of his transfer fee.' Davis had scored as many goals with one less start from his position at the heart of the defence. I rest my case.

Heath, God-like though he undoubtedly was, hadn't managed a league goal all season. His saving grace was that he had created quite a few (Sheffield United, Millwall, Luton, Tranmere) which for me was one of the joys of having someone like Heath playing for you. When Inchy played well, (which he usually did), it almost always had a beneficial effect on the rest of the team.

Unlike Tony Philliskirk, whose inclusion in the squad was guaranteed to fill the opposition's hearts with an uplifting mixture of joy and hope, yet sent Burnley fans scrabbling for their Thesaurus in an attempt to find new ways of expressing their despair.

Phyllis was brought to the club the previous season on the strength of his reputation for having scored goals wherever he had played. The fact that he had just recovered from a hernia operation, and couldn't even command a place in the first eleven of the all-conquering Peterborough, who were relegated from Division One at the end of that season, didn't seem to deter Jimmy in the least.

His initial lacklustre performances (no pace, no positional

118

sense, no bloody idea) were attributed to the fact that he was still recovering from his injury. However, as the passage of time worked its way, it became heart-sinkingly clear that the phrase 'wholly inadequate' would be permanently and inextricably linked with Phyllis. The highlight of his stay at the club to date was an Eyres-assisted hat-trick which finally relegated Barnet, who with all due respect, could probably have been given a thumping by eleven, bed-ridden geriatrics.

Nathan Peel was a local lad who had always wanted to play for Burnley. When he finally got his wish, he came on as a sub and banged two in against Plymouth (well, he actually bundled them over the line, but goals is goals). 'Yes!' we all thought, 'A star is born.' The sad truth was, he was more of a shooting star than a permanent one.

Denied a regular first team slot, that brace was Peel's last significant contribution to the team, and he seemed destined to spend the majority of his footballing career travelling with the reserves to all-but-empty stadia every other Wednesday evening to play in the Pontins League.

My thoughts on David Eyres are to be found in my scribblings about the Stoke game, so on to Graham Lancashire, who was something of an enigma. Whenever we loaned him out to other clubs, he would go goal-crazy. However, put a claret and blue shirt on him, and apart from an impressive spell in the 91/92 Fourth Division Championship season, he would struggle to score into a goal as wide as his surname. His supporters may have argued that he had only had a limited number of starts. I would argue that in those limited starts, he looked a very limited player. The Middlesbrough game marked his last week on Burnley's wages list, as we inflicted him on Preston North End and gained £55,000 into the bargain.

I liked John Gayle. He always put 110 per cent in, looked as though he wanted to do well, and had that rare quality in a foot- baller – an appreciation of the fans. His other endearing feature was his never-failing ability to make the opposition turn white with fear, through his sheer physical presence. However, huge fan though I was, even I had to concede that Big Bad John was never going to get more than ten a season. Which wasn't good enough for your top striker. A good man to have in a storm, and an even better man to have going for a 50/50 ball with just about anybody.

John Mullin, like Nathan Peel, was from the Burnley area. He, too, had come on and scored as a sub for Burnley the previous season; his moment of glory being away at fellow promotion winners, Port Vale, where he rifled a dramatic late goal for the Clarets which earned us a point.

Unlike Peel, Mullin looked quite promising, scoring in just about every game he played in for the reserves. And therein lay the fly in the ointment. Although he was more than capable of regularly finding the net for the second string, it was unknown (due to his having been given only a handful of starts) if he could fulfil his undoubted potential in the first eleven.

The good thing for him was that at nineteen, he had plenty of time on his side. The bad thing was that promotion the previous season seemed to have all but killed off his chances of getting a regular start. Mullen seemed loathe to throw Mullin into First Division action as anything but a last-ditch substitute, an attitude which suggested that he didn't believe the youngster was up to the grade.

Personally, I believed Jimmy had adopted a far too over-protective attitude and should have given him a chance. He was young, enthusiastic, and probably possessed of some of that ridiculous self-belief bordering on arrogance which accompanies many footballers under the age of twenty-one. He could certainly have done no worse than Robinson, and might even have surprised one or two people.

And finally, John Francis, who I believed on his day was amongst the top five players at the club. His speed was his great asset, and he had shown in the two games where he had briefly appeared as a sub that he had got faster, if anything. Unfortunately, he was injured until at least February, so that particular avenue of attack was temporarily closed.

And so, as John Hendrie carved up the Christmas Turkey that was the Burnley defence for his third goal of the afternoon and his fifth of the season against us, I shook my head, gritted my teeth and made a mental note to ask Santa to bring Burnley a goal-scorer of the Scotsman's calibre.

Steve Coppell, speaking of the 'bung' allegations in his role as a member of the Premier League Commission, suggests that George Graham accepted the money and then repaid it. Arsenal's board announce their unanimous support for Graham.

Ray McHale becomes Billy Ayre's replacement at Scarborough, less than two years after he was sacked from the job to make way for Ayre.

Leyton Orient are put up for sale by their chairman, Tony Wood – with an asking price of just £5.00. Phillip Wallace, an Essex businessman, is to take over.
Doncaster part company with their management team of Bruce McLellan and Jimmy Neighbour.

Monday 26/12/94
Turf Moor

BURNLEY 1v2 PORT VALE *(McMinn 6)* *(Foyle 25, Burke 26)*

MATCH ABANDONED AFTER 55 MINUTES
DUE TO WATERLOGGED PITCH
League position before and after match: 20th . . . 21st

Attendance: 13,775

BURNLEY: Beresford, Parkinson, Dowell *(Harrison 50)*, Davis, Winstanley, Randall, Hoyland, Heath, Gayle, Robinson, McMinn.
Subs (not used): Mullin, Russell.

PORT VALE: Musselwhite, Aspin, Sandeman, Porter, Griffiths, D. Glover, Burke, Van der Laan, Foyle, L.Glover, Guppy.
Subs (not used): Kent, Naylor, Van Huesden.

Referee: W. Burns

Yellow Cards: Gayle, Winstanley (Burnley)
Sandeman (Port Vale)

121

Red Cards: None

It hadn't been what you might call a sparkling Yuletide. A couple
of days before Christmas Eve, my doctor diagnosed me as having
acute bronchitis and an ear that required syringing. The latter he
could do nothing about until the district nurse paid a visit – six
days later. (This was particularly infuriating, as I couldn't hear a
damned thing through it.) For the bronchitis, he prescribed me a
course of antibiotics, which meant alcohol was out of the
question for seven days. Consequently, I had spent the festive
period coughing my lungs up, swilling back gallons of orange
juice and saying 'Merry Christmas!' to people who had just asked
me what I thought of the new Oasis single. I wasn't happy.

It was in this dilapidated state, then, that I coughed and
spluttered my way to Turf Moor on Boxing Day, hoping for the
kind of high quality Claret-tinged entertainment that would
raise my considerably jaded Christmas spirits. I got
entertainment alright. I got (appropriately enough for the time of
year) pantomime.

The first act in the pantomime was the appearance of the new
club mascot – Bertie Bee. Apparently he had made his debut the
previous week against Middlesbrough, but as I had only just made
it to the ground in time for kick-off for that match, (and
regretted it for the couple of hours which followed), I had missed
out on the experience.

With a physical appearance not unlike the result of an explo-
sion in a fuzzy-felt factory, Bertie had presumably been inspired
by an individual who had suffered a very bad experience, whilst
under the influence of a particularly potent cocktail of hallucino-
genic drugs. Bertie briefly lumbered about in front of the
Endsleigh Stand, waved at a couple of kids, and then buzzed off
down the players' tunnel to escape the adverse weather
conditions.

It had in fact, been raining heavily and steadily for the past
twenty-four hours or so, but from the Longside, the pitch looked
to be in fine nick; until, that is, some of the players who were
warming up, attempted to pass the ball more than two yards
along the deck to each other, in which instances the ball rolled
a difficult six inches and then just sat there, adamantly refusing
to move any further.

And indeed, as the rain fell in even vaster quantities, a golden hour of Christmas comedy unwrapped itself in front of those soggy souls who were lucky enough and stupid enough to be there. Passes along the ground fell some yards short of their intended target, whilst their airborne counterparts zipped off the slippery surface at incredible speed. Every time a player's boot made contact with the pitch, it gave the effect of them having just trodden on a water-filled balloon, so huge were the puddles thrown up in their wake.

But the two most memorable moments of the first half belonged to Ted McMinn, recalled for the suspended Eyres. The first occurred when the Tinman went behind the goal to retrieve the ball for a corner. Finding himself submerged up to his ankles in rainwater, he grimaced, then uttered aloud a few words which made clear his abject displeasure at the situation.

The second incident was pure theatre. An attempted back-pass by a Port Vale midfielder from the half-way line (which given the inclement conditions was audacious in the extreme), completely bypassed a statue-esque Valiant's defender, who stood motionless as the ball trickled past him. It was as if he had remained too long on one spot, and, having sunk ankle deep into the mud, now found himself unable to move.

Ted was alive to the possibilities and without hesitation, touched the ball forward, before hammering it home past the advancing Musselwhite. The Tinman, intoxicated with a heady mixture of joy and mirth, celebrated by diving chest-first onto the rain-soaked surface and aquaplaning towards the Longside. Great finish – great celebration.

This was what I'd come to see. One-nil up, playing a below-par Port Vale and Ted McMinn throwing himself all over the Turf with gay abandon. I was feeling better already.

My reprieve from sickness lasted all of twenty minutes, when Martin Foyle picked the ball up about twenty-five yards out and unleashed the shot from hell towards our goal. Marlon dived, but it proved to be an entirely pointless exercise, the ball speeding past him into the top corner.

'How the hell did he manage to do that?' I thought, as I stood there open-mouthed. I was still doing a fair impersonation of a Venus fly-trap sixty seconds later, as Mark Burke thundered an unbelievable thirty-yard effort into the bottom left hand corner to give Port Vale the lead. Marlon unnecessarily muddied his jersey for the second time in as many minutes.

In the space of one hundred and twenty seconds, I had been toppled from the snowy peaks of ecstasy and now found myself flailing around in the wind-swept valley of despair. I cannot think of many other aspects of existence where you can experience such a *sudden* turnaround in such extreme emotions, as you can watching football.

I was absolutely distraught. It just didn't seem fair. We had practically played Port Vale off the park for forty-three minutes, only for all our craft and guile to be undone by two top-drawer strikes in two minutes. But like I said; since when has 'fair' ever had anything to do with football?

Half-time saw the weather deteriorate into Monsoon-like conditions. I half-expected the players to re-emerge after the break sporting not only the usual kit, but also galoshes and a sou'wester. In fact, I firmly believe that there would only have been a modicum of head-scratching, had a Polaris submarine surfaced in front of the Bob Lord Stand.

The referee however, deemed the pitch playable (or at least surfable), and so we were invited to indulge in yet more high jinks, as players slid, slipped and splashed in synchronisation around what was becoming less and less a pitch, and more and more a paddy-field.

One player who didn't find it all quite so amusing was young Wayne Dowell, who, having gone in with one of his customarily clumsy challenges, lay writhing in agony and was stretchered off with cruciate ligament damage by a couple of St John's Ambulancemen, to be replaced by Gerry Harrison.

At that point Mr Burns really should have called the match off, but instead allowed the farce to continue for another five minutes, during which time Adrian Randall received an eyeful of mud and both Inchy and Steve Davis proved they really were Gods, as they genuinely walked on water.

As Gerry Harrison tried to shake off the attentions of two Port Vale players, whilst scuba-diving down a left flank that could easily have been mistaken for Lake Windermere, the ref decided enough was enough, giving three long blasts on his whistle and pointing to the changing rooms.

'You're not singing anymore!' came the chant from the

Longside, as hundreds of Vale fans gloomily traipsed off home, believing themselves robbed of three points by an unfortunate combination of ridiculous weather and a swine of a referee. As for myself, I was both relieved and worried. As we sat in a traffic jam listening to the other results filtering through, I mentally worked out that we had dropped a place. That put us back in the relegation zone for the first time since mid-November. As the game had been abandoned, (and therefore no points awarded to Port Vale), I comforted myself with the fact that at least we would have another bite at the cherry, and we still had between one and three games in hand on some teams.

The problem was, we had to win those games in order to climb out of trouble. The other cause for concern was the points situation. Whereas a few weeks previously two consecutive wins would have propelled us into the top ten, a gap was now beginning to develop, which meant that six points would now see us climb a mere five places to sixteenth place. It was essential we got some points – quickly. Two or three more defeats would see us fighting a bona fide relegation battle. Like I said, it hadn't been such a Merry Christmas.

Manchester United's 3-2 victory at Chelsea, coupled with Blackburn Rovers' 3-1 win at Maine Road over Manchester City, put the pair five points clear of the chasing pack.

Tuesday 27/12/94

11.30 am Board coach to travel to Baseball Ground, only to hear over local radio that torrential rain in Derby means pitch is waterlogged, and game has been postponed.

11.31 am Go home.

17.00 pm Results roll in. Portsmouth beat Barnsley, Bristol City beat Stoke City. As a result of not having a game today, we drop to third bottom, our lowest league position this season since mid-October.

17.02 pm Wish I wasn't on these antibiotics; I could do with a bloody drink right now.

Aston Villa's 3-0 defeat of Chelsea gives Brian Little his first win since taking charge at Villa.

Northampton sack John Barnwell.

Saturday 31/12/94
Turf Moor

BURNLEY 5-1 SOUTHEND UNITED (*Saville 27, Gayle 34, Bressington 51* [og]*, Davis 85, Robinson 90*)
(*Willis 71*)
League position before and after match: 22nd . . . 19th

Attendance: 10,561

BURNLEY: Beresford, Parkinson, Armstrong, Davis, Winstanley, Harrison, Saville, Heath, Gayle (*McMinn 57*), Robinson, Deary.
Subs (not used): Joyce, Russell.

SOUTHEND UNITED: Sansome, Hone, Powell, Gridelet, Edwards, Bressington, Hails, Whelan, Willis, Ansah (*Sussex 19*), Thomson.
Subs (not used): Royce, Tilson

Referee: R. Furnandiz

Yellow Cards: Gayle (Burnley)

Red Cards: Harrison (Burnley)
            Gridelet, Bressington (Southend United)

You will occasionally get matches like this: matches which far exceed expectations, matches which remind you exactly why you fell in love with the game in the first place, matches which yield

126

six goals, a triumvirate of sendings-off and three timely points, which lift you out of the relegation mire just in time for the New Year. These are in fact more than matches. These are gifts from the Gods, and should be cherished as such. That having been said, I was simply thankful that we had a game at all. Whereas the majority of fans up and down the country had feasted on a footballing banquet of three games in six days, Burnley supporters had been forced to survive on a meagre diet of fifty-five minutes of what might as well have been water-polo; a situation which had many of us spooling through old video tapes, in a desperate attempt to remember just what it was like to watch the Clarets in action. It was, then, with enormous appetites, that the soccer-starved hordes turned up at Turf Moor, hoping to have their hunger satisfied.

Proceedings got off to a bizarre start, with the visitors taking to the field wearing our jade and black change strip from the previous season. I interpreted this as a good sign, for two reasons. Firstly, the strip we had loaned to Southend that afternoon, had been utterly useless for Burnley. We had only won once whilst wearing it – away at York, in the FA Cup. There was no reason to assume that it should produce any kind of luck other than bad, for anybody else who pulled it on. Secondly, how difficult was it going to be to beat a team whose foresight was so limited that they had failed to notice that their red and blue kit would clash with our claret and blue number?

The previous forty-eight hours had seen Jimmy sign two loan stars, for a month apiece. With Chris Vinnicombe out until mid-March with his fractured jaw and Wayne Dowell side-lined with cruciate ligament damage, Craig Armstrong had arrived from Nottingham Forest to fill the injury-jinxed left-back position. Newspaper reports had suggested that the nineteen-year-old was being groomed as a replacement for Stuart 'Psycho' Pearce, and was therefore not for sale. That didn't bother me in particular; it simply made a pleasant change to have somebody playing in that position who looked as though they knew what a football was. Armstrong proved to be an adequate replacement for Vinnicombe and prevented my knuckles from going white every time somebody broke down our left flank, which hadn't been the case in previous weeks.

Mullen had also read my mind about the striker situation and had swooped for Birmingham City's Andy Saville, one of those players who will be perpetually associated with the journalistically lazy tag, 'lower division journeyman'. With the signing of Ricky Otto from our opponents that afternoon, Birmingham were top-heavy with goalscorers, (a fact underscored by the Midland club's 7-1 massacre of Blackpool that same day), and were quite happy to let Saville play his first team football with us.

When, with less than half an hour on the clock, he received an inch perfect, defence-splitting ball from Heath and slammed it past Paul Sansome in the Southend goal, I too was more than happy for him to be playing his first team football with us. True, he did drift in and out of the game at times, but it would have been more than unfair to expect him to run the show on his debut with us. Besides, he showed more positional awareness and all-round understanding of Heath's game than either Robinson or Phyllis had managed in most of their outings.

Big Bad John, who had been having one of his less effective games, was determined not to be outdone by the new kid in town. Inchy rifled in a cross from the right and Gayle met it with one of the most brilliantly-executed scissor-kicks I have ever seen. Sansome didn't have time to move, less still attempt to save the big man's effort. I was suitably awed. So much so, in fact, that I found myself unable to cheer the goal and just stood open-mouthed, pointing at Gayle, and laughing with the joy of it all.

The Heath-Gayle axis was to have a hand in knocking another, by now inevitable, nail into Southend's New Year's Eve coffin, six minutes into the second half. A dink through from Inchy found Gayle in space, just inside the left hand side of the box. His attempted shot was heading for the corner-flag. Until, that is, Graham Bressington got his clumsy size tens in the way and diverted the ball into his own goal. Three sides of the ground became a claret and blue expression of human joy.

At the same time, I envisaged hundreds of Shrimpers fans who had made the long trek northwards wondering why the hell they had bothered, when they could have been sat in a Southend boozer getting quietly steamed as New Year approached. (Not that I suppose Southend's supporters were cock-a-hoop when they first learned that the FA's computer had, in its infinite wisdom, decided they should make the short ten hour round trip to local rivals Burnley on that afternoon of all afternoons.)

Ten minutes of token resistance followed, in which Roger Willis grabbed one back for United and the impressive Julian Hails should really have put us on the rack by firing home instead of wide, when he was clear through on goal with just Marlon to beat. However, we hung on and were soon back in the driving seat, with the Tinman, who had come on for Gayle, terrorising Southend's right back, without even the merest hint of a reprieve.

There was one black spot. Harrison, clearly not satisfied with beating Southend at football, wanted to take them on at fighting, too. As he stood up after having left a twelve stud impression on Keith Dublin's shin, Gerry seemed intent on locking himself in mortal combat with Phil Gridelet. The flamboyantly-monickered Mr Furnandiz decided that a bout of fisticuffs was doing nothing to enhance the seasonal philosophy of 'Goodwill To All Men', and sent them both packing.

From that moment on, Burnley went about exploding the frankly absurd myth that it is often easier to win when you have less players than your opponents. (Why do those who espouse this view think that the two teams start with eleven players each?)

A few moments later, Inchy, who was having his game of the season to date, put Andy Saville through on goal again. Own goal hero Graham Bressington had other ideas though, and scythed the debutant down as he attempted to twist and turn away from his marker. The ref had little choice but to send him to the dressing-room, to keep fellow bad-boy Phil Gridelet company. From at least twenty-five yards out, Steve Davis sent a fireball of a free-kick towards the Southend goal. Poor Sansome looked on helplessly as the speeding sphere whizzed past him and buried itself in the corner.

There was just enough time for one more, as Robinson dramatically slid onto the end of a Parkinson cross to poke the ball high and handsome into the roof of the net. Five-one. Which was wonderful; to me, such a scoreline suggests total superiority for the winning side and complete humiliation for the losers. If there was a better way to finish the footballing year, then I was struggling to think of what it might have been.

And so, I did what anybody would do after winning 5-1 at home on New Year's Eve. My course of antibiotics completed, I went out, had far too much to drink and told everybody, including a visibly bemused taxi-driver, how Burnley were going to stop in Division One and have a very Happy New Year.

Jimmy Hill is awarded an OBE, whilst Alex Ferguson is the recipient of a CBE.

Spurs' transfer-listed Romanian international, Ilie Dumitrescu, goes on loan to Seville of Spain.
Crystal Palace end the year not having scored a single league goal in their last seven attempts.

Monday 2/1/95
Fratton Park

PORTSMOUTH 2-0 BURNLEY *(Preki 26, Creaney 86)*
League position before and after game: 19th . . . 20th

Attendance: 9,097

BURNLEY: Beresford, Parkinson, Armstrong *(Brass 45)*, Davis, Winstanley *(Philliskirk 76)*, Harrison *(Russell 37)*, Saville, Heath, Robinson, Eyres, Deary.
All subs used.

PORTSMOUTH: Knight, Gittens, Daniel, McGrath, Symons, Butters, Pethick, Preki, Powell, Creaney, Wood *(Hall 70)*.
Subs (not used): Reeds, Flahavan.

Referee: T. Holbrook

Yellow cards: Brass, Deary, Robinson (Burnley)

Red cards: Beresford (Burnley)

The front cover of the 1992 edition of 'The Concise Oxford Dictionary of Current English' boasts 120,000 entries. [12] This is unquestionably impressive, staggering even; yet I seriously doubt if any single one of those entries is able to describe just how abysmal our performance was that afternoon.

Following our 5-1 obliteration of Southend, I had seen the green-eyed monster shine brightly in many people's eyes as I told them that I would be undertaking the long trek to deepest Hampshire to witness the mighty Burnley slaughter ailing Portsmouth, before throwing the bloodied corpse to the South Coast seagulls.

As it happened, it didn't quite turn out that way. And as Gerry Creaney turned in Robbie Pethick's 86th minute centre, I found it hard to resist the logic of the argument that I would have been better off back home, rushing around Burnley town centre in a frantic attempt to track down that all-important bargain in the January Sales. If this wasn't the nadir of the season, then I didn't relish the prospect of being there when it happened.

The long haul down to Portsmouth had been a tense affair. Overnight, Jack Frost had been busy ruining the Bank Holiday of many a footer fan by randomly freezing pitches or laying blankets of snow on football grounds up and down the country. Those on the coach with Walkmans tuned into Radio 5 every half hour, and relayed to the rest of us a list of all those fixtures that had fallen foul of the weather. 'Barnet v Exeter's gone . . . Orient's off . . . Swindon v Sunderland, that's off too.' Each dispatch would end with a calming phrase, such as, 'Nah, we're OK yet,' or 'No mention of Portsmouth in there.'

Listening to those half-hourly bulletins, reminded me of being back at school, when a particularly sadistic schoolteacher would randomly select the names of four or five unfortunates, who would have to go out and pick up all the litter in the yard, on a freezing winter's afternoon. All you could do was hope and pray that your name didn't pass his lips.

When we arrived in Portsmouth, it became instantly clear why so many fixtures had been postponed. It was bloody freezing. An anaemic midwinter sun seemed to hang reluctantly in the sky, and offered us precious little warmth as we tried to think of novel, yet interesting ways of killing the two hours that stood between us and three o'clock. Unfortunately, a combination of no local knowledge, no pub and no imagination thwarted our attempts. As a consequence, we spent the majority of the time

131

repeating the ten minute walk between ground and coach, debating what the odds might be on contracting listeria, should any of our number be tempted into buying one of 'Mick's Monster Burgers' from one of the many mobile food stalls dotted around Fratton Park.

Our boredom was temporarily relieved by the arrival of the players' coach. I stood and watched, filled with the same feelings of awe and reverence I had experienced as a twelve-year-old, when I had seen my then hero, Billy Hamilton, walk into the players' tunnel before a home game. Now, as then, there seemed to be something very strange about seeing my footballing heroes in civvies.

I only ever saw them running around a football pitch and as far as I was concerned, that pitch and the mysterious area forbidden to mortals known as 'the dressing room' were the only places where they existed. They had no other life, no other function, except running out on that pitch at three o'clock on a Saturday afternoon, or half-past-seven on a Tuesday or Wednesday evening, and entertaining me. Similarly, the only clothes they possessed, (because they were the only ones they needed), were the home and away kits. What else would footballers wear? Footballers aren't like other people, they're . . . well . . . *footballers*.

Fratton Park wasn't the most attractive ground I'd ever visited. In fact, you could say it was downright ugly. Huge, intimidating banks of perimeter fencing, chicken wire and more perimeter fencing, succeeded in giving the impression that Alcatraz would have been a more inviting place in which to spend a couple of hours. The hitherto reluctant sun had all but given up as we passed through the turnstiles, and dismal patches of light grey cloud provided our ceiling. It started getting colder – much colder. At ten to three, I lost practically all feeling in my feet, and it pretty much stayed that way until we were about half way up the M6, later on that evening. It was bitter and obviously had been long before our arrival, a fact emphasised by the state of Pompey's pitch, which would have been better employed playing host to 'Holiday on Ice', rather than an important Division One fixture.

The first indications that the match was to be played on an ice rink came when two or three of our lads took to the field. As they ran towards us, small powdery clouds of frost, maybe ice, flew up in their wake. Marlon and Inchy slipped and skidded around the penalty area, before retiring to the dressing-rooms to select footwear which might be more appropriate to the surface; skis or skates for example.

Mr Holbrook, however, had no qualms about allowing the game to be played. So at 3.00 pm, our twenty-third Endsleigh League Division One fixture of the season (exactly half-way through the league programme) got under way. The decision to play having been made, the team should have been professional enough to get their heads down and get on with it. It wasn't as if they weren't getting paid for their efforts. Sadly, certain members of the team didn't share my philosophy.

It was evident from the opening five minutes that Burnley, and Eyres and Heath in particular, simply didn't want to know. Their challenges bore all the clout of wizened powder-puffs, as they gingerly minced around the periphery of the game, trying their best not to get involved, lest they fell over and got their legs cold. They were, in short, a bloody disgrace.

It was, in fact, our lack of willingness to put in anything that bore even a passing resemblance to a challenge that on twenty-six minutes, allowed Preki to skip around three 'tackles' and fire in a shot from the right hand side of the area, which ricocheted off Beresford's far post and into the back of the net. One-nil to Portsmouth – and the famous Pompey Chimes rang out. Well, I say the famous Pompey chimes, but what they actually consisted of was somebody ringing a cow-bell and another half-witted individual blowing on a hopelessly out-of-tune hornpipe now and again. Hardly the stuff of legend, I'm sure you'll agree.

Preki, by now having twigged that he could pass anyone wearing a Burnley shirt without fear of recrimination, took the game by the scruff of the neck. The Portsmouth number eight knocked crosses over, forced saves out of Beresford, and generally took the rise out of a back line which offered less resistance than a paper bag in a monsoon.

With ten minutes to go to half-time, the former Everton man knocked a high ball over our static midfield for Gerry Creaney to chase. With no defensive cover, Marlon had little choice but to come for the ball. As he did so, Creaney lobbed him. With the ball heading for that space in between the two goal posts, Beresford instinctively threw his hands up and palmed the ball to safety. Which was fine, apart from the fact that this all occurred about ten yards outside our penalty area. It was Oldham all over again. I shuddered to think what our disciplinary record must have looked like. We'd now had four sendings-off in as many games. (Eyres at Stoke, Dowell against Middlesborough, Harrison in the Southend massacre, and now Marlon.)

As the referee produced his red card, (although to be honest, it looked pink – maybe the cold weather had turned it that way), I admit to feeling a soupcon of sympathy for our number one. Mullen stood on the touch-line, shouting the odds and openly berating Beresford's 'faux pas', as he made his way to the dressing-room. But what had Jimmy *expected* Marlon to do? During the incident, the closest thing the goalkeeper had to any form of protection was the condom machine inside the pub down the road.

It seemed almost inconceivable that the situation could worsen, but it did. Two minutes before the break, Craig Armstrong, the only player to emerge from the half with any credit, suffered an innocent but painful clash of heads with Robbie Pethick. As the nineteen-year-old lay on the deck, receiving treatment for concussion, (proof positive as if it were needed, that the number three shirt carried a definite jinx – this was the third victim it had claimed in as many months), Jimmy was to be seen playing merry hell with Mr Holbrook over the state of the frozen pitch.

He went about proving his point not by talking calmly to the referee and suggesting that the players might be in danger, but by pulling nasty faces, shouting at Mr Holbrook and jumping up and down on the ground, like a deranged Zebedee. Unfortunately for Jimmy, this highly embarrassing, yet somehow strangely amusing tantrum, failed to impress the man in black, and as soon as a dazed Armstrong had found his head again, play continued. The half drew to a close with the concussed left back wandering round, looking as if he wasn't sure what country he was in, let alone what position he was supposed to be playing in – a state of affairs which summed up the pitiful forty-five minutes to which 1,000 travelling Clarets had just borne witness.

Half-time was a dismal experience. It is indescribably difficult to be at all cheerful when you're ten minutes away from hypothermia, 1-0 down away from home, having had your first choice keeper sent off, and the only player worth his salt is looking highly unlikely to re-emerge for the second half.

We'd been treated to many surreal sights and sounds on our travels away from home already during the course of the season: unfeasibly large cloth creatures at Middlesbrough and Swindon, calypso rhythms at Sunderland, and Luton's unforgettable exhumation of Morecambe and Wise's 'Bring Me Sunshine'. Portsmouth's contribution to this seemingly never-ending carnival of the bizarre was to have a young chap dress up in a nineteenth century sailor's suit and parade around the perimeter of the pitch, sporting a large placard, upon which was inscribed the legend, 'Play Up Pompey!'

As the mariner strolled round to the Burnley end, a mass chorus of 'Rent boy, rent boy, give us a wave!', reverberated around the terraces. The matelot duly obliged, before rubbing sea-salt into our wounds by pointing to the nets with a huge grin on his face and mouthing 'One-nil' to the travellers. Having made his point, Jolly Jack Tar scuttled off to the safety of the Portsmouth enclosure.

The first fifteen minutes of the second half saw Burnley approach their task with a little more determination (however, considering their attitude in the first forty-five, they could hardly have approached it with less). Eyres, Saville and Davis all had efforts saved by Alan Knight in the Portsmouth goal. The best chance for the Clarets came when Lovely Legs directed a hard low ball into the Pompey six yard box. The ball arrived straight at Eyres' feet, but instead of ramming it over the line, he unbelievably hesitated and in doing so allowed Pethick to tickle the ball off his toes and away for a corner.

Eyres' mind-boggling miss was the last real opportunity that we had to get ourselves back in the game. With the clock ticking away, Heath decided that the only thing for it was to get the match abandoned. He went about this by performing a series of skating moves under Mr Holbrook's nose, that were so sophisticated, I feel sure they would have brought a complete set of 6's from any panel of judges. Apart from being extremely embarrassing, it was also highly unprofessional. Interestingly enough, none of the Portsmouth players seemed to have encountered any problems with the surface.

Mr Holbrook was immune to Heath's pathetic theatrics and

allowed the game to continue. In the last twenty minutes, Portsmouth missed a hatful of gilt-edged opportunities, before Creaney put the result beyond doubt. Immediately the ball crossed the line, scores of Burnley fans drifted past me and out of the gate at the top of the terrace, chuntering, muttering and cursing. And to be quite honest, who could blame them?

Any football supporter knows it always hurts like hell to watch your side lose, but when you've given up a Bank Holiday to make a 600 mile round trip, starting at 8.00 am, which means you won't be home until 11.00 pm, the team has played like donkeys, and it has cost you somewhere in the region of thirty pounds, that pain is more acute than usual.

To say I felt let down as we travelled back home later that evening would be understatement of the highest order. I wondered how could they do what they had done that afternoon? How could they go to a team two places below them who were in the relegation zone and allow them to walk (or perhaps skate) all over us? How could they refuse to get involved in a game they could have won, and which could have lifted them further away from the bottom four? How could they sell both themselves and the supporters so short? But the question that required the most urgent answer, was how were we going to get ourselves out of the mess we were rapidly getting ourselves into? I had no answers – did Jimmy?

Birmingham City celebrate the New Year, as they smash seven past Blackpool.

Crystal Palace would be grateful for just one of those goals. They have now failed to make the opposition's net ripple in their last nine league fixtures.

Blackburn Rovers extend their lead at the top to six points, as they beat West Ham 4-2.

The police inform Bruce Grobbelaar that it will be at least another month before he discovers whether or not he will face criminal charges over allegations of match-rigging.

Peter Shilton is suspended as Plymouth manager after he fails to pay £50,000 to the club. The money Shilton owes is for an outstanding tax bill on his signing-on fee. Jimmy Quinn and Mick Gooding are appointed as Mark McGhee's successors at Reading.

The Premier League deny a newspaper report that they are planning to buy Wembley Stadium for £100 million.

Saturday 7/1/95
The Abbey Stadium

FA CUP SPONSORED BY LITTLEWOODS POOLS. THIRD ROUND.

CAMBRIDGE UNITED 2-4 BURNLEY *(Butler 17* [pen.]*, 85) (Eyres 24* [pen.]*, Robinson 44, Randall 72, Gayle 76)*

Attendance: 6,275

BURNLEY: Beresford, Parkinson, Eyres, Hoyland, Winstanley, Randall, Harper, Heath, Gayle, Robinson, McMinn *(Deary 77).* Subs (not used): Russell, Philliskirk.

CAMBRIDGE UNITED: Sheffield, Joseph, Barrick, Heathcote, Jeffrey, O'Shea, Hyde, Lillis, Butler, Corazzin, Hay *(Hunter 66).* Subs (not used): Kriehn, Granville.

Referee: N. Barry

Yellow cards: O'Shea, Corazzin (Cambridge United)

Red cards: None

As it turned out, Jimmy didn't have any answers. Or rather, he didn't have the answers to any of the questions I wanted answering after the Portsmouth game. As Heath had skated around the pitch at Fratton Park, so Mullen skated around the

137

shortcomings of the Clarets, choosing instead to rant about how the game should never have been played in the first place. 'It's absolutely disgraceful that we were asked to play on a frozen pitch,' [13] he complained, conveniently ignoring the fact that Portsmouth had been asked to play on exactly the same area of turf.

This was becoming a disturbing trend. Every time we didn't get the result we were after, or whenever the side played badly, you could guarantee that JM would avoid the difficult questions the game had thrown up, by appearing in the local papers the following week and raging against some secondary issue or incident that had occurred during the match. Bryan Robson's foul on Inchy during the Middlesbrough match, the referee in the West Brom game and countless others, John McGinlay's bad sportsmanship when we played Bolton: all of these were convenient smokescreens which served to cloud the main issue, ie sometimes we weren't very good at football.

Any Burnley fans familiar with the local press knew that following a poor display or result, a 'MULLEN BLASTS . . .' headline was inevitable. And although the points he made were quite often valid, I wished he would stop talking exclusively about them, and confront the more pressing matters.

The Cambridge game was unique, in that Jimmy created a side-issue about the game before a ball had even been kicked. Obviously believing defeat was a distinct possibility, (highly likely, even), he pre-empted any criticism of the team and/or his tactics by letting it be known through the local press of the massive injury crisis he was facing, with fifteen of his first-teamers receiving some form of attention from Andy Jones, Burnley's physio.

Tactically, this was a stroke of genius. If we lost, defeat would be seen as the inevitable consequence of having a depleted squad from which to select a team. If we won, hero-status would be secured for players and manager alike, as they would be perceived as having overcome tremendous odds to emerge victorious. Jimmy Mullen – the shrewdest cookie in town.

The superb irony of all this was that in spells, the performance was one of our finest of the season. Nobody had a bad game. Randall came as close to convincing me that he was a genuinely gifted player as he had ever done, Eyres, who slotted in as a makeshift, attacking left back, looked as though he was capable of freezing Graeme Le Saux out of the England team in that position, and even Alan Harper gave such an assured first-half performance that he could easily have been mistaken for Barcelona's play-maker, Bakero. (Except, of course, the Spanish number six didn't sport a crap moustache.)

The alleged injury crisis proved to be something of a sham (quelle surprise!). The only notable absentee was Steve Davis, which meant that the defence needed some fine tuning. As at Sunderland, Jamie Hoyland dropped back to partner Winstanley at the heart of defence and did a fine job, whilst Eyres, as mentioned, moved to left back.

Having said that, the defence looked anything but solid, when United's Steve Butler ran straight through the middle of it after seventeen minutes and was halted only by the four-legged barrier of Winstanley and Lovely Legs, whose joint challenge on the striker earned the home side a spot-kick. Despite going through my penalty routine, (miss it, miss it, miss it), Cambridge's number nine squeezed the ball in between the post and Marlon's fingertips to give the U's the lead.

At which point I started to worry. My thoughts turned to that evening's 'Match Of The Day'. I imagined Gerald Sinstadt providing the chilling voice-over for this game in the goals round-up, saying something like, 'At the Abbey Stadium, struggling Cambridge United made easy work of beating a lacklustre Burnley side who have failed to make the fourth round for over a decade . . .'

I needn't have worried. Seven minutes after their penalty, we got one, as Danny O'Shea sent Eyresie into orbit, after he'd left a trail of Cambridge defenders in his mazey wake. The keeper went right, the ball went left, we went wild . . . with relief.

Then we turned it on, playing some gloriously flamboyant football. I couldn't remember a twenty minute period that season when we'd been so in control of a game. We eventually got our reward, when Eyres picked out an unmarked Robinson on the far post and the number ten, who had been re-christened 'The Fat Shearer' by certain sections of the crowd, nodded over the line with a minute to half-time. This considerably settled my nerves, and my nightmare 'Match Of The Day' scenario began to recede.

After having calmed me down by being Brazil '70 for the last twenty minutes of the first half, the Clarets set my nerve-ends jangling again, by pretending to be Exeter '95 for the opening fifteen minutes of the second period. As we hacked, hashed and scrambled to safety a succession of Cambridge corners, the spectre of Gerald Sinstadt loomed menacingly overhead. 'I don't like him,' I thought, 'Make him go away, Burnley.'

Adey 'Spaceman' Randall must have heard my plea, because two minutes later, a slide-rule pass from Inchy had sent him clear of the U's back four. With just the keeper to beat, Adey coolly slotted it under his diving body and into the corner of the net behind which we were stood. 'Pick that out!' yelled Andy, his voice rich with joy, as United's goalie stooped to retrieve the ball right under our noses.

Four minutes later, the Tinman nonchalantly twisted and turned, before knocking over the kind of cross that Ryan Giggs could only dream of delivering. Big Bad John was waiting on the far post, and from two yards out, tapped the ball over the line. As 2,000 Burnley fans celebrated our passage into the Fourth Round, Gayle did what he always did after he scored: he walked over to the cock-a-hoop Clarets fans and just stood there nodding, with an enormous grin on his face. We were through.

Not even a Steve Butler consolation in the dying minutes could take the gloss off what had, by and large, been a marvellous display. The coach journey home was spent listening to the results on Radio 5, wondering who we'd get in the next round.

Twenty-four hours later, we'd been drawn at home to whoever would triumph in the Liverpool v Birmingham replay, on Wednesday week. Much though I admired the inventive, mercurial qualities of the Reds, (twice already that season at close quarters), I quite fancied making it into the next round. So I crossed my fingers and hoped that the loveable arch-nutter who was Barry Fry, could motivate his side into performing their one and only giant-killing act of the season.

Peter Shilton threatens to sue Plymouth, unless he is reinstated as manager.

Gary Charles and Tommy Johnson move to Aston Villa from Derby, for almost £3 million the pair. Derby boss Roy

McFarland is unhappy he wasn't consulted about the sales, sanctioned by chairman Lionel Pickering whilst on a Paris break.

The only real upset of the FA Cup Third Round is Wrexham's 2-1 defeat of Ipswich. Meanwhile, replays are needed for Birmingham and Liverpool, Notts County and Manchester City, Carlisle and Sunderland, and Arsenal and Millwall, where there are reports of crowd trouble. Crystal Palace finally end their goal drought, hammering five past Lincoln.

The PFA step in to help Gillingham, who are in administrative receivership, following the collapse of a financial package put together by club chairman Bernard Baker.

Tuesday 10/1/95

BURNLEY v CHARLTON ATHLETIC

MATCH POSTPONED – TURF MOOR WATERLOGGED

'We'll be alright,' people kept saying, as we slid further and further into relegation trouble, 'we've got games in hand.' But games in hand did not necessarily equal points in the bag; and I, for one, was starting to become just a little nervous.

Andy Cole becomes Britain's most expensive footballer, when he moves from Newcastle to Manchester United in a shock deal worth £7 million. As part of the deal, Keith Gillespie leaves Old Trafford for St. James' Park.

The Coca-Cola Cup Quarter Finals see Crystal Palace ease past Manchester City 4-0, and Bolton dispose of Norwich by a single goal. The same scoreline separates Liverpool and Arsenal, whilst Swindon's 3-1 victory over Millwall solicits one of the footballing quotes of the year from

Millwall boss Mick McCarthy, who, speaking of Fjortoft's goal, says 'If he meant it as a shot, I'll drop my trousers in Burton's window.' Fjortoft quips back, 'If the Millwall manager likes, I will come with him to Burton's. It should make a good picture.'

After months of unrest, Plymouth Argyle and Peter Shilton finally part company. Steve McCall is his successor.

Howard Kendall is appointed manager of Notts County . . . seventy-two hours before Burnley are due to visit.

Steve Wignall is appointed manager at Colchester.

Saturday 14/1/95
Meadow Lane

NOTTS COUNTY 3-0 BURNLEY
(*White 50, Devlin 69, McSwegan 87*)
League position before and after match: 20th . . . 20th

Attendance: 8,702

BURNLEY: Beresford, Parkinson, Eyres, Davis, Winstanley, Randall (*McMinn 55*), Harper, Heath, Saville, Robinson (*Deary 68*), Hoyland.
Subs (not used): Russell.

NOTTS COUNTY: Cherry, Mills, Legg, Turner, Murphy, Johnson, Devlin, Butler, White (*Agana 86*), McSwegan, Matthews.
Subs (not used): Sherlock, Reece.

Referee: G. Singh

Yellow cards: Hoyland (Burnley)

Red cards: None

142

Twenty minutes prior to kick-off, the Red Cross gave a marvellous demonstration of how to pump life back into a corpse. The manoeuvre was known as the Recovery Position. As the ref blew for full-time a couple of hours later, I hoped for Jimmy's sake that he had been watching and taking notes.

This was truly awful. Every time I managed to convince myself that we'd hit rock bottom and we couldn't possibly get any worse, we somehow did.

I told everybody that we were unbelievably bad against West Brom. I publicly doubted that we could play with less ability and enthusiasm than we had against Middlesbrough. I confidently informed all and sundry that we could only get better following the shenanigans at Portsmouth. What the hell was I going to tell people about this one – a Burnley performance in front of 3,000 travelling Clarets' fans, who had each forked out £12.00 to get into Meadow Lane, that was so bad, it would necessitate the invention of a new language in order to express the soul-destroying terribleness of it all?

To lose by a three goal margin is rarely acceptable, but to succumb 3-0 to the division's basement team, who had won only four times all season, having been beaten in their last five league outings, with a meagre eighteen points from twenty-five games, borders on the scandalous. Granted, Howard Kendall had taken over as manager thirty-six hours previously; many of his charges were no doubt trying to impress their new boss, but the fact remained that this was one of the games we should have been looking to take maximum points from, and we should have been able to raise our game accordingly. But we didn't. We failed. What hurt more though, was that we failed because we didn't even try.

Although Beresford, playing his last game before suspension, made a stunning contribution to our defeat, (gifting County their opener, by blasting a back-pass straight at the static frame of Devon White, who looked on gleefully as the ball ballooned over Marlon into the empty goal), the game was lost in midfield. You could have been forgiven for thinking that somebody had told Randall, Harper, Heath and Hoyland that there was an exclusion zone in operation ten yards either side of the half-way line, such was their reluctance to get involved in said area. Randall was outrageously lazy, Hoyland was unfit and overweight, and Heath sulked (as he was prone to do when the going got tough) for the entire ninety minutes.

Heath had let many people down, including myself. I had hoped that he would be the one player who would dig in and lead by example. Instead, he dug a hole and hid in it for ninety minutes.

Harper meanwhile, was in a class of his own – the remedial class. He possessed the unerring and unhappy knack of being able to break down any move we had, simply by being in a two yard radius of the ball. I wasn't alone in my belief. My dad, who had watched Burnley sides in five different decades, (and therefore must have been subjected to an awful lot of crap, as well as the good stuff), claimed that never had he seen any Burnley player give the ball away in midfield with such ease and frequency as did the man they called Mooncat.

Of course, having a midfield as static as ours was that afternoon, meant that our strikers didn't get much of a look-in either. Then again, anybody who seriously believed either Robinson or Saville capable of posing a threat to Steve Cherry's goal would presumably have had little trouble lending credence to the theory that the moon was made of cheese.

The Fat Shearer performed his usual trick of chasing everything yet winning nothing, and it seemed that in Andy Saville, Jimmy had achieved the unlikely feat of unearthing another Philliskirk; a realisation that hardly left me fizzing with delight.

The lack of any real firepower was a problem that had dogged us since the beginning of the season. The longer the problem went unsolved, the more likely it was to play a huge part in getting us relegated.

Other clubs were in a similar predicament. Other clubs managed to take steps to sort it out. The week of the Notts County game proved particularly frustrating. Lee Nogan, who had been banging them in for Watford, moved to Reading for £250,000 – a sum not beyond Burnley's budget. Lee Chapman, who had been considered good enough to be a part of West Ham's plans earlier that season, (and who had trained with and expressed an interest in the Clarets), went on a month's loan to Southend – and scored. Robert Fleck, another Premiership player, moved to Bristol City, not a club renowned for its wealth. The players were obviously there. The players were obviously available.

Meanwhile, *we* were content to take on loan a striker who was not considered good enough to be included in the plans of Barry Fry's ambitious Birmingham City side.

It was, in fact, a lack of ambition,('Back Where We Belong' proclaimed the posters of the team in the club shop, following our promotion to only the second highest division in England), coupled with a lack of inspiration, which was at least partially responsible for our league position. Reading, Southend, Bristol City; none of these clubs were bigger than us, yet they seemed awake to the transfer market and the bargains that there were to be had therein, if only you looked closely enough. Burnley, however, dabbled with a player from the reserve team of one of the clubs in the division below us. Like that afternoon's performance, it wasn't good enough.

And as County's second and third goals rolled in, it was obvious that I wasn't alone in my feelings of frustration. Many of the 3,000 fans who had made the trip were on their feet for the last ten minutes. Some were shouting abuse at the players, others chose Mullen as their target, the rest of us just sat there, – watching our (at one time) promising season come apart at the seams, wondering just what the hell was going on both on and off the pitch, and hoping beyond hope that this really was as bad as it could get, and normal service would be resumed within the week.

The Notts County game woke a few people up. It provided proof, if proof were needed, that unless we got our act together very soon and started to win some games, then phrases such as, 'relegation dog-fight' and, 'threatened with the drop', would become synonymous with Burnley Football Club for the remainder of the season.

Twenty-four hours later, Port Vale beat Tranmere and Swindon defeated Middlesbrough – two results that saw us drop to third bottom in the league. With twenty-two league games remaining, it seemed a little premature to be panicking *just* yet. However, many more performances like that . . .

George Graham signs Luton's John Hartson and Ipswich's Chris Kiwomya for a total of £4 million.

Such is the ill-feeling amongst Newcastle fans about Andy Cole's recent departure that Manchester United's record signing is advised to stay away when the two clubs clash at St. James' Park. The game ends in a 1-1 draw, a result that means Blackburn Rovers' 3-0 victory over Nottingham Forest takes them five points clear atop the Premiership.

Labour leader Tony Blair hits out at the commercial aspect of football, using Manchester United's introduction of a new away kit as an example. He says, 'There is a fine line between fashion and exploitation.'

Ken Ramsden, United's assistant secretary, hits back, calling Blair's comments 'ill-informed'.

Roy Evans signs a new 3½ year deal to keep him at Anfield.

In the FA Cup Third Round replays, Middlesbrough are toppled by Swansea and Millwall see off Arsenal, as Birmingham push Liverpool all the way before going out 2-0 on penalties.

Debt-ridden Gillingham are put up for sale, as are Portsmouth.

Ghanaian striker Tony Yeboah joins Leeds on loan to the end of the season, for around £3.5 million.

Saturday 21/1/95
Turf Moor

BURNLEY 1v2 READING (*Viveash 56* [og])
(*Nogan 5, Taylor 10*)
League position before and after game: 22nd . . . 22nd

Attendance: 9,841

BURNLEY: Russell, Parkinson, Armstrong (*Saville 81*), Davis,

Winstanley, Randall, Harper *(McMinn 57)*, Hoyland, Gayle, Robinson, Eyres.
Sub (not used): Siddall.

READING: Hislop, Bernal, Jones, Holsgrove, Hopkins, Viveash, Gilkes, Gooding, Nogan, Quinn *(Lovell 79)*, Taylor.
Subs (not used): Thorp, Sheppard.

Referee: G. Cain

Yellow cards: Taylor (Reading)

Red cards: None

'As a fan,' reflected Jamie Hoyland, in the wake of our third straight league defeat in as many weeks, 'you don't think about how goals are given away, you're just desperately disappointed that you are 2-0 down.' [14]

Apart from being patronising in the extreme, (his words implying that supporters merely look at the scoreline and smile or frown, as the poor things aren't quite able to get to grips with such heady and complex concepts as tactics), his post-match comment was nearly as wide of the mark as one of his many wayward passes that afternoon.

I, for one, thought about how the goals were given away. In fact, I couldn't *stop* thinking about how Russell, in for the suspended Beresford, had mis-controlled Parky's back pass with a hard to believe degree of ineptitude, and looked on in horror as Lee Nogan rounded him to walk the ball into the net after just five minutes.

I experienced similar difficulties when trying to erase the memory of Winstanley gifting the ball away in midfield to Mick Gooding, who released Scott Taylor on the right hand side. With ten minutes on the clock and not a defender in sight to hamper his progress, Taylor raced forward to the edge of the area and cracked one in off the underside of the crossbar.

So you see, Jamie, us fans *did* think about how the goals were given away, that wet and windy afternoon. To be honest, I thought about them to the exclusion of practically everything else for the remainder of the weekend. Yes, it's silly, yes, it's probably very unhealthy, but hell, it *gets* you that way sometimes. If truth be told, it gets me that way *every* time.

'Obviously,' continued Jamie, warming to his theme, 'it's not a nice feeling to be booed during a home game.' [15] No. Jamie – it probably isn't. I'll tell you something else that isn't 'a nice feeling' – standing soaking wet on the terraces, with wind and rain blowing into your face, watching the same invertebrate midfield display that you thought you had seen the back of, seven days previously.

Standing on the Longside, with ten minutes gone and two goals to make up, I really couldn't believe what I was seeing. 'How can they do this?' I thought. 'How can they play like they did against Notts County and dare to show their faces again, let alone put in an identical performance?' Yet, with the exceptions of Russell for Beresford, and Gayle for Saville, there they all were; the same disorganised back four, the same clueless impotent forward line, and worst of all – the same lumbering midfield, more gutless and static than a disembowelled hippopotamus.

Not for the first time that season and almost certainly, I suspected, not for the last, I had to exercise great restraint from preventing myself from leaping over the Longside fence, rushing across the pitch to JM and asking him what sick, twisted perversion it was that drove him to repeatedly pick the fantastically inept Alan Harper.

I could live with his hairdo from hell. I could even find it within myself to excuse his naff moustache, which looked as though it was comprised solely of those bits of orange rind you find in jars of 'Robertson's Marmalade'. But it was becoming more and more difficult to forgive his on-the-pitch antics.

Not that the failure of midfield was entirely Mooncat's fault. He was only symptomatic of the general malaise in that area. Hoyland, for all his post-match bluster, had done nothing all afternoon, other than scythe down Jimmy Quinn on one occasion and clap his hands together in a feeble and utterly futile attempt to rouse the team from its somnambulism, following the second goal. It is hard to believe that a player so overweight should be invisible from a game for so long; but invisible he was.

Adrian Randall, the untouchable darling of many a Burnley fan, was desperately in need of a sharp, swift kick up the rear. For a player who allegedly liked to run at defences and score goals,

Spaceman rarely did either. In fact, such was his predilection that afternoon for avoiding forward movement, by means of running around and around the same square yard of turf, that there were those who suggested that perhaps young Adey was responsible for the Corn Circles of a few years back. It was not inconceivable.

What was inconceivable was that whoever played up front would get any service from such a bloodless and lacklustre trio as the manager employed in midfield week in, week out. Of those on display in that first forty-five, only Eyres, (surprisingly enough), put in an acceptable performance, showing the kind of invention and spirit that was needed.

Mullen had to take a lot of the rap for this. Whilst it wasn't his fault that Russell couldn't trap a ball, or that Winstanley surrendered possession on the half-way line, it was he who picked the team, and he who decided on what system to play. When the ball was in midfield, the only wide man, and therefore the only outlet, was Eyres. Cut him off, and you cut off our supply of balls into the box. We were screaming out for another option, someone to play out on the right wing for example: someone like Ted McMinn . . . who was on the bench for fifty-five minutes.

What was worrying and suggested that not for the first time that season Mullen was tactically unaware, naive, out of his depth, call it what you will, was that whilst many fans, certainly those around me, had sussed that the only way we were going to break Reading down was to attack them with wingers, it took nearly an hour for Jimmy to reach the same conclusion. Why? Wasn't it, after all, part of his job to be alive to these situations?

When the Tinman eventually did replace Harper, we scored within a minute, thanks to a fortuitous deflection, after Lovely Legs had lobbed a hopeful ball into the box. Almost instantly we looked a different side. Suddenly, Reading had their backs well and truly against the wall, as they were bombarded with hellishly difficult crosses from either flank.

With Eyres and McMinn reaping a twenty minute spell of havoc down either wing, we actually looked as though we might *win*. The former of the two wide men had three or four chances, a Winstanley header crashed against the bar, and Mick Gooding stretched out what must have been a telescopic limb in order to deny Steve Davis, by clearing off the line.

149

The best chance fell to Big Bad John, who, unbeknown to us at the time, was making his last appearance in a claret and blue shirt, as he was transferred to Stoke forty-eight hours later. Randall chipped over a cross which met an unmarked Gayle lurking on the Royals' goal-line. The ball was about chest height. All the big man needed to do was to fall over and his momentum would have forced the ball in. Unfortunately, his parting gift to us was to chest the ball off Reading's goal-line and out for a goal-kick. A sad way indeed to end a reasonably successful six month spell at Burnley which saw him win his way into the heart of many a Claret, myself included – but not that afternoon.

Nevertheless, for all our pressure, we came away with nothing. At ten to five we were still stuck with the same number of points that we had on New Year's Eve, with just one more goal to add to our tally. We now found ourselves one place higher than Bristol City, the Division's second bottom team, by virtue of goal difference. A win for bottom club Notts County meant they now trailed us by a mere three points.

That sort of form wasn't going to see us get ten more goals before the end of the season, let alone keep us up. And whilst the half-time voices of dissent against Jimmy Mullen might have been temporarily stifled by a spirited twenty minutes in the second half, it wouldn't take much to set tongues wagging again.

The top two in the Premiership meet at Old Trafford. Manchester United run out 1-0 winners, thanks to a late goal from Eric Cantona.

Seventy-two hours later, hero turns villain, as Cantona is sent off against Crystal Palace. Abused by the crowd, he launches himself over the advertising hoardings to deliver a two-footed, chest-high kick at one spectator, which he follows up with a flurry of punches. Paul Ince also appears to get involved.

The FA issue a statement saying, 'charges of improper conduct and of bringing the game into disrepute will inevitably and swiftly follow'.

A random dope test at Crystal Palace's training ground reveals that Chris Armstrong has taken cannabis.

Wimbledon boss Joe Kinnear lands himself in hot water with the FA, after calling referee Mike Read 'a cheat' when he disallows an injury-time equaliser in the Dons' 2-1 defeat at Newcastle.

Saturday 28/1/95
Turf Moor

FA CUP SPONSORED BY LITTLEWOODS POOLS. FOURTH ROUND.

BURNLEY 0-0 LIVERPOOL

Attendance: 20,551

BURNLEY: Russell, Parkinson, Eyres, Davis, Winstanley, Randall, Harper, Hoyland, Mullin, Robinson (McMinn 75), Saville.
Subs (not used): Deary, Siddall.

LIVERPOOL: James, Jones, Scales, Ruddock, Babb, Matteo, McManaman, Redknapp, Barnes, Rush, Fowler.
Subs (not used): Stensgaard, Walters, Thomas.

Referee: K. Morton

Yellow cards: Parkinson, Winstanley, Robinson, Davis (Burnley)
Scales, Babb (Liverpool)

Red cards: None

'I saw 'em on 'Match Of the Day'. They played OK, didn't they?'

The above comment, made by a colleague at work the Monday after the game, has to stand as one of the understatements of the season. What did he mean,'played OK'? Following his line of

151

logic, I can only assume that Vincent Van Gogh would be 'a painter' and the Notre Dame Cathedral might be described as 'a church'.

Make no mistake – Burnley were fantastic that afternoon and whilst we never outclassed the Reds, we were never overwhelmed, as could easily have been the case. And sure, there was every chance we'd get a towsing come Tuesday week in the replay – but to match Roy Evans' charges over ninety minutes was no mean feat. This was, after all, Liverpool, and lest we forget just how mighty our opponents were, let's consider a few facts.

We were third bottom of Division One. They were third top of the Premiership. Our defence cost somewhere in the neighbourhood of £500,000. Jones, Scales, Ruddock and Babb were valued in excess of £10,000,000. Of the side Liverpool fielded that day, only Dominic Matteo was without international experience. Within the Burnley ranks, John Mullin had played one Youth international for England. Get the picture?

Given the above facts, a 0-0 draw was a fine result and those same facts made certain moments in the game that much sweeter. Moments such as the Tinman dispossessing a begloved John Barnes deep in our own half and leaving him for dead as he raced down the wing. Moments such as the relatively inexperienced John Mullin, leaving £10,000,000 of international defence in his youthful wake, as he nearly snatched it for us at the death. And moments such as Wayne Russell, saving at the feet of McManaman, foiling Rush in a one-on-one, and making a superlative one-handed catch to deny both Rush and Fowler as they bore down on the Welshman's goal.

Although there were many memorable individual performances, what impressed most was the way that the team as a whole approached their task. A tactical switch saw Jamie Hoyland in the role of sweeper. As at Sunderland and Cambridge, he adapted to his defensive duties superbly. Alan Harper never looked anything less than in complete control at the heart of midfield, and Saville and Robinson's zeal, endeavour and tireless pestering of the Reds' back four very nearly paid dividends for the pair of them.

Strange to report then, that as Kelvin Morton brought proceedings to a halt at 4.45 pm, I had mixed emotions. My initial response was one of delight, having held Liverpool to a

152

goalless draw. But that feeling quickly waned, to be replaced by one of mild disappointment. It was probably petty on my behalf, but I was genuinely frustrated that we had failed to shatter Liverpool's FA Cup aspirations for another season. So instead of my Saturday night being a celebration of the Endsleigh League David refusing to succumb to the Premiership Goliath, I spent most of it thinking about what could have been.

'What if Davis' last-minute header had gone a yard either side of David James?' I thought to myself. 'What if Saville's shot hadn't taken that cruel deflection off Phil Babb's boot and gone out for a corner?' and so on and so on. Us football fans, eh? We're never satisfied.

Manchester United ban Eric Cantona from playing for the club until the end of the season. He is also fined £20,000.

Matthew Simmonds, the Crystal Palace supporter who hurled abuse at, and was subsequently assaulted by Cantona, is banned from Selhurst Park for the rest of the season and is to be interviewed by the police.

There are no giant-killing acts in the FA Cup Fourth Round. Manchester United have to come from behind to beat Wrexham 5-2, Everton squeeze through 1-0 at Bristol City, and Spurs ease past Sunderland 4-1.

Labour MP Kate Hoey's demand that the Government investigate corruption in football, is rejected.

Arsenal's Paul Merson declares himself fit to return to playing football.

Portsmouth dismiss manager Jim Smith. Less than 24 hours later, Terry Fenwick takes his place.

Following Blackburn Rovers' stormy 1-1 draw with Leeds United, one Blackburn fan runs on to the pitch to confront referee Roger Gifford, and has to be restrained by Rovers' keeper Bobby Mimms.

Inbetween the Liverpool and Swindon games, John Deary was sold to Rochdale for £25,000, a deal which struck myself and many other Burnley supporters as absolutely absurd. If there was one player at the club who gave the impression that if you cut him he would bleed claret and blue, then it had to be Deary. That isn't to say that commitment alone is sufficient in a footballer, but the man who played a large part in winning us promotion to Division One, had been in fine form whenever he had been called upon in the 94/95 campaign.

My favourite memory of Deary was in the 93/94 season, when we played Hull City away. The thousands who had made the journey stood getting soaked to the skin on the uncovered terraces of Boothferry Park. With the score at 1-1 and both the game and the weather getting grimmer by the minute, Inchy touched the ball back to Deary on the edge of Hull's penalty area. He then unleashed one of the most ferocious right-footed drives I have witnessed, which fairly screamed into the bottom right-hand corner of City's net, to give us one of only four away victories that season; splendid stuff indeed. He would be sadly missed.

Saturday 4/2/95
Turf Moor

BURNLEY 1-2 SWINDON TOWN (Harrison 85)
(Thorne 43, 72)
League position before and after match: 22nd . . . 23rd

Attendance: 10,960

BURNLEY: Beresford, Parkinson, Armstrong (McMinn 45), Davis, Winstanley, Randall, Harper, Hoyland, Mullin, Robinson (Harrison 78), Eyres.
Sub (not used): Russell.

154

SWINDON TOWN: Hammond, Robinson, Murray, Culverhouse *(Gooden 45)*, Nijholt, Taylor, Horlock, O'Sullivan, Fjortoft, Thorne, Ling.
Subs (not used): Mutch, Digby.

Referee: N.S. Barry

Yellow cards: Murray (Swindon)

Red cards: None

> 'We have still got a very long way to go before the end of the season and I am sure that we are not going to have anything to worry about in the final analysis.' [16]

Thus spake Jimmy Mullen in his programme notes before the Swindon game. But as 10,000 Clarets traipsed dejectedly off Turf Moor after our fourth consecutive league defeat, his words looked almost as ridiculous as the 'BURNLEY ARE BACK!!' [17] logo, boldly emblazoned across the top of every page of 'Claret News', the official matchday programme.

Zero league points out of a possible twelve in January of 1995 told its own story; and if Jimmy seriously expected us all to believe that such form would give us nothing to worry about come the beginning of May, then we might as well have called the funny farm there and then.

This was a genuine six-pointer. Before kick-off, Swindon were two points and one place ahead of us. Victory would have lifted us to the fringes of safety, one point above the Robins and with a game in hand on them. Instead we lost, a result that meant we dropped down to second bottom. Swindon (experiencing only their second away win of the season) climbed out of the mire, and we found ourselves five points away from escaping the relegation zone. As if that wasn't bad enough, the man who did the damage was Peter Thorne, whom Swindon had bought from Laughing Boy Dalglish just down the road. That small matter aside, things were looking grim, to say the least.

As with the defeats against Portsmouth, Notts County and Reading, it was the way we lost which gave the greatest cause for concern. It seemed that in order for us to start playing, we had to

155

go at least 1-0 down. Then, and only then, did we seem to raise our game and consider having a go back, by which time it was invariably too late.

This in turn had to reflect on the man in charge. Why was it that Jimmy was able to raise the players to face Liverpool in the FA Cup, yet obviously found it enormously difficult to instill any passion in them when it came to the less glamorous, yet infinitely more important task, of disposing of fellow relegation candidates Swindon?

Another worry in this game was that, once again, I believed Jimmy had got his tactics in a twist. In substituting Armstrong for McMinn at half-time, we had two wingers on the pitch. But instead of putting one on either flank, he opted to switch Eyres to left back and have the Tinman operate down the same side of the field. Surely, at 1-0 down, it would have made more sense to move Parky to left back, put Harper at right back, push Hoyland into midfield, and have two wingers knocking in crosses from either side for Mullin and Robinson.

Even the one bright spot of the afternoon, an 85th minute strike from substitute Gerry Harrison, failed to cheer me. His goal was the first in the league this year to be scored by a Burnley player, (the one which Reading conceded against us having been self-inflicted), and only served to highlight our increasingly desperate need to sign someone who was capable of putting the ball in the net. In the rest of the division, only the fans of West Brom and Bristol City had seen their team score less times this season, than had Clarets supporters.

Jimmy seemed particularly clueless when it came to acquiring somebody who could rustle the onion-bag. His latest folly was to believe that Brighton's Kurt Nogan, who hadn't scored in twenty or so games for a team who were in the division below us, was capable of moving up a division and providing the killer instinct in front of goal. Expecting JM to find an effective striker was like expecting snow in June – it could happen, but it seemed highly unlikely.

Even if we did sign a quality striker, you had to wonder about the quality of service he would receive from the midfield we had, particularly as the one genuine play-maker we did possess – Adrian Heath – was out injured. Randall's form was far too erratic to rely on, Gerry Harrison was a battler, but little else, whilst Harper and Hoyland were more comfortable occupying defensive roles. With Warren Joyce on loan to Hull City and John Deary scandalously sold to Rochdale, that was your lot as far as midfield went.

I personally believed it was worth going into serious debt (say £1,000,000 plus) in order to secure both a quality striker and a midfield playmaker. This may have seemed a drastic move, but the long term future of the club was at stake. Various rumours were doing the rounds that Premiership Division Two was on the way. It was mooted that the new set-up would see automatic promotion and relegation from Division Two to Division One (and vice-versa) become things of the past.

In light of this potential restructuring of the Football League, it was absolutely imperative that Burnley Football Club got its act together and made damn sure it didn't go and get itself relegated. A return to Division Two would be nothing short of catastrophic for the club. If ever the board needed to pin its colours to the mast, it was now; because without some serious money for a playmaker and a striker, the club was heading for Division Two, with no guarantee of a return to the game's higher echelons.

Not that any Burnley supporter ever got to know much about the faceless mute that was Burnley's board. The average fan, such as myself, knew little of its composition, and the only time it ever issued statements of any kind, was to placate the fans when the club was going through a bad spell, (early 1995 being a case in point), by saying how wonderful we all were, turning up week in, week out. Which was exactly the kind of patronising nonsense we could have done without at the time.

Commitment was the buzzword – both on and off the field. It was amply demonstrated week in, week out, by those supporters who turned up at Turf Moor and undertook gruelling trips to Millwall, Portsmouth, Swindon and Notts County. If we could be relied upon to show such a level of commitment, then so could the players and the board – couldn't they?

As Sunderland fans prepare a protest ballot against their board, Bob Murray, the club's majority shareholder, claims the board are prepared to step down to let new owners come in.

Blackburn Rovers' lead at the top of the Premiership is reduced to two points as they lose 3-1 at Spurs, and Manchester United beat Aston Villa 1-0.

Birmingham top a tight Division Two, whilst Carlisle's draw against Doncaster means that the Cumbrians' cushion at the top of Division Three is a meagre 16 points.

Tuesday 7/2/95
Anfield

FA CUP SPONSORED BY LITTLEWOODS POOLS. FOURTH ROUND REPLAY.

LIVERPOOL 1-0 BURNLEY *(Barnes 44)*

Attendance: 32,109

BURNLEY: Beresford, Parkinson, Eyres, Davis, Winstanley, Randall, Harper, Hoyland *(Peel 75)*, Mullin, Robinson, Harrison *(McMinn 64)*.
Sub (not used): Russell.

LIVERPOOL: James, Jones, Bjornebye *(Walters 64)*, Scales, Babb, McManaman, Thomas, Rush, Barnes, Fowler, Ruddock.
Subs (not used): Clough, Stensgaard.

Referee: K. Morton

Yellow cards: Harper, Harrison, Parkinson (Burnley)

Red cards: Ruddock (Liverpool), McMinn (Burnley)

Twenty weeks and twenty-three fixtures had elapsed since Jimmy Mullen's Claret and Blue Army last descended on Anfield, to give the home fans a first-class lesson in how to support your team. As we took our seats prior to our fourth and final meeting of the season with Liverpool, it struck me just how much things had changed since that late September evening.

Our previous trip to Anfield had seen us fourth bottom of the division, after eight league games. However, we had been buoyed by two fantastic away wins at Luton and Millwall, coupled with a home defeat against the then table-toppers Wolves – a game which we not only could, but should have won. That night, players and supporters were brimming with confidence, and it showed, as we gave the Scousers a run for their money and were more than a touch unlucky to lose 2-0. There was an optimistic air about events. We'd had a tough start to the season, but we seemed to be finding our feet. We'd stop up.

Five months down the road, however, and the mood and outlook were distinctly bleaker – second bottom, no league win since New Year's Eve and an ever-increasing gap between ourselves and safety. Things were going very wrong. Still, that evening was a chance to forget our dismal league form – a night off, if you will. It was a game where we had the chance to go out, play our hearts out and give it our best shot. Hell, with a slice of luck, who knows, we might even have won it.

For a short while, things looked good. In a tremendous three minute spell, Robinson thundered a thirty yard piledriver against the crossbar, Davis chipped the keeper from the edge of the box and rippled the back of the net, and Eyres slotted home from the penalty spot. It was unfortunate, then, that the warm-up had to end, and the match begin.

Despite what various papers might have said, Liverpool *were* a cut above. McManaman's strong, fluent and purposeful running terrified me. Ruddock, far from being the thug portrayed by the media, (his 82nd minute indiscretion excepted), was solid in defence and visionary in his passing. But if you were looking for elegance, then John Barnes was the man. In truth, he didn't have a brilliant game, but he was good enough. If ever a footballer's style of play has deserved the label of 'eloquent', then it was surely this man. The way he seemed to wrap his boot around the ball, caress it and almost effortlessly lay it off to perfection time and again, would have been a joy to behold, had he been weaving his subtle magic around anybody else's midfield, save ours.

159

Not that I can say I was exactly singing his praises, when in the 44th minute, he rose unchallenged in our area to meet Bjornebye's corner and power it past Beresford to ensure Liverpool's passage into the next round.

That goal, coupled with the prospect of Liverpool knocking us out of a second Cup competition, proved too much for Andy and Mick, both of whom spent the majority of half-time attempting to bribe the refreshment stall staff into opening the crates of Carlsberg piled high behind them. Unfortunately, licensing laws forbade any sale of alcohol for midweek matches, so the pair of them skulked off to their seats to watch the the remainder of the game stone cold sober.

The first part of the second half was practically a repeat of what had gone on in the first forty-five; Liverpool in control, Burnley trying, but always failing to hit them on the break. The problem was that we looked to be devoid of ideas, passion and all those other ingredients that you need to win Cup ties – goals for example. And as we tried in vain to find a chink in Liverpool's seemingly impenetrable armour, I thought of Burnley as that duff Roman Candle that you always seem to get in boxes of fireworks. Like the Roman Candle we coughed, spluttered and threatened to explode into life; but deep down, you knew that this particular firework was never going to go off in Liverpool's face.

There were momentary flashes of resistance. Davis tried his luck from thirty yards once or twice, the same player put a great through ball to Mullin, who, one-on-one with the Reds' 'keeper, was unable to find a way past his imposing figure, and Kelvin Morton decided that it was well within the laws of the game for John Scales to whip Robinson's legs from beneath him in the penalty area.

With eight minutes remaining, Burnley hearts leapt into mouths, as Robinson raced clear of the Liverpool defence and bore down on goal. Razor Ruddock had other ideas and sent the number ten sprawling. Seven thousand Clarets rose to their feet to voice their indignation. The man in black produced a card to match the colour of the home team's strip, pointed to the tunnel, and number 25 took no further part in the proceedings.

As the resultant free-kick glided safely over the bar and into the top tier of the now almost complete and mightily impressive Kop, you sensed that that was it, kaput, goodnight Vienna; and it was. It was all too much for the Tinman, who immediately the final whistle sounded, was over remonstrating with the linesman about something he'd done, or said, or God knows what. His indisciplined outburst earned him a red card. Well done, Ted; with a relegation battle looming, what we really needed was to have experienced professionals getting themselves sent off for no good reason, and therefore suspended for vital games.

It was a somewhat deflated Burnley following that drifted out into the streets of Liverpool that evening. There was, tellingly, no twenty-five minute version of 'Jimmy Mullen's Claret and Blue Army', and precious little wisecracking. Which was hardly surprising, given the largely dispassionate performance.

'Ah, well,' someone said, 'That's the season over, then.' Whilst I knew what he meant, he couldn't have been more wrong. Given our distressing league position, the season was just about to begin. We had twenty league games to save ourselves from the drop. Sixty points were up for grabs. Given that a reasonable target for survival was fifty-four points, we needed to be looking to pick up another twenty-seven to finish fifth bottom. Having already amassed twenty-seven points from twenty-six games, we needed to step things up a little. It was quite clearly do-able, but did we have the stomach for the battle ahead? We would soon find out, with a trip to a rejuvenated Watford who were loitering on the fringes of the play-offs, that Saturday.

Snooker impresario Barry Hearn expresses an interest in the purchase of struggling Leyton Orient.

Birmingham goalkeeper Ian Bennett claims he was offered £20,000 to throw his side's FA Cup Third Round replay against Liverpool.

Terry Venables drops Dennis Wise from the England squad for the forthcoming game against the Republic Of Ireland, after the Chelsea player is found guilty of assaulting a London taxi driver and causing criminal damage to his cab.

An exciting night of FA Cup football, as Wolves take

Sheffield Wednesday to penalties, and trail 3-0 before eventually running out 4-3 winners.

Another penalty shoot-out is required at Stamford Bridge, where Millwall triumph 5-4 over London rivals Chelsea. Their victory is marred as more than 30 arrests are made, when fans and police clash on the pitch after the match.

Le Tissier scores two and makes two, as Southampton demolish Luton 6-0 in their Fourth Round F.A. Cup replay.
Milan beat Arsenal 2-0 in the Super Cup.

Eric Cantona fails to turn up for police questioning about the incident at Selhurst Park.

Saturday 11/2/95
Vicarage Road

WATFORD 2-0 BURNLEY (*Ramage 52, Bazeley 71*)
League position before and after match: 23rd . . . 23rd

Attendance: 9,297

BURNLEY: Beresford, Parkinson, Eyres, Pender, Winstanley, Harrison (*McMinn 69*), Harper, Hoyland, Heath, Robinson, Mullin.
Subs (not used): Russell, Peel.

WATFORD: Miller, Lavin, Bazeley, Foster, Millen, Ramage, Holdsworth, Payne, Moralee (*Jemson 69*), Porter, Gibbs.
Subs (not used): Digweed, Johnson.

Referee: A.P. D'Urso

Yellow cards: Payne (Watford)
 Winstanley, Parkinson (Burnley)

Red card: Payne (Watford)

'Did you know,' inquired Mick as our coach sped down the M6 on its way to Watford, 'that bananas can predict the future?' As it happened, I didn't know, but was sufficiently intrigued to ask just how it came to be that a lump of bent fruit could succeed where 1,001 fortune-tellers had failed.

Mick explained that first of all, it was necessary to ask the banana a question, (well, obviously). That having been done, its tip should be sliced off. This in turn would apparently reveal either a 'Y' or an 'N' in the fruit's seed patterns and thus your question would be answered. Not wholly convinced, I told Mick not to 'be so bloody stupid', and returned to reading the newspaper.

Half an hour later we were sat on the back of the coach, debating what questions we should ask the pair of bananas we had just purchased from Newport Pagnall Services. Andy wanted to know whether or not Mooncat would shave off his crap 'tache, Chris was more interested in how long Mullen had left in charge, whilst Steve was desperate to find out if we would be getting a proper striker, ('you know, like other teams have'), before the end of the season.

As we only had two bananas, we decided to ask, a) would Burnley win that afternoon, and b) would the Clarets avoid the drop, come May? We waited with bated breath as Mick interrogated the curvaceous yellow fruit as to Burnley's short and long term future, before feverishly cutting into it with Andy's banker's card. A large grin spread across Mick's face, indicating that our questions had been answered in the affirmative. That was it then, everything was OK . . . THE BANANA HAD SPOKEN!

It was perhaps a measure of how desperate we had become, that we were prepared to invest more faith in the random seed patterns of a couple of West Indian Class A's, than we were in the eleven players who would turn out for us that afternoon. But desperate times invoke desperate actions, particularly amongst football supporters like myself, who will cling to any kind of hope, from any kind of source – and that includes exotic fruits.

Unfortunately, what the banana had failed to tell us was that we would miss the first twenty minutes of the match, which with the benefit of hindsight was probably no bad thing, but at the time was frustrating to the nth degree.

163

Arriving in Watford town centre just after 2.00 pm, it took our coach the best part of an hour to carve its way through the monster traffic jams that choked the streets leading to Vicarage Road. It is almost impossibly difficult to explain the frustration of being able to see the ground, yet being too far away to jump out of the coach and leg it towards your intended destination. Clutches of Watford fans calmly saunter past your static vehicle, confident in the knowledge they'll get there on time, the traffic seems to be moving slower than Alan Harper's thought processes, and the digital clock at the front of the coach ticks and tocks irrevocably towards 3.00 pm, as your blood pressure threatens to go through the roof.

Eventually, along with about twenty other coaches, we parked up at the foot of a hill, atop of which sat Vicarage Road. 'Five to three,' I thought as the Claret and Blue Army yomped in unison up the hill, 'We might just make it.' However, any thoughts of getting into the stadium for kick-off were suddenly and cruelly dashed, as our gaze fell on another thousand or so Clarets queuing at the turnstiles – which was, of course, when the heavens decided to open.

The frustration felt on the coach that had temporarily ebbed away, returned with a vengeance. As the game got under way, there were hundreds of Burnley fans still outside the ground. Initially, the crowd was good-humoured enough, greeting what should only have been a five minute delay with chants of, 'Come on you Clarets'. However, with the problem still not sorted out after ten minutes or so, a certain and wholly understandable agitation began to creep in.

'Why won't they open them other turnstiles?' asked a Claret, indicating three of the seven entrances shut for no apparent reason. 'It happens every week, mate. It's always like this,' replied a police officer with an apathetic shrug of his shoulders. 'Oh well, that makes everything alright, then,' I thought to myself, as a young lad in front of me, who was visibly worried, asked his dad what was happening. 'Shut up, and don't ask questions,' he might have replied, 'You're only a football fan, after all.'

The remaining turnstiles remained closed. People pushed, people shoved and I recall the crowd being packed so tightly that I was unable to move in any direction. The initial good humour was beginning to evaporate at a fair old rate of knots. Fortunately, (and it was fortunate), it was at precisely this point that the queues began to move. Five minutes and a whole lot of pushing, shoving and cursing later, we eventually stormed Fort Watford.

The point remained however, that either the police or the club, or perhaps both, seemed perfectly prepared to allow this to happen, when the opening of another three turnstiles, or the delaying of the kick-off, would have completely defused the situation. That afternoon, the relevant authorities got lucky. I am not being in the least dramatic when I say that if the situation had taken much longer to resolve, then the police would have had at best a mild case of crowd disorder, or at worst some *very* serious injuries. And all for the want of a little common sense . . .

The remainder of the first half was frustrating, both on and off the pitch. As we struggled to find a decent place to sit in the Stanley Rous Stand, Burnley experienced their own difficulties in attempting to break down Watford's rearguard. Taking our seats at the front of the stand, we had a worm's-eye view of proceedings, as the Clarets struggled (and by Christ, it *was* a struggle) to create decent openings on a pitch which could easily have passed for the original set of 'Swamp Thing'.

As Mick tucked into his half-time 'Hornet-Burger', priced at a stinging £2.40, I caught sight of the friend I had last seen at the Charlton game, (no, not Neil Kinnock). 'This is bollocks,' he said, gesticulating in the general area of the swamp, as Watford's fluffy mascot, which I presumed was supposed to be a hornet, yet bore a closer resemblance to a three-day-old piece of soggy bacon-rind, passed us by. 'We're as good as down, y'know.' I was about to tell him not to be so over-dramatic, but was hit by the realisation that, given our current form, I didn't have a leg to stand on.

It took Burnley just seven second half minutes to prove my friend right. A cross from the left swung across our defence and out to the right wing. As Eyres seemingly couldn't be bothered to chase after the ball to clear our lines, Gerard Lavin seized the initiative and knocked a cross back over to the far post. Craig Ramage propelled himself forwards and thundered a diving header past Beresford, to the obvious delight of the yellow and red masses assembled behind Marlon's goal.

'You're shit, and you're going down!', came the chorus from

Watford's North Bank. It was noticeable that no-one bothered to contradict the statement, probably because of the large element of truth it contained. Although at that point of the season it was debatable whether or not we would be relegated, there was no doubt that we were, as Watford's terrace analysts had observed, 'shit.'

The Hornets then proceeded to slaughter us. Jamie Moralee slammed a shot straight at Marlon, who a couple of minutes later pulled off a fabulous save from Nigel Gibbs. Ramage picked out Moralee in roughly five acres of space, who was somehow unable to work a decent angle, and ended up firing a tame shot at Beresford. The killer blow was provided by Darren Bazeley, who finished off a neat Watford build-up by cracking an angled drive past what must have been a thoroughly dejected Marlon.

Even that failed to spark us into life. We seemed content to knock balls into the corner for an increasingly knackered Liam Robinson to pursue; balls which were almost invariably snaffled up and cleared by the Watford defence. With seventeen minutes left, Jamie Hoyland was sent sprawling five yards outside the box. Derek Payne, having been booked already, took no further part in the game.

But even with ten men, Watford still looked the more likely to score, even going so far as to hit the post. This was due to the fact that they had a midfield, whereas we had Harper and Harrison. Whilst the latter at least tried, (but was unfortunately not really up to it that afternoon, and was subbed for McMinn during the second half), the former was a dead loss, or perhaps just dead. A classic example of this occurred late in the second half. Watford were awarded a throw-in, which Mooncat believed should have been Burnley's, but instead of getting on with the game, he stood and argued the toss with the linesman, as a Watford midfielder raced past him; unprofessional, unbelievable and unacceptable.

The situation was growing more serious by the game. Had nine-man Southend not performed major heroics, by equalising with the last kick of the game against Notts County, we would have been lying bottom of the table that evening. We hadn't picked up one point out of a possible fifteen in our last five league fixtures, and were scoring at the rate of one every three and three-quarter hours. 'Every team goes through a lean spell,' a fellow football fan had tried to console me. But this wasn't so much lean, as anorexic.

Mullen's post-match reaction was nothing short of staggering. Apart from the inevitable blasting of the pitch, (a pitch on which Watford managed to score twice, and look more than comfortable with), JM's comments betrayed more than a touch of desperation, as the man in charge showed seriously worrying signs of losing the plot. After saying that he didn't feel under pressure, which given our recent form and perilous situation was as good as official confirmation that he was living in la-la land, he went on to exhibit distressing traits of paranoia. Berating the officials, he moaned, 'The referee was from Essex and one of the linesmen was a Cockney – that's too close to Watford in my book.' [18] What book might that be, Jimmy? 'The Desperate Football Manager's Book Of Excuses', maybe?

Not satisfied with this outburst, he took a vicious sideswipe at the 'Burnley Express' newspaper, practically accusing them of running a 'Mullen Out' campaign, saying, 'I know the local Press are waiting for the answer to the situation because they succumb to the pressure of the supporters out there – certainly the Burnley Express does, anyway.' [19]

So there we had it; a team who looked more and more clueless with every passing game, managed by a man whose grasp on reality seemed tenuous, to say the least.

By now, an increasing number of Burnley supporters were becoming more and more disenchanted with the manager, citing what they perceived as his lack of tactical nous at Division One level, his seemingly unmotivated sides, and his inability to sign a goalscorer of any calibre as reasons for him to stand down.

The voice of discontent, first heard at Notts County, was getting louder and louder. It was a voice you could hear in the 'Mulen Out!' chants on the terraces. It was a voice you could listen to on the local radio phone-in on a Saturday evening. It was a voice you could read about in the many passionate letters sent into the 'Burnley Express', by supporters who had quite simply had enough, and wanted to voice their concern at the prospect of the club they loved slipping back into the footballing wastelands, from which it had taken eleven seasons to escape.

It hadn't always been like this. For the majority of his managerial reign, Jimmy had been the toast of the town.

The former Blackpool boss arrived at Turf Moor in April 1990, as assistant to Frank Casper. Following a poor start to the 1991/92 campaign, Casper was sacked. After an extremely successful spell as caretaker manager, Mullen was offered the post on a full-time basis.

In his first season as boss, there can be no doubt that he worked wonders. He turned a mediocre Fourth Division outfit into a passionate team that tore through the division, breaking records and winning hearts, as Burnley ended the season as worthy Champions, having played some highly entertaining football along the way. The seven-season-wait to escape the Football League's basement division had ended. In achieving what he had, Jimmy became an instant hero.

The 1992/93 season was one of consolidation, the Clarets finishing the campaign in mid-table after having briefly threatened to grab a play-off place, which was exactly what they did in the season which followed. No Clarets supporter who was at Wembley Stadium on 29/5/94 for the Division Two play-off Final will ever forget that afternoon. North London became Burnley for the day, as 34,000 of the town's inhabitants descended on the capital to watch their team overcome Stockport County 2-2, in a Final which although falling some way short of being a great match, was one of the most thrilling pieces of theatre I have ever borne witness to.

At that time, the general feeling seemed to be that although Jimmy had no management experience in Division One, he should at least be given the chance to prove himself, in the light of what he had achieved for the club. But on the evidence of what he had accomplished after twenty-seven games in Division One, the only thing he was proving was that he really didn't appear to be up to the job.

'You're talking to someone who has achieved two promotions in three seasons,' [20] he said after the Watford game; very true, very true indeed. But all the indications were that if this appalling sequence of results was allowed to continue, Jimmy would be well on the way to achieving something else; something he might not be quite so keen to boast about.

Eric Cantona appears to be in yet more trouble, following allegations by ITN cameraman Terry Lloyd that the

Frenchman, holidaying in Guadeloupe, kicked him in the ribs.

Peter Shilton is back in action again, appearing as substitute goalkeeper for Wimbledon, in their FA Cup tie at Liverpool.

Manchester United complete the derby double, triumphing 3-0 over City at Maine Road.

Blackburn Rovers remain top with a 3-1 victory against Sheffield Wednesday.

In the first leg of the Coca-Cola Cup Semi-Finals, Swindon beat Bolton 2-1 and Liverpool have a 1-0 advantage over Crystal Palace.

Phil Neal is no longer manager of Coventry City. He leaves by 'mutual consent'. Twenty-four hours later, Ron Atkinson is appointed boss.

Keith Burkinshaw, sacked by West Bromwich Albion earlier in the season, is to sue the club for £300,000 plus.

Twenty-seven minutes into the Republic of Ireland v England friendly at Lansdowne Road, rioting England fans cause the match to be abandoned. Forty are arrested and twenty treated in hospital, as rumours of National Front involvement abound. England's hosting of the 1996 European Championships will not be called into question, according to FIFA President Joao Havelange.

Doncaster Rovers have severe financial problems, so much so that they tell the Football League they may have to resign.

Saturday 18/2/95
Turf Moor

BURNLEY 0v2 GRIMSBY TOWN *(Mendonca 25, 81)*
League position before and after game: 23rd . . . 23rd
Attendance: 10,511

BURNLEY: Beresford, Harrison *(Robinson 86)*, Parkinson, Pender *(Heath 74)*, Winstanley, Randall, McMinn, Hoyland, Stewart, Mullin, Eyres.
Sub (not used): Russell.

GRIMSBY TOWN: Crichton, McDermott, Jobling, Handyside, Rodger, Groves, Watson *(Laws 83)*, Dobbin, Woods, Mendonca, Gilbert.
Subs (not used): Pearcey, Childs.

Referee: K.Leach

Yellow cards: Stewart, Harrison, Hoyland (Burnley)

Red cards: None

After the Watford game, Jimmy Mullen was travelling back to Burnley up the M6. Eager to get home early, Jimmy put his foot down and was soon flying up the motorway. Unfortunately, a hidden police car clocked the Burnley boss doing 100 mph.

The police car gave chase and eventually caught up with Mullen, and signalled that he should pull over. In the ensuing conversation, the officer warned JM about speeding, strongly advised him not to do it again, and told him to be on his way.

'What,' said Jimmy, 'Is that it then?'

'How do you mean?' replied the officer.

'You're not going to book me, or report me, or anything, then?'

'No.'

'Oh, go on,' moaned Jimmy, 'Please book me.'

'Why?' asked the visibly bemused officer.

'Well,' answered Mullen, 'It's just that this is probably the closest I'll come to getting any points this year.'

No, I know it's not particularly funny, but then, neither was the predicament we found ourselves in, following the Grimsby match. Forty-nine days into 1995 and we had still to collect a single point. In the six straight league defeats we had suffered since the turn of the year, only one Burnley player, Gerry Harrison, had managed to get his name on the scoresheet.

Only those Burnley fans with brave hearts dared to look at the league table. Second bottom, with twenty-seven points from twenty-eight games, we found ourselves five points adrift of Swindon, the team above us, on whom we had just one game in hand. Sunderland, fourth bottom, had collected thirty-three points from thirty games. Twentieth place in the league, and with it, safety, lay seven points away, which was where Bristol City found themselves, having played thirty-two matches.

In January, victories from our games in hand would have seen us escape the relegation zone. Now, however, maximum points from our spare fixtures were required, simply in order for us not to lose touch with the rest of our fellow-strugglers.

'My gut feeling is that we are good enough to survive,'[21] Jimmy was reported as saying at the post-match press conference. My gut feeling was telling me something quite different, something not nearly as optimistic.

However, as the teams were announced before the game, I must admit to feeling a little more confident than in previous weeks. (Not that I ever allowed myself to think we would romp home, but I thought that we might just nick it with a bit of luck.) On paper at least, it looked as though Jimmy might have got it right, with regard to team selection. The sweeper system was abandoned, Mullen choosing instead to push Hoyland into midfield. Harper was out, (a decision which led to calls for a local holiday), and Harrison was brought in at left back. This meant that Eyres and McMinn could play as out-and-out wingers, hopefully supplying crosses to Mullin and the on-loan Paul Stewart, whose inclusion demoted the Fat Shearer to the subs' bench, where he kept Inchy company. We were certainly going all-out for three points; not that we had much choice in the matter.

The fans were certainly going for it. In the week leading up to the game, Mullen had attempted to engender a sense of we're-all-in-this-togetherness, urging Burnley's followers to 'shout the house down'[22] on the Saturday, to help spur the players on into grabbing our first points of the year. On the day, the supporters were nothing short of magnificent, singing and chanting from before the first whistle. But it was always going to take more than a few hearty choruses of 'No, Nay, Never' and 'Come On You Clarets' to see off our promotion-chasing opponents that day. As it transpired, the effort and passion of the home fans was not reflected in Burnley's performance.

It was clear from the off that the players were on edge; poor ball control, misplaced passes and a general lack of cohesion made for a nerve-jangling opening ten minutes both on and off the terraces. Matters were not helped by our defensive line-up. The combination of Parkinson at left back, Harrison at right back, and a central defensive pairing of Winstanley and Pender (playing his second match in place of the suspended Davis) was one which had never played together before; and it showed.

Twenty-five edgy minutes had elapsed, when from a Dave Gilbert corner, an unmarked Clive Mendonca rose unchallenged in the area and headed Grimsby ahead. Marlon, who should have come to claim the ball, chose instead to berate Gerry Harrison, who returned his fiery invective . . . with interest. Finger-pointing and on-the-field bickering was just what we didn't need, but the scene somehow seemed to sum up perfectly the tension felt by all connected with the club. Everybody was looking for a scapegoat.

The scapegoat for many Clarets supporters was the manager, as patience continued to run short on the terraces. Never was this more evident than at the start of the second half. The cheers of encouragement that greeted the players' return to the pitch suddenly changed to loud boos, as Jimmy Mullen re-emerged from the tunnel and headed for the dugout.

The forty-five minutes that followed had a mightily familiar air about them. As against Swindon, Burnley turned it on for half an hour. But in the same way that either bad finishing or bad luck denied Burnley an equaliser against the Robins, so it was to be against the Mariners. Mullin dragged his shot wide of goal, Eyres missed by a coat of paint, McMinn thwacked his effort into the side-netting and from one of eight second half corners, Grimsby's Tommy Watson was grateful for the opportunity to clear Jamie Hoyland's goal-bound header off the line.

But the most depressing similarity between the two games was the seemingly inevitable second goal for the opposition. With ten minutes remaining, Marlon failed to get to grips with a tame effort from Graham Rodger. As the ball slipped from his grasp, Mendonca was on hand to waltz the ball around the despairing figure of Beresford and tap into an empty goal to double Grimsby's lead.

Unlike the Swindon game, there was to be no late consolation goal from an unexpected source, and as Mr. Leach blew for time, both players and manager headed for the dressing-room with a crescendo of boos and 'Mullen Out!' chants ringing in their ears.

You had to feel for the fans. They'd been asked to give the team their full vocal support during the game, and they'd given it. What had we got in return? We'd got Parkinson disinterestedly tying up his boot-lace as Mendonca celebrated his first goal. We'd got Hoyland, who had less bite in midfield than a muzzled poodle. We'd got some team members who looked as if they were giving it substantially less than everything. We'd got, in short, let down.

Not that it was the first time this year. Over 1,000 of us had given up a Bank Holiday and the best part of forty pounds to spend twelve hours on the road, just so we could freeze on the Fratton Park terraces. Roughly the same number had undertaken a 400 mile round trip to stand outside Vicarage Road for twenty minutes the week before the Grimsby game. Sandwiched in between these matches was the Notts County episode.

And *still* the supporters demonstrated unswerving loyalty, above and beyond the call of duty, by turning up in their droves at Turf Moor: 9,841 against Reading, 10,960 against Swindon, 10,511 against Grimsby, an average of just under 10,500. You had to marvel at the sheer number of people who cared about their club so much that they would return week after week, to be repeatedly slapped in the face. (This point was underlined in a survey published a few weeks after the end of the season, which showed that with an average gate of 12,058, [23] the Clarets were the tenth best-supported club outside the Premiership. Just think what attendances *might* have been, had we been pushing for promotion.)

I wasn't entitled, (nor did I expect us), to win every week. What I *was* entitled to, (and *did* expect), was my passion, pride and commitment to be reflected by whichever player pulled on a claret and blue shirt and ran out to represent Burnley Football Club.

'For the five seasons I have been here, first as assistant and then as manager, I have grown to admire the fans for the loyalty you display. Thousands of you follow us wherever we play, and you really are a credit to the club.' [24] So had written Jimmy in his programme notes for the Grimsby game. It was about time some of that loyalty received more than lip service. The first opportunity would be in front of the many supporters who would take time off work to travel to Bramall Lane on Tuesday evening to watch the Clarets take on high-flying Sheffield United.

In the FA Cup Fifth Round, Everton thump five past Norwich, Manchester United beat Leeds 3-1 and a goal from Wolves' David Kelly knocks out Premiership club Leicester.

Ron Atkinson gets off to winning ways, by lifting Coventry away from the relegation zone, with a 2-0 win over West Ham.

Tuesday 22/2/94
Bramall Lane

SHEFFIELD UNITED 2-0 BURNLEY *(Blake 44, 90)*
League position before and after match: 23rd . . . 23rd

Attendance: 13,349

BURNLEY: Beresford, Parkinson, Eyres, Davis, Winstanley, Harrison, Harper *(Peel 74)*, Hoyland, Heath, Stewart, Mullin. Subs (not used): Robinson, Russell.

SHEFFIELD UNITED: Kelly, Gage, Blount, Gannon *(Anthony 77)*, Scott, Beesley, Rogers, Veart *(Starbuck 85)*, Ward, Flo, Blake. Sub (not used): Mercer.

174

Referee: J. Brandwood

Yellow cards: Blake (Sheffield United)
　　　　　　　Stewart (Burnley)

Red cards:　　None

I regard myself as having been lucky enough never to have had my head repeatedly smashed against a brick wall. However, if a football supporter's equivalent of this experience ever existed, then it was to be found in watching the Clarets' dismal form of early 1995.

The 2-0 defeat at Bramall Lane meant that Burnley had achieved the decidedly unenviable feat of equalling the club's worst run of league defeats in the twentieth century. In the 1904/5 season Burnley had succumbed to Gainsborough Trinity (twice), Burton United, Liverpool, Burslem Port Vale, Bristol City and Manchester United in consecutive league fixtures. Ninety years on, the names had changed, but the story remained the same.

Under the guidance of Spen Whittaker, the 1904/5 squad had turned things around, eventually finishing 11th in Division Two. As Nathan Blake notched his, and Sheffield United's second goal of the evening, I wondered if Jimmy Mullen could perform a similar feat, by keeping Burnley in Endsleigh League Division One. It was looking increasingly unlikely.

On the night the team battled well and another, perhaps kinder time, might have seen them come away with a point. There wasn't an awful lot to choose between the two teams, apart from the fact that they had a striker who could score goals. Two superlative efforts by the Welsh international condemned Burnley fans to yet another cheerless journey home.

It was hard to believe that this was, give or take a Vinnicombe here and a Hoyland there, the same side that had gone undefeated in the league from October 1st to December 10th. It was scant consolation to Clarets fans that that ten match unbeaten run was a record for 1994/95, in Division One.

It might have seemed a terrible thing to say, but the way things were going, that run would count for nothing in the final reckoning. With seventeen games remaining and an estimated

175

twenty-five points required for survival, we could still do it, but it would require a massive turnaround in form. If we were to stop up, drastic action was required *immediately*.

After eight and a half successful years at Highbury, George Graham is dismissed as manager, as the FA Premier League Commission find that the Arsenal boss was guilty of accepting 'bungs', in the transfers of certain players brought to the North London club. Graham vows to clear his name.

Southend United relieve manager Peter Taylor of his duties, telling him to take a holiday and come back in a month. Steve Thompson takes charge.

Aston Villa go 4-1 up against Leicester with thirteen minutes remaining, only to be pegged back to 4-4 by full-time. It is Steve Thompson's last game for Leicester before joining Burnley.

Manchester City record their first win in eleven games, with a 2-0 home victory over Ipswich.

Eric Cantona appears before the FA, who suspend him until the end of September and fine him a further £10,000. Cantona is due to appear before Croydon Magistrates within the month, to answer a charge of common assault.

Saturday 25/2/95
Prenton Park

TRANMERE ROVERS 4-1 BURNLEY
(Muir 16, 79, Nevin 48, Aldridge 90) (Garnett 89 [og]).
League position before and after match: 23rd . . . 24th

Attendance: 9,909

BURNLEY: Beresford, Parkinson, Eyres, Davis, Hoyland,

Harrison, Harper (*Robinson* 56), Thompson, Heath, Stewart, Nogan.
Subs (not used): Dowell, Russell.

TRANMERE ROVERS: Nixon, Stevens, Thomas, McGreal, Garnett, O'Brien, Morrisey, Muir, Malkin (*Aldridge 80*), Brannan, Nevin.
Subs (not used): Coyne, Irons.

Referee: T. West

Yellow cards: Thomas (Tranmere Rovers)
              Harrison (Burnley)

Red cards: None

What a bloody shambles.

Half of me didn't want to write about this, our eighth consecutive league defeat, (if the players couldn't be bothered, then why should I?), but the other half of me told me I must do, if only as some form of personal catharsis. Having said that, I found it very difficult to know where to start, how to begin describing the debacle that meant come full-time that afternoon, Burnley had slumped to the bottom of Endsleigh League Division One.

We should have known it wasn't going to be our day. All the signs were there. Travelling through Liverpool City centre, en route to Birkenhead, we were given countless 'V' signs, informed that we had extremely small genitalia, and were mooned at from the front window of a Vauxhall Astra – all in the space of ten minutes. These welcoming Scouse gestures were all, no doubt, born out of that natural aptitude that Liverpudlians are said to possess, when it comes to wit.

Our nerves were further unsettled by our coach driver, who had marginally less directional sense than Alan Harper. Having embroiled us in countless traffic jams the length and breadth of Merseyside, the hapless courier announced to the coach that he 'didn't fancy' going through the Mersey tunnel, and anyway he knew 'another way' (not a better or quicker way, you note, simply 'another way'). His alternative route involved driving away from Liverpool, getting to within twenty miles of Manchester and then with half an hour to kick-off, turning around and heading in the vague direction of Birkenhead. It was Watford revisited – almost literally.

There is something strangely unsettling about arriving in a ground after the game has started. It's as if you are interrupting a ceremony; and I suppose that in a way, you are. The build-up to the match has passed you by. You don't have time to do the normal things: casually buy a programme, find your seat, familiarise yourself with the layout of the ground. As a result you find yourself plunged in at the deep end, trying to find out who's playing, and where they're playing.

Eyresie certainly didn't appear to know where he was playing. Ever since Vinnicombe had been injured, Mullen's make-do approach to football management had meant that we had been without a decent left-back since Bonfire Night. Since that fateful day, Harrison, Brass, Armstrong, (who by this time had returned to Nottingham Forest), Dowell, and more recently Eyres, had all had a go at it. All had failed in varying degrees. It was then little wonder that Tranmere's opening goal was created down that side.

Nobody had the inclination, wit or wherewithal to get out to Tony Thomas, in order to stop him getting a cross in. An unmarked Ian Muir threw himself at the ball, directing his header past Marlon. Frustration wasn't in it. How many times had that happened that season? More depressingly, why was it still happening in our thirtieth league game?

As Muir ran off to celebrate, Tranmere's Tannoy treated us to a short, sharp and, given the context, highly surreal blast of James Brown's 'I Got You, I Feel Good'. The sight of Tranmere's number eight gyrating to the Godfather of Soul's good-time anthem in the middle of Birkenhead had to count as one of the most ridiculous sights of the season to date; but not nearly as ridiculous as Burnley's near post marking.

Going 1-0 down in a game is a bewildering experience for the average football supporter. It's bad enough being in arrears, but it's at that precise moment that your psyche splits in two. The sane rational half knows that you've seen it all before, and there is no way back; you're on for a right hammering, and that's that. But the other half, the half which believes that Mooncat is a

178

gifted player and Santa Claus exists, tells you that it's only 1-0, you can easily pull things round, and there's every chance you'll win. And whilst it's true that the latter of these scenarios *does* occur, it never seems to involve your team.

Up until the point that Rovers took the lead, it had been pretty much honours even, but the goal shattered Burnley's all-too-brittle resistance. It didn't take the home side long to cotton on to the Clarets' confidence crisis, and tin hats became the order of the day as Tranmere pulverised us with some dazzling wing play. Muir's twenty-yarder shaved the post, Malkin's header was hacked off the line by Jamie Hoyland, and they were winning corners for fun. Quite how we managed to reach the interval without conceding another goal is a mystery to rank alongside anything to be found in an Arthur C. Clarke book.

Of all those congregated inside Prenton Park, I felt a more than usual degree of sympathy for Steve Thompson and Kurt Nogan, the two players making their debut for the Clarets that afternoon. During the week, the board had backed Mullen, both verbally and financially. After telling the press that Jimmy's position was not under review, (although if they'd sauntered around the Away Kop that afternoon they would have encountered many who would have urged them to reconsider), Frank Teasdale et al had put their money where their collective mouth was, and allowed JM to go on a £500,000 spending spree.

So on Friday, Thompson and Nogan had arrived at Turf Moor, signed on the dotted line and spent the rest of the afternoon doing what all new signings everywhere do – singing the praises of their new club to the local media, which I must admit is a particular *bête noir* of mine. It happens at every club – and I'm sure there are thousands of fans up and down the country who bang their heads against the wall in frustration, as the latest new signing rambles on about how delighted they are to come to the club, how much bigger the club is compared to their previous one, and how much they are looking forward to the challenge that lies ahead.

I for one would have unbridled respect for a player who came to Burnley, saying that his decision was swayed by bigger wages/better bonuses/the lack of first team opportunities at their previous club, or indeed any other *genuine* reason for moving to Turf Moor.

Steve Thompson had arrived for £200,000 from a Leicester side, who if truth be told, had been relegated since Christmas '94, and were now only playing their remaining fixtures to fulfil their obligation to the rest of the Premiership. The latest and badly-needed boost to Burnley's midfield, was largely ineffectual. This owed much to the fact that he was probably shell-shocked at just how naff his new team-mates were. Rumour had it that the ex-Bolton player was spotted later that evening, begging his agent to find a loophole in his contract that would allow him to move back to Filbert Street.

Signing Kurt Nogan for a club record £300,000, struck me as a marginally less ridiculous thing to do than sticking your head into an industrial cement mixer. Jimmy had put this vast amount of money and faith in a striker who hadn't scored since October '94 in the division below us, had a hairline fracture in one of his shoulder bones, and perhaps worst of all, spoke with an accent which had the undesirable effect of making him sound like the bastard offspring of Wurzel Gummidge. This, we were asked to believe, was the new Messiah – the man who would end Burnley's goal famine and deliver us from relegation, Amen. I thought not.

Not that 'Noggin', or 'The Nog', had much chance to show us what he could do. In fact, as a friend pointed out, it would have been remarkable if Andy Cole, Alan Shearer or Jurgen Klinsmann would have found the back of the net, with the lack of service from our midfield.

As the second half got under way, it became apparent that Jimmy's half-time talk had been less than inspirational. Just three minutes after the interval, O'Brien's pull-back from the byeline eluded everybody apart from Pat Nevin, who found himself in the kind of space normally encountered in aircraft hangars. Nevin slid the ball over the line, then stood to salute the Tranny faithful seated in the Prenton Road West Stand, as we were treated to another snatch of James Brown.

I certainly didn't 'feel good'. They hit the bar, had a goal disallowed, missed sitters and generally humiliated a Burnley side whose glaring inadequacies were all too embarrassingly highlighted. The introduction of The Fat Shearer to the proceedings made little difference. It was no use him running his socks off, only for the disgracefully lazy Paul Stewart (who was at

Burnley simply to get match-fit and nothing else) to make no attempt to chase any ball that went anywhere other than straight to his feet.

It had to get worse, and it did. Twelve minutes remained, when Muir shot from twenty yards. Marlon looked to have it covered, but Robinson decided to help him anyway. Unfortunately, his idea of help was to stick his boot in the trajectory of the ball, which had the disastrous consequence of deflecting it past the utterly stranded Beresford. Which was when a huge section of the travelling support decided they'd get an early start on the traffic.

Which meant that they missed another two goals. The first came as Robinson cut into the box and fired a lethal shot which was going one place and one place only – the corner flag. Taking pity on the Clarets, Shaun Garnett became the epitome of generosity, as he put through his own net to make the score 3-1. I can't say I punched the air and whooped with delight. It was far too late for that. Besides, what was so good about being the only team in the league whose 'Goals For' column for 1995 contained more own goals than goals scored by Burnley players?

James Brown was given one more airing in the last minute as John Aldridge, on his return from injury, atoned for his penalty miss from earlier in the season at Turf Moor, latching onto the end of a Morrisey cross to make the score 4-1.

Come the final whistle, there was a strange atmosphere in the Burnley end. The anger that had manifested itself at Notts County, at Watford, and at Sheffield United, had given way to a palpable air of resignation. Between them, Mullen and the team had ground us down. Every week we were losing. Every week Jimmy lectured the players for forty minutes in the dressing-room after the game before spinning us the same old line about his 'gut feeling' that we'd survive. Every week the players trotted out the same, lame cliches, vowing to try harder next time. The problem was, we were fast running out of 'next times.'

Nobody – the players, the manager, or the board – appeared to realise the seriousness of our plight, or if they did, they were merely playing lip-service to it. (After this match, one director rang the local radio phone-in, saying that all we needed was a change of luck!) I felt as if they all knew we were going down, but didn't really care all that much, didn't really care that we'd be playing Shrewsbury, and not Sunderland, the following season. I felt as if I was being let down – badly.

More bad news came as we sat in silence at the back of the coach, and learned via the radio of Notts County's victory over Reading, a victory which meant that for the first time that season, Burnley Football Club had sunk to the bottom of Endsleigh League Division One. The final blow came with news of Manchester United's defeat a few miles down the road at Everton, a result which put Blackburn Rovers three points clear at the top of the Premiership. This was shaping up to be the season from hell.

'You've got to laugh, haven't you?' asked someone a couple of seats in front of us. 'No,' I thought to myself, 'No, not really.'

There are minor scuffles and a handful of arrests, as Chelsea go down 1-0 in the first leg of their European Cup-Winners' Cup Quarter-Final in Bruges.

Liverpool make it to the FA Cup Quarter-Finals with a 2-0 victory over Wimbledon. In the game Ian Rush scores, to equal Denis Law's record of 41 FA Cup goals.

Gillingham's manager Mike Flanagan is made redundant by the administrators. Neil Smillie takes charge.

George Ndah's injury-time header knocks Watford out of the FA Cup and puts Crystal Palace through to the Quarter-Finals.

Also through are Spurs, at the expense of Southampton, courtesy of a hat-trick from super-sub Ronnie Rosenthal.

Everton agree to pay Mike Walker £300,000, for what was left of his 3½ year contract when he was dismissed last November.

Arsenal can only manage a 1-1 draw at home to Auxerre, in the first leg of their European Cup-Winners' Cup Quarter-Final.

Darlington sack manager Alan Murray.

Saturday 04/03/95
Turf Moor

BURNLEY 1-1 WEST BROMWICH ALBION
(Robinson 89) (Hunt 63)
League position before and after match: 24th . . . 24th

Attendance: 11,885

BURNLEY: Beresford, Parkinson, Dowell *(Robinson 45)*, Davis, Hoyland, Randall, Harper *(Heath 15)*, Thompson, Stewart, Nogan, Eyres.
Sub (not used): Russell.

WEST BROMWICH ALBION: Naylor, Burgess, Agnew, Phelan, Strodder, Raven, O'Regan, Smith, Rees, Hunt, Hamilton. Subs (not used): Lange, Taylor, Ashcroft.

Referee: J. Kirby

Yellow Cards: Stewart (Burnley)
Burgess (West Brom)

Red Cards: None

In the 1889/90 season, Burnley lost eight consecutive league matches. This feat was equalled in 1895. A hundred years and thousands of fixtures down the line, the Clarets squad of 1995 found themselves in the unenviable position of being 1-0 down in the eighty-ninth minute and therefore moments away from breaking this century old record.

With the whistles from the visitors' section growing louder with every passing second, Steve Thompson raced over to take a corner kick from the left hand side of the Endsleigh Stand. His deep cross was headed away by a West Brom player. Jamie Hoyland picked up the rebound, and his deft chip back into the area bounced across the path of Liam Robinson. In one flowing movement, The Fat Shearer, with his back to goal, swivelled his considerable bulk around and fairly lashed the ball past a crowd of defenders and into the Baggies' net to level the score.

If you were one of those people who invested their faith in omens, then you would have left Turf Moor that afternoon with hope in your heart, the reason being that the 1895 run of eight consecutive league defeats also came to an end against West Bromwich Albion. That season, Burnley survived in their division. It wasn't over yet . . .

Admittedly, we'd only managed to salvage a point, when really we had needed to grab all three and we were still in one hell of a hole. But the important thing was, the rot had been stopped; we hadn't lost. Our share of the spoils from this game meant that the gap between ourselves and 21st place in the table had been reduced by one point. Eight points now lay between the Clarets and safety.

Tuesday night's visit to Barnsley was the first in a gruelling programme of seven games in twenty-two days. Given this information, it was evident that the month of March would have an enormous bearing on the club's survival in this division.

Manchester United rattle nine past a thoroughly humiliated Ipswich Town. The scoreline is a Premiership record. With the score at 8-0, Ipswich fans are heard to chant, 'We want one!'

Snooker impresario Barry Hearn agrees to buy a controlling interest in Leyton Orient.

Tuesday 07/03/95
Oakwell

BARNSLEY 2-0 BURNLEY (*Taggart 41, Payton 89*)
League position before and after match: 24th . . . 24th

Attendance: 5,537

184

BURNLEY: Beresford, Parkinson, Winstanley, Davis, Vinnicombe, Randall, Thompson, Hoyland, Stewart, Nogan *(Peel 65)*, Eyres.
Subs (not used): Brass, Russell.

BARNSLEY: Watson, Eaden, Fleming, Wilson, Taggart, Davis, O'Connell, Redfearn *(Snodin 39)*, Payton, Liddell, Sheridan *(Bullock)*.
Sub (not used): Butler.

Referee: K. Lynch

Yellow cards: Liddell, Davis, O'Connell, Watson (Barnsley)
Beresford, Hoyland, Eyres. (Burnley)

Red cards: Stewart, Parkinson (Burnley)

Following this excursion into deepest, darkest Yorkshire, I would not have been at all surprised to discover that REM's 'It's The End Of the World As We Know It' was inspired by a trip to the distinctly less-than-glamorous surroundings of Barnsley. If the universe possessed a scrag-end, then this was surely it.

It had just started to get dark when we parked up on the hill-top mess of mud and gravel that passed (but only just) as our car park for the evening. A chill wind struck up, as we reluctantly left the warmth and safety of the Supporters Club coach. Peering through the darkness and tree branches which partially obscured our view, a meagre yet nevertheless discernible light was visible at the foot of the hill, about a quarter of a mile in the distance. 'That,' said Andy, adopting a chilling Hammer House of Horror voice, 'must be the ground.' At which point it would have been wonderfully poetic, had a crack of thunder ruptured the silence.

Of course, there's never a thunderstorm around when you need one, and so we made our way towards the light, half-expecting to find human skulls tied to primitive poles, and crudely painted signs reading, 'ABANDON HOPE, ALL YE WHO ENTER HERE'. The unenthusiastic programme sellers we encountered outside the ground provided a clue as to what Barnsley folk did with their dead.

The theme of doom and gloom was continued inside Oakwell.

The black, decaying brickwork at the back of the visitors' enclosure was more in keeping with a Victorian workhouse, rather than the rear of a football terrace. 'I bet they sell bloody gruel here,' commented Andy.

Looking around, (probably for the exit subconsciously) I saw a couple of friends chatting to someone I didn't recognise at first. Moving closer, it became evident that the stranger was none other than Paul Mariner – one-time England international, and expert summariser for Radio Lancashire that evening.

So there we were, on a chilly Tuesday night in Barnsley, casually chatting to this guy who'd seen it all, (English league football at the highest level, FA Cup finals, World Cup Finals – the lot), about whether or not The Nog was a good buy and what our chances were of surviving the drop. Who'd have thought it?

As Paul Mariner made his apologies and left to 'do a bit for the radio', we faced up to the fact that with only ten minutes to kick-off, we were going to have to be brave and seek out our seats in The Victorian Workhouse Stand. The West Stand, to give it its proper name, was (worryingly) built almost entirely from very old-looking, very dry-looking wood, and appeared to have been designed by somebody who had a particularly virulent hatred of football fans.

I don't know who was in charge of the lighting budget for the West Stand at Oakwell, (going from the Dickensian feel of the place, possibly a descendant of Scrooge), but their balance sheet must have made very favourable reading at the end of the season, judging by the woefully inadequate lighting facilities therein. I kid you not, when I say that when looking downwards, I was unable to see as far as my feet.

Mention should also be made of whichever sadist designed the seats in which we were expected to sit for the game's duration. I regard myself as being neither fat nor thin, but as I attempted to get comfortable, it soon became evident that only the most emaciated of super-waifs would have been able to fit into one of these devices of torture. Our discomfort was doubled by casting our gaze to the other side of the pitch, where stood the highly impressive East Stand. Superbly illuminated, with spacious seats, it was hard for Clarets fans not to feel a little put out – particularly as the home stand was practically empty up to five minutes before kick-off, and didn't fill up much thereafter.

The last time Burnley had ventured over the Pennines had been a fortnight previously, for the Sheffield United fixture. On that occasion, our performance had ranked amongst the most impressive of the season, in terms of grit and determination. More of the same was called for in the grim surroundings of Oakwell, as the Clarets went in search of their first win of the year.

One encouraging sign was the return to action of Chris Vinnicombe, after four months out. He had been badly missed since he broke his jaw at Reading, and his restoration to the side at Barnsley gave the team a more balanced look overall. Indeed, as the first half worked its passage, and I fidgeted in my seat trying to find a position which didn't necessitate severe curvature of my spine, the lads were doing well, and with a modicum more composure in front of goal, might have been in front. Stewart somehow bungled a free header wide of the target, and twice The Nog fluffed chances with only the 'keeper to beat. Still, the signs were good, and with Barnsley on the back foot for most of the half, the idea of leaving Oakwell with all three points seemed a lot less ridiculous than it had done before kick-off that evening.

Then it all started to go horribly, horribly wrong. With four minutes of the half remaining, Danny Wilson swung in a corner, which Gerry Taggart headed goalwards. Steve Thompson was the man on the line, and he rose to head the ball away to safety. 'Christ,' I thought, 'That was close.' It was, in fact, a lot closer than I had imagined. The next thing I knew, the Barnsley players were jogging back to the centre circle, congratulating each other, after the ref had somehow convinced himself that the ball had crossed the line.

He had a much more difficult job convincing Beresford and Hoyland, who joined the Claret and Blue Army in The Victorian Workhouse Stand in a vociferous protest against his decision. Mr. Lynch wasn't amused, and illustrated his displeasure by letting them both have a look at his yellow card. Worse still was to come.

Paul Stewart, having witnessed the whole episode from the less than ideal position of the half-way line, voiced his concern vis-a-vis the quality of the eyesight of the two officials, who were a good thirty yards closer to the action. 'If your eyesight's so bloody good, laddie,' thought Mr Lynch, 'You'll have no bother seeing what colour this card is,' and flourishing a bright red rectangle from his pocket, pointed in the direction of the players' tunnel.

I won't bother putting into print my exact thoughts at that time. Suffice to say that I was less than pleased with the on-loan star. To be honest, his dismissal wasn't entirely unexpected. In his previous four appearances for the Clarets, he had done little save get himself booked three times, most recently for deliberately stamping on the head of West Brom 'keeper, Stuart Naylor. Most refs would have sent him off for that, and tonight he had got his comeuppance. As our tubby number nine lumbered gracelessly from the field of play, I hoped never to see him wearing a Burnley shirt again. The player himself probably felt the same way.

The half-time whistle provoked loud booing noises all around me as the Burnley fans rose en masse from their painful sitting positions and spent the fifteen-minute interval attempting to straighten out their twisted vertebrae and the even more twisted refereeing decision that had left us one goal down.

Much to Burnley's credit, they came out fighting in the second half. The determination to get something from the game was evident throughout; rarely did we look as though we had one less man than the Tykes. Spaceman's performance was particularly exemplary. Of all the players out there, I had earmarked Randall as one of the ones who wouldn't have the stomach for a battle. But there he was, winning every ball, tackling back and beating his man, or men, as the situation required. His performance was symbolic of the team's collective display. Had we played like this all season, we would have been pushing for the play-offs, not fighting for survival.

Eleven minutes after the interval, it looked as if the hard work had paid dividends. From ten yards out, Eyresie slotted home from a cross on the left hand side. The Victorian Workhouse Stand was transformed into a joyous, writhing claret and blue mass. Until, that is, the ref decided it was offside, or not particularly nice or something, and awarded a free kick to Barnsley. At which point, the entire travelling contingent launched into a spontaneous round of 'One nil, to the referee.'

Five minutes later, Eyres was haring away down the left wing, when former Claret Steve Davis invited our number eleven to take a closer look at the poor quality of Barnsley's playing surface, helping him on his way with a particularly nasty-looking elbow.

Mr. Lynch didn't see too much wrong with the Barnsley number six's ad lib attempt at reshaping Eyresie's face, and found it deserving of a mere yellow card.

Undeterred, the Clarets continued to press forward. With a quarter of an hour to go, Parkinson was impeded by Brendan O'Connell on the edge of the Barnsley area. Lovely Legs was not enamoured of the former Burnley man's challenge. His reaction was a two-handed shove to O'Connell's chest. Poor Brendan staggered away, as though a prize fighter had lamped him one round the temples. This particularly hammy piece of theatre from O'Connell was enough to convince the clearly addled mind of the match official that Lovely Legs was a menace to society in general. Following a stern lecture, Mr Lynch sent him packing. As Parky made for the dressing-rooms, his parting shot for the evening was to kick out at a bucket of water adjacent to the Burnley bench, which kersploshed impressively over a nearby police officer.

'What next?' I innocently inquired of Andy. 'Next,' arrived in the eightieth minute, when Burnley's Steve Davis was through on goal with only Dave Watson, the Barnsley keeper, to round. As he attempted to do this, Watson quite blatantly flung himself into Davis' path, sending the Clarets' skipper sprawling. The only way in which this could possibly have been a more obvious sending-off, was if Watson had then paraded around his eighteen yard box with a huge placard bearing the legend, 'IT'S GOT TO BE RED, REF! IT'S GOT TO BE RED!'

In producing only a yellow card, Mr Lynch was either demonstrating an unrivalled capacity for understanding the finer points of irony, or was, as one fan put it, 'a bald, cheating git.'

This latest piece of hair-brained refereeing seemed, perhaps understandably, to be the signal for the Clarets to fold. Burnley born Andy Payton sealed the points, after Steve Davis had allowed the Barnsley number nine to get in front of him and nod in a free header from Martin Bullock's corner. It was a final blow which the nine-man Clarets really didn't deserve.

Making our way off The Victorian Workhouse Stand that evening, with the chants of 'Two-nil, to the referee' bouncing off the rafters, I reflected to myself that it was games like that evening's, that made you think your name was not just pencilled in, but indelibly inked into one of the relegation spots. Well, that and the fact that we were bottom of the league, ten points away from safety, having picked up just one point out of the last possible thirty, and having netted just four times in the last ten league fixtures.

'We've got Oldham on Saturday,' said one man as we made our way back to the coach, 'They'll do us no favours.'

'We don't want no bloody favours,' replied his mate. And whilst I understood that what he said was borne out of pride, I was more than willing to accept any favours coming our way between now and the end of the season, if it meant the Clarets would still be in Division One, on the first day of the 95/96 campaign.

The FA refuse to lift the ban imposed on Chris Armstrong, after he was found guilty of taking cannabis. The refusal means Armstrong will miss the second leg of the Coca-Cola Cup Semi-Final against Liverpool.

The FA charge George Graham with misconduct, as they launch their own investigation into the 'bungs' allegations. Graham remains confident about clearing his name.

Joe Kinnear has a pop at yet another referee, as Robbie Hart sends him off in what Kinnear describes as, 'his usual Hitler fashion.'

Bolton and Liverpool will meet in the Coca-Cola Cup Final, as they see off Swindon Town and Crystal Palace respectively, with aggregate scores of 4-3 and 2-0, in the second legs of the competition's Semi-Finals.

Saturday 11/04/95
Turf Moor

BURNLEY 2-1 OLDHAM ATHLETIC
(Nogan 7, Vinnicombe 75) (McCarthy 47)

League position before and after game: 24th . . . 24th

Attendance: 11,620

BURNLEY: Beresford, Parkinson, Winstanley, Davis, Vinnicombe, Randall, Hoyland, Thompson, Stewart, Nogan, Eyres.
Subs (not used): Peel, Harrison, Russell.

OLDHAM ATHLETIC: Gerrard, Snodin, Pointon, Bernard, Moore, Redmond, Halle *(Holden 79)*, Ritchie, Eyre *(McCarthy 46)*, Richardson, Brennan.
Sub (not used): Hallworth.

Referee: A. Dawson

Yellow Cards: Randall, Davis, Beresford (Burnley)
Snodin (Oldham)

Red Cards: None

On 11/04/95, Tory MP Robert Hughes came under pressure to resign following revelations of his affair with his Commons assistant Janet Oates, British fishermen sided with Canadians in their trawler war against Spain, and the dust was beginning to settle in the wake of the Barings Bank collapse.

The news that Burnley Football Club had recorded their first victory of 1995 might have been small potatoes in the grand scheme of things; but for the majority of the 11,620 people gathered inside Turf Moor that afternoon, Burnley 2 Oldham Athletic 1, *was* the news.

This was more than just a victory. It was a lifeline, a reason to believe, three precious points closer to safety. For the first time in seventy days and just under one thousand minutes of league football, the Clarets had come out on top.

As the crowds flooded from the terraces and spilled out into Brunshaw Road, I saw people smiling and laughing about a game for the first time since New Year's Eve. Fair enough, a tough battle lay ahead – nobody was under any illusions about that. But those supporters who had been following the Clarets since the

191

beginning of the year had had a pretty rough time of it, and so we had a right to savour the moment, and bask in the glory of a wonderful victory. We'd earned it.

What was most pleasing about the victory was the style (and style was the watchword that afternoon) in which the points were secured. Had somebody unfamiliar with Burnley's predicament witnessed the superlative performance of the home side, they would have had difficulty in believing that we were bottom of the division. Because whilst the Clarets displayed all the qualities usually associated with teams involved in relegation battles – passion, commitment, desire, etc – there was also plenty of high quality, skilful football on show.

Thompson's raking, twenty yard passes were the very definition of precision, finding feet every time. Spaceman, with his frequent, powerful and purposeful running, destroyed a midfield that a few months earlier had been competing in the Premiership. Jamie Hoyland proved once again that if ever a player was born to defend, then it was he. And quite aside from his winning goal, Chris Vinnicombe belied the fact that he had been out for four months, with the kind of performance that made many Burnley fans realise just how badly our first choice left back had been missed.

With the benefit of hindsight, our opening goal should have served as an indication that the pendulum of fate might be swinging in Burnley's favour. Just seven minutes had elapsed when Kurt Nogan chased a hopeful punt forward by Steve Davis. Noggin was clearly a mile offside, but both the linesman and the referee seemed immune to the fact and allowed The Nog to advance into the penalty area, round Gerrard and his awful haircut, and tuck the ball into the corner, despite the attentions of Neil Moore and Steve Redmond.

I don't know how he celebrated opening his goal-scoring account with the Clarets. I was lost under a heap of other Burnley supporters, shouting, 'Get in!', 'He's bloody done it!' and other expressions of unbridled joy which usually greet your record signing's debut goal. 'Cometh the hour,' I yelled down Andy's earhole, 'Cometh The Nog!'

With the Latics clearly rattled, Burnley streamed forward in search of a second. The lacklustre Stewart hit the post from five yards, Nogan nearly doubled his tally for the afternoon, and Paul

Gerrard was caught out and almost ended up carrying a David Eyres shot over the line. Other than the goal, the outstanding moment of the half was produced by Chris Vinnicombe, who streaked down the left hand side, weaving in and out of the challenges of four thoroughly bewildered Oldham players, before forcing a great save from their keeper.

The Latics offered little in the way of resistance, and half-time saw the Clarets leave the pitch with the sound of applause, rather than boos, ringing in their ears, for the first time in many a match. Not since the 5-1 drubbing of Southend on New Years's Eve had we gone into the interval with a lead to defend in a league match. It felt just fine.

The introduction of Sean McCarthy into Oldham's front line early in the second half made the desire to beat the Latics even greater than it already was. Here was the man who earlier in the season at Boundary Park had come close to inciting trouble in the Burnley crowd, after spectacularly celebrating the last of Oldham's three goals, right in front of a Burnley contingent already wound up by some diabolical refereeing decisions, including one which led to McCarthy's last goal.

With his first touch of the ball, the Latics' rotund substitute proved that history had a (in this instance, nasty) habit of repeating itself. Brennan's chip into the area found McCarthy in space. This was not because he had used cunning and guile to lose his marker. It was because he was even further offside than Nogan was for his goal. Not one to look a gift horse in the mouth, the lardy Latic lobbed the advancing Marlon, to level the scores.

His goal prompted a volley of abuse towards the linesman from Lovely Legs and 10,000 Burnley fans. Which was strange really. Maybe I was too carried away with my celebrations, but I couldn't remember a single voice of dissent when The Nog was in such an advanced offside position for our opener that you could have parked any number of double deckers lengthways twixt him and the nearest Oldham defender. 'Unfair, linesman! Unfair!' yelled an OAP stood alongside me. 'If you want fair,' I thought to myself, 'go play chess'.

Whatever, the chips were now well and truly down. It was time for the Clarets to show their mettle, and by Christ they showed it. Wave after wave of Burnley attacks followed the visitors' equaliser, as the Clarets pressed forward in search of a winner. Davis blasted a shot straight at Gerrard, whose ridiculous hairstyle, (as if he had a curtain either side of his face), began to irritate me more with every passing minute. From the edge of the area, Randall trickled a feeble shot towards Oldham's gaping net, allowing Moore ample time to clear off the line. I put my head in my hands and let out a cry of anguish.

'You think *that* was bad?' asked The Nog, as Randall pulled back the ball to the unmarked number ten, who, standing a matter of feet away from an open net, committed the greatest act of profligacy ever witnessed on a football pitch *anywhere*, by slicing the ball across the goalmouth and away to safety. Stewart missed an easy header, Noggin went down under a challenge in their box as the ref waved play on, and that horrible feeling began to get a grip on me – that feeling which tells you that there is more likelihood of world peace breaking out, than there is of you scoring a goal.

With fantastic support from the terraces, the Clarets continued to push forward. Fifteen minutes remained when Nogan broke down the right hand side and slotted a ball across the area to Eyres. With his back to goal, it was clear he was going nowhere. Releasing the ball to the unmarked Vinnicombe on the left hand edge of the area, a voice from behind me screamed out: 'HIT IT!' Vinny took on board this timely piece of advice and, pulling back his left foot, fired the Clarets into the lead with a crisply struck effort, which never rose more than a couple of inches off the ground, from the moment it left his boot, to the instant it hit the back of Oldham's net. Perfection.

As 10,000 Burnley fans let out eleven league games-worth of frustration, anger, tension and depression in one almighty primal scream, the diminutive left back raced over to the Burnley bench and jumped into Mullen's open arms, before dancing a jig with him on the touchline, much to the obvious bewilderment of the nearby linesman. Now all we had to do was hang on.

Burnley however, had no intentions whatsoever of merely hanging on, and poured forward in search of a third killer goal. Stewart lumped a shot into Mr Curtain-Hair's midriff, The Nog somehow contrived to put a simple one-on-one six feet wide of the post, and then . . . and then the ref decided that was it. Which meant that myself and thousands of others could all go home happy for a change.

Other results that afternoon meant that we remained bottom, nine points adrift of safety, the next two games being tricky away fixtures at Derby County on Wednesday, and Bristol City on Saturday. However, if the Clarets could reproduce the same kind of performance that had secured our first league win of the year, then survival was far from a lost cause. Come on, you Clarets!

Peter Shilton is again in demand. This time the much-travelled goalkeeper's services are required by Bolton Wanderers. He is drafted in as cover until the end of the season.

Manchester United, Spurs and Everton are through to the FA Cup Semi-Finals, as QPR, Liverpool and Newcastle United fall by the wayside. Crystal Palace and Wolves must try again.

Blackburn Rovers extend their lead at the top of the Premiership to four points, as they earn a draw at Coventry.

Dennis Wise is sentenced to three months imprisonment for assault and criminal damage, but is released on bail pending appeal.

Chris Armstrong is given clearance to play again by the FA.

The FA decide that both FA Cup Semi-Finals will be played away from Wembley. Tottenham will play Everton at Elland Road, whilst either Crystal Palace or Wolves will meet Manchester United at Villa Park.

Wednesday 15/03/95
The Baseball Ground

DERBY COUNTY 4-0 BURNLEY
(*Mills 28, Trollope 51, Simpson 55 {pen}, Gabbiadini 90*)

League position before and after match: 24th . . . 24th

Attendance: 13,922

BURNLEY: Beresford, Parkinson, Winstanley, Davis, Vinnicombe, Randall, Hoyland, Thompson, Mullin *(Peel 72)*, Nogan, Eyres.
Subs (not used): Harrison, Russell.

DERBY COUNTY: Hoult, Yates *(Sutton 56)*, Wassall, Trollope, Short *(Wrack 51)*, Williams, Harkes, Pembridge, Mills, Gabbiadini, Simpson.
Subs (not used): Quy.

Referee: G. Cain

Yellow cards: None

Red cards: None

With a quarter of an hour remaining, a Burnley fan I recognised from previous away games and whose state could reasonably be described as 'extremely disgruntled', brushed past me. 'I've had enough of this crap,' he said. 'I'm sodding off back to the coach.' With those well-chosen words, he yelled something unintelligible at Parkinson, who had just sliced his umpteenth easy clearance of the evening up, up and away into Row Z for a throw-in, and stormed off in the direction of the exit.

Given the circumstances, 'sodding off back to the coach' struck me as being a thoroughly commendable course of action. He wasn't the first to leave. Hundreds of other Clarets had already turned their backs on the eleven clowns who were masquerading as professional footballers on Derby's gluepot of a pitch, and had got an early start on the two and a half hour haul back to Burnley.

And who could blame them? Not I. There was certainly no logical reason to be there for the last thirty minutes. We were three-nil down, for heaven's sake! The team were playing like doped-up donkeys in what was, without a shadow of a doubt, Burnley's most pathetically inept and utterly disgraceful showing

196

of the season. To cap it all, a vicious blizzard which had struck up, immediately the players took the field for the second half, was blowing so fiercely into one side of my body, that part of my left cheek was literally frozen at one point, and to this day remains a good five minutes younger than the rest of me.

It's not easy to explain why I and many others decided to stay on and watch, as Burnley's already fragile hopes of survival took yet another hammering. Well, I say 'decided', but maybe that's the wrong word to use. 'Decided' implies that I had some choice in the matter – which I'm not altogether sure that I did. Something inside me, a perverse mental flaw, a subconscious desire for masochism perhaps, kept me holding onto the pain, and made damned sure I was as firmly rooted to the spot as the Clarets were to the foot of the table. As Lee Mills and Marco Gabbiadini combined to complete the embarrassment (backed by The Derby Choristers with a soulful reading of 'You're Shit And You're Going Down'), I found myself more depressed than I had been all season.

It was a depression that lasted into work the following day. 'What's wrong with you this morning?' a colleague had asked. 'You've been as grumpy as hell.' I apologised, and tried to explain. I told her we'd lost 4-0, the players were lousy, we were stuck in the middle of a blizzard, the results hadn't gone our way, we were looking more and more likely to be relegated; in short, I told her all the facts. She was very understanding. She made all the right noises, nodding and tutting sympathetically in all the right places. But as her eyes slowly took on the sort of glaze more normally seen on Melton Mowbray pork pies, it was obvious that my attempt to communicate my misery had failed. As I continued with my tales of woe, it struck me that I was coming across less and less like a troubled soul, and more and more like a spoilt child, sulking because he couldn't have his own way. So having thoroughly embarrassed myself, I forced a laugh, muttered something about, 'never mind, there's always next week', (or some other ridiculous lie I didn't believe), and just shut up.

The problem was, of course, that I had tried to convey three months of frustration, anger, despair and bewilderment, in three minutes. I had tried to convey passionate emotions, using logic. I had tried the impossible. Really, I just wanted to shout at her: 'YOU DON'T UNDERSTAND! YOU CAN'T UNDERSTAND! YOU'RE NOT A FOOTBALL FAN!'

Without wishing to sound at all patronising to those who don't follow what many consider to be the finest game in the world, it is nigh-on impossible to explain how and why the lives and emotions of millions of people throughout the world, are controlled and dominated from mid-August to mid-May by eleven men kicking an inflated lump of leather around a rectangle of grass. I could have a go at explaining – but that's another book altogether.

Maybe I couldn't explain. Maybe I daren't. Maybe I wouldn't want to discover what lies at the heart of a human being who spends his Sunday mornings scouring the 'goals for' and 'against' columns of Notts County and Bristol City. Perhaps it's not such a good idea to seek out what motivation drives a seemingly normal human being, to give up a day's leave in order to make a 600 mile, ten hour round trip, just so they can witness their side grind out a tedious 1-1 draw on a chilly Tuesday night in November. It's probably inadvisable to delve too deep into the psyche of someone who is still prepared to debate, (with passion), whether it was Paul Comstive or George Oghani who got the Clarets' injury-time winner against Swansea . . . eight years after the event itself. (By the way, it was George Oghani.)

The truth of the matter is that, over the past two decades, Burnley Football Club have come to mean more to me than they ever should have been allowed to. Quite how this state of affairs has been arrived at, I'm not sure. What I am sure of, is that the Clarets have permeated my heart and soul, on a scale that is both massive and worrying.

BFC impinges on almost every area of my existence. Members of my family know that any conversation they conduct with me between the months of August and May must be prefaced with an inquiry as to the state of Burnley's midfield. At work, it is understood that I am unable to engage in verbal intercourse on a Monday morning, until the words, 'How did they do at the weekend?' have passed a colleague's lips. I regard myself as lucky, in so much as most of my friends also view everything through claret and blue-tinted spectacles, which makes life (and conversations) that much easier.

Frighteningly, results have a very definite bearing on my personality. A win, for example, more often than not induces a good mood that can last for days at a time. Lose, however, and

I'm dark, withdrawn, moody, difficult, and any number of morose adjectives. (A draw, depending on the context, could tip the scales either way.)

And so this is how it is. This is how I am unable to think, speak, move, live, without Burnley Football Club having a say in things. You might have reasonably thought that over the years, this considerable burden would have proved too much for me, and I might have jettisoned the Clarets and all the baggage they bring, in favour of a fuller, more satisfying life. But no.

There have been several occasions when the link between myself and the football club might have been severed: the fickleness of my teenage years, the death of relatives, relationships I've been involved in, and my years away at university. These are major milestones in a person's development, yet my unbridled, often unhealthy passion for all things Claret and Blue never waned during any of these times. Why?

Part of the answer might lie in the fact that although all of the above events have had varying degrees of impact on my life, they haven't been around for twenty years, like the club have. Other than certain members of my family, Burnley Football Club have been the only constant since I was seven. In that respect, it's a cornerstone, one of the foundations upon which my life is built. I think it always will be. I'm not altogether convinced that this is necessarily a good thing, but that's the way it is.

It's also quite possible that the club fills a void in my life – a void that could (and in all probability should) be filled by something with more substance, more meaning. Having said that, I find it impossible to envisage a time when the club will cease to be an important part of my life – only time will tell.

For richer, for poorer, for better, for worse. There's no escaping the frightening fact, I'm practically married to Burnley Football Club. Which I believe goes at least part of the way to explaining why I stood and froze on the terraces at Derby County, and why I would be undertaking the mammoth journey to Bristol City that coming Saturday, to give the club the support it was going to need if we were to have any chance at all of avoiding the drop – a drop which seemed to become more and more imminent with every passing game.

Bruce Grobbelar, Hans Segers, John Fashanu and his girlfriend, and a Malaysian businessman are arrested by police as they investigate allegations of match-rigging.

Chelsea win through to the Semi-Finals of the European Cup-Winners' Cup, as they defeat Bruges 2-0 at Stamford Bridge and 2-1 on aggregate. Arsenal are also through. Their 1-0 win in Auxerre gives them a 2-1 aggregate victory.

Coventry go to Liverpool and win 3-2, as Peter Ndlovu becomes the first player to score a hat-trick at Anfield since Norwich's Terry Allcock, 33 years previously.

Saturday 18/03/95
Ashton Gate

BRISTOL CITY 1-1 BURNLEY
(Partridge 12) (Eyres 65)
League position before and after match: 24th . . . 24th

Attendance: 6,717

BURNLEY: Russell, Harrison, Winstanley, Davis, Vinnicombe, Randall *(Parkinson 82)*, Hoyland, Thompson, Nogan *(Robinson 66)*, Pender, Eyres.
Sub (not used): Beresford.

BRISTOL CITY: Welch, Hansen, Munro, Dryden, Bryant, Edwards, Khul, Bent, Baird, Partridge *(Wyatt 73)*, Owers.
Subs (not used); Kite, Shail.

Referee: M. Pierce

Yellow cards: Bryant, Edwards (Bristol City)
              Pender (Burnley)

Red cards: Vinnicombe (Burnley)

Monday morning; and as I arrived at work, mentally prepared to fend off the inevitable volley of abuse from some of my non-Burnley supporting colleagues, I chanced to bump into the Works Security Officer. Before I had so much as a half-chance to offer him the traditional, 'Good morning', he tutted loudly and shook his head. 'They're down now,' was his opening gambit, 'You do know that, don't you?'

It wasn't the first time that he'd speculated on Burnley's demise. In fact he had been positively revelling in his role as The Angel of Death ever since we'd lost 2-0 at Middlesbrough on the opening day of the campaign. Then, I'd laughed it off, as I had done for most of the first half of the season. But as the Clarets' dismal post-New Year's Eve form plummeted them closer and closer to the trap-door marked 'RELEGATION', I had laughed less and less.

'A point's no good,' he continued, a grim expression fixed upon his countenance. 'They needed three.'

'Ah, it's not over yet,' I replied, only half-believing myself, and with that darted between the open doors of the lift, making good my escape from the Harbinger of Doom before he had a further chance to depress my spirits.

Under different circumstances, the result against Bristol might have provided cause for celebration. One-nil down, away from home, and having been reduced to ten men, Burnley had dug in and salvaged a point. But it wasn't enough. Like the Security Officer had said – they really had needed three points.

The game had been a dour affair, living well down to expectations. Two sides fighting for their First Division lives rarely produces high-calibre football, and this was no exception.

Obviously unimpressed with certain of his charges' performances against Derby, Mullen had seen fit to radically rejig the team. Parkinson, whose recent form had fully justified the cries of a spectator at the Baseball Ground, ('Don't try and play football, Parky! You know it's not your sport!'), made way for Gerry Harrison at right back. In one way, this was no bad thing. Harrison would soon have to deputise for Lovely Legs anyway, as he was due to serve his suspension brought about by his dismissal against Barnsley at the hands of the psycho-ref-from-hell. Hoyland was taken out of the heart of defence and pushed up into midfield. John Pender filled his vacated space.

Most alarming of all was Jimmy's decision to axe Beresford, and replace him with Wayne Russell. I couldn't see why. Granted, Marlon had had a stinker against Derby, but in that respect he was no different to most of the eleven who had been on duty that evening. Besides which, the number of games which Beresford had kept us in, far outweighed those that he had lost us.

Twelve mundane minutes of scrappy soccer had elapsed when Rob Edwards pushed an innocuous-looking ball down the left hand side for Scott Partridge to chase. His speed took him free of Winstanley, whose 'tackle' consisted of falling on his back and waving a hopeful leg in the general direction of the Robins' number ten.

Sensing imminent danger, Russell hared out to the edge of the area. 'Don't bugger this up, or we'll be in real trouble,' I thought, as young Wayne buggered up and put us in real trouble. Attempting to clear the ball, the Clarets' second choice keeper thwacked it against the attacker's legs. The ball ballooned up in the air and seemed to hang there for a lifetime. Sat at the opposite end of the ground, it was impossible to tell whether or not it was going in. The roar which went up from home fans in the bizarrely-monickered and wholly unpronounceable 'Atyeo Stand' answered my question. One-nil, City.

For the next ten minutes or so, ex-Claret Junior Bent terrorised Vinnicombe down our left hand side. Cross after cross flew in, and were it not for some spectacular impotence in front of goal from City's forwards, the Avon side could have run up a rugby score in a matter of minutes.

City continued to push forward and it was no surprise when Bent showed a clean pair of heels to Vinnicombe and raced goalwards, with just Russell to beat. 'Oh no you don't, Junior.' thought Vinny, and brought the tricky winger's run to an abrupt end, a yard or so outside the area, with a challenge that was the very definition of 'professional foul'. In terms of accuracy and effectiveness, I rated it second only to Davis' juggernaut of a challenge on Ged Brannan, which led to his dismissal at home to Tranmere. Mr Pierce took a dim view of Vinny's tactless tackle, and our number five became the twelfth Burnley player to be sent off in the 1994/95 campaign.

Our disciplinary record made ugly reading. In thirty-five

league games, we had ammassed ten red cards. This meant we had incurred the wrath of an official once every 3.5 games. Early baths taken up and down the football grounds of England by Beresford (Oldham and Portsmouth), Davis (Tranmere), Hoyland (Charlton), Eyres (Stoke), Dowell (Middlesbrough), Harrison (Southend), Parkinson and Stewart (both Barnsley) and Vinnicombe that afternoon, meant that so far that season, Burnley held the unenviable record of having the most players sent off in the Football League or the Premiership, not just in the 94/95 campaign, but in *any* season.

Add to this a more than liberal sprinkling of bookings, and it was clear the Clarets were unlikely to be invited to any 'Fair Play Awards' ceremonies, come the end of the season and there were still eleven games left. Even in the event that another team overtook our tally by the end of the season, there was still every chance that the club would be hauled before an FA Disciplinary Committee.

The latest red card had the beneficial effect of sparking the Clarets into life. Before the interval, Davis had a shot turned over the bar and both Nogan and Eyres should have done better with headed efforts. But half-time arrived with Burnley still trailing by the single goal.

Looking around during the interval, it was clear that this was Burnley's lowest away following of the season – somewhere in the neighbourhood of eight hundred. Not that I was too surprised. After the flame of hope, lit following the victory against Oldham, had been so cruelly and emphatically extinguished at the Baseball Ground in mid-week, the prospect of a nine-hour round trip to the West Country could hardly be said to be one worth getting excited about. These were trying times for Burnley fans.

The first twenty minutes of the second period were so unutterably dull, that if someone had had the wit to video that particular section of the match, they could have become the market leader in the cure for insomnia, practically overnight.

Enter Adey Randall, who up until this point had been invisible in midfield. His twenty-five yard shot looked to be easy enough for Keith Welch, Bristol's keeper. Obviously aware that the majority of the 6,717 crowd were on the brink of sleep, good old Keith decided to inject some excitement into the game by dropping the ball right at the feet of David Eyres. 'Go on, Davey,' said Keith, 'You can't miss from there!' Too right.

As Eyresie lashed the ball into the net, (his first goal in open play of the 94/95 campaign – and about bloody time too), the travelling support set about celebrating Burnley's first away goal in the league since Parky's dramatic last-gasp equaliser at Grimsby at the end of November the previous year. By no means was it as spectacular as Lovely Legs' effort, but it was just as important.

At this point, Jimmy clearly fancied all three points and decided that the best way to collect them was to introduce a bit of pace, in the shape of the Fat Shearer. The man for the chop was Nogan, who up to that point had performed with less clout than a soggy slice of bread.

This prompted an irascible display of petulance from The Nog, who illustrated his displeasure by steadfastly refusing to leave the field of play. As Clive Middlemass signalled to him to get a move on from the bench, Noggin stamped his feet a bit, pulled off his shirt and began walking off the pitch at such a slow pace, that had he continued at that rate, he may well have aged a week or so by the time he reached the touchline. Uncle Clive's blood was up by this point, and we were treated to the most absurd piece of pantomime.

Poor old Uncle Clive, angry at being woken from his afternoon nap, shuffled onto the pitch, and, grabbing The Nog by the wrist and elbow, had to quite literally wrestle him to the touchline, where the *enfant terrible* had a further fit of pique, throwing his shirt into the dugout. 'Words' were exchanged, twixt the record signing and Uncle Clive, with the result that Noggin The Nog remained on the bench for the rest of the game.

The whole affair (which earned Nogan a new nickname, 'Kurt the Shirt') wore a faintly ridiculous air. It resembled nothing so much as a seven-year-old who had been playing football with his mates, and who, having been told that his tea was ready and it was time to come in, decided to throw a particularly juvenile tantrum.

As a spectacle, it must be said that there was more than an element of humour to the whole episode. I'm sure if a Bristol player had done the same, a wry smirk might have crossed my lips. But it wasn't a Bristol player, and so it wasn't nearly so amusing. Like so many of the needless sending-offs over the past few months, it served to highlight the lack of discipline in the side. As the moaning child sat and sulked on the bench, I felt a mixture of shame, disgust and anger. How dare he behave like that? How dare he insult the players, staff and supporters of Burnley Football Club?

There were Burnley fans there that afternoon who would have given an arm and a leg to don the famous claret and blue. It should also be noted that even without these two vital limbs, they could in all probability have turned in a better performance than Kurt Nogan had in the hour or so he'd been on the pitch.

Kurt the Shirt's childish *tête-à-tête* with Uncle Clive proved to be the last action of the afternoon which could have been reasonably described as entertainment. And so as the referee blew for time and the home supporters booed their team from the pitch, we made our way through the grey drizzle back to the coach.

Another game, another draw; with just eleven games left, time was running out. That result meant that a win against Luton on Tuesday night was of the utmost importance. Not only would three points hopefully close the ten point gap between ourselves and safety, it would also mean I could face The Angel Of Death on Wednesday morning, with my head held high.

The FA announce a campaign against sleaze, which will be unveiled at the beginning of next season.

Manchester United reveal plans to rebuild and extend their North Stand, at a cost of £28 million.

Many believe this is the weekend that Manchester United's bid for the Premiership grinds to a halt, as they go down 2-0 at Anfield, and Blackburn beat Chelsea 2-1 to go six points clear at the top.

Notts County triumph over Ascoli to win the Anglo-

Italian Cup Final at Wembley. A mere 11,704 turn up to watch.

Tuesday 21/03/95
Turf Moor

BURNLEY 2-1 LUTON TOWN
(Mullin 73, Harrison 83) (Marshall 61)
League position before and after match: 24th . . . 23rd

Attendance: 9,541

BURNLEY: Russell, Harrison, Winstanley, Davis, Pender *(Mullin 68)*, Vinnicombe, Randall, Robinson, Thompson, Nogan, Eyres.
Subs (not used): Brass, Beresford.

LUTON TOWN: Sommer, James, Johnson, Waddock, Thomas *(Harvey 45)*, Peake, Telfer, Matthews, Dixon, Preece *(Woodsford 80)*, Marshall.
Sub (not used): Davis.

Referee: R. Poulain

Yellow Cards: None

Red Cards: None

The newspapers spoke about many things following this game. They talked about the passion and commitment of the Clarets, they waxed lyrical over Mullin's equaliser and Harrison's late winner, and they discussed the improvement in Burnley's chances of survival. What they didn't mention was the backing that Burnley received from the terraces that evening. This was a crying shame, because the 9,000 home fans were nothing short of fantastic. The only person to make any sort of comment on the subject was Luton's stand-in-manager, John Moore, who was quoted as saying, 'Their backs are up against the wall, but they have a magnificent crowd behind them here. They helped lift the side in the second half.' [25] Nice one, John.

Crowds don't win games. I have yet to see a supporter make the back of the opposition's net billow with a twenty-yard volley, or make a vital last-ditch challenge to deny their number nine. What crowds can do is make the kind of noise which inspires the home team to perform heroics, whilst simultaneously putting the absolute fear of God into the visitors. Which is exactly what happened in the last half-hour of this game.

The first hour can be forgotten. The only purpose it served was to remind all those gathered inside Turf Moor that watching the game we love can, at times, be a stupefying and crushingly mediocre experience. A minute later, Dwight Marshall put Luton ahead, and suddenly a stupefying and crushingly mediocre contest seemed incredibly appealing.

But it was at this precise moment that the crowd realised the importance of the role they had to play, and set about raising the roof as one. Any differences of opinion about the manager, the team, or the tactics, were wholly irrelevant. What mattered for the last half-hour, was the 9,000-strong Claret and Blue Army yelling themselves hoarse and communicating their passion for victory to their eleven representatives on the pitch – something they did superbly.

For the next twelve minutes, the Clarets poured forward, looking for an opening, a moment of inspiration, a chink in the armour of the side with the best away record in the the division, whilst all the while being urged on by the fabulous vocal support from the sidelines.

Seventeen minutes were left when Juergen Sommer failed to clear his lines properly. His mis-cued punch fell nicely for John Mullin, who had a quick look up, steadied himself, and buried the ball from ten yards out to level the scores. We were half-way there.

After getting the equaliser, Burnley had to make it count. A point was practically worthless. We had to score. As the seconds ticked away, Turf Moor became a cacophony of claret-tinged noise as Burnley pushed forward, desperate for the winner. Eyres forced a brilliant one-handed save from Sommer. 'COME ON YOU CLARETS!' Randall's swerving, dipping shot just cleared the bar. 'COME ON YOU CLARETS!' Steve Thompson had a snap-shot whizz over the top of Sommer's goal. 'COME ON YOU CLARETS!' Could we do it?

Seven minutes remained when Steve Davis, on one of his many elegant runs of the evening, stormed through midfield, bisected two defenders and slid a ball through to The Nog, who dummied and allowed it to roll on to the unmarked Harrison on the right hand side of the area. Gerry took three or four strides towards goal and smashed his shot past Sommer and into the corner of Luton's net.

I can't remember exactly what happened next. It's all a blur. I have vague recollections of leaping up and down, as though my jeans were coated with fiery jack, hugging my sister, hugging my mates and yelling, 'We've bloody done it! We've bloody done it!' It was without doubt the celebration of the season.

An incredibly tense last five minutes then ensued, during which roars of encouragement mixed with whistles of frustration, as the Clarets stood firm and kept the Hatters at bay. Anything that came within five yards of our penalty area, was met with a firm Burnley boot, sending the ball back from whence it came. One Steve Davis clearance was packed with such venom that when it struck goal-hero Gerry Harrison full in the face, it temporarily concussed him, adding yet more nerve-jangling minutes to the game.

Eventually, a shrill blast from Mr Poulain's whistle brought the game to a full stop. The cheers of relief were almost as loud as they were for Harrison's winner. I must have stood here for a good couple of minutes, applauding the team from the field and trying to calm down and take in the last gripping, exhausting, seventeen minutes.

I couldn't stand many more games like this. I was already half-way to a nervous breakdown having watched this one. Seven points was now the gap between ourselves and twentieth position. If fifty-four points was the end-of-season target, which seemed to be the received wisdom, we needed nineteen points from our last ten fixtures.

It was a tall order, no question about it, but nevertheless, it was also an achievable one, especially if the next game – away at Wolves – saw the supporters and players display the same passion and determination to succeed as they had that evening.

Comedian Freddie Starr is thought to be one of a group
seeking to buy Gillingham Football Club.

Crystal Palace earn the right to meet Manchester United
in the Semi-Finals of the FA Cup, after they demolish
Wolves 4-1 at Molineux.

Gordon Strachan leaves Leeds for Coventry, to become
assistant manager to Ron Atkinson.

Friday 24/03/95
Molineux

WOLVERHAMPTON WANDERERS 2-0 BURNLEY
(Bull 11, Emblen 59)
League position before and after match: 23rd . . . 23rd

Attendance: 25,703

BURNLEY: Russell, Harrison *(Brass 68)*, Winstanley, Davis,
Vinnnicombe, Randall, Hoyland, Thompson, Nogan, Robinson
(Shaw 45), Eyres.
Sub (not used): Beresford.

WOLVERHAMPTON WANDERERS: Stowell, Blades,
Venus, Rankine, Law, Shirtliff, Goodman, Kelly, Bull, Emblen,
Dennison.
Subs (not used): Smith, Wright, Jones.

Referee: P. Foakes

Yellow Cards: Venus (Wolves)

Red Cards: None

Friday night in the Black Country; and another defeat to add to
the seventeen we had already accrued in the course of the
campaign. You might have thought that having suffered so many

losses during the season, I would have learnt to come to terms with the feeling by now, or managed to find a way of stifling the pain; not so. Leaving the ground that evening, I was filled with the same depressing combination of disappointment, dejection and frustration that I had experienced every time we had lost, that, or indeed any season.

This defeat was cruel – more so than most. Coming just seventy-two hours after our considerable heroics against Luton, almost 2,000 Clarets had undertaken the trip to Wolverhampton, buoyed up with a feeling of cautious optimism.

However, as our coach came to a halt in the middle of a Wolverhampton car park, the feeling of optimism soon become a feeling of apprehension, largely due to the presence of what looked like two-thirds of the West Midlands Police Force. Evidently, the boys and girls in blue (or rather, the boys and girls in fluorescent yellow jackets) were not at all happy with the idea of hundreds of Burnley fans making their own way to the ground, and had very kindly turned up to give us an escort to the stadium.

As we were being route-marched, I couldn't help thinking that there was something a little bit daft about it all. I looked around me. A large part of the crowd was composed of parents with their kids, thirty and forty-somethings, and a fair contingent of women. Yes, there were some single males under the age of thirty there, but they weren't acting like nutters (I know, because I was one of them). These were football fans, going to a football match.

Maybe the police thought they were protecting us from the massed ranks of psychopathic Wanderers' fanatics. The thing was, I never saw any. Nor did Andy, nor did my sister, nor did Steve or any of the others with whom I'd travelled down. In fact, I don't recall feeling at all threatened. Nor did I see the good people of Wolverhampton screaming in fear, dropping their goods and chattels and fleeing for safety as the Claret and Blue Army trooped over the crest of the hill.

It would have been nice to have been trusted, that's all.

Within a few minutes, we were outside the stadium; and what a stadium. A couple of years earlier, I'd visisted Molineux with a Wolves supporter whom I'd met at university. Then, the foot-balling arena in which I stood in awe of with many other Clarets that night, was still being built and could only hint at the grand structure that it would become.

The all-new Molineux was a wonder to behold. The concourse beneath our stand was warm, spacious, well-lit and clean. There were food stalls which sold that most rare of commodities at football grounds – edible food. And if you're reading this and thinking 'What's so special about that?', then you should try visiting some other, less accommodating grounds up and down this green and sometimes not-so-pleasant land. Nowhere else was Wolves' generosity towards visiting fans better exemplified than at the in-house betting kiosk – where else would you get odds of only 11/1 on The Nog being the first goalscorer?

Taking our seats in the Upper Tier of the Jack Harris Stand, the ground somehow didn't seem real. In fact, so pristine and perfect did it look, that it rather put me in mind of one of those Subbuteo sets with all the accessories, which I'd craved as a kid – a craving which, incidentally, the advent of early adulthood has yet to to curb.

It had the lot. Four magnificent stands, all of them filled to capacity, surrounded the pitch. Gone were the tall, spiralling floodlights, such as those at Turf Moor. In their place, built into the roofs of the stands, huge rows of spotlights shone down, illuminating Sir Jack Hayward's theatre of dreams. Two corners of the stadium housed forty foot metal structures; perched atop of each one, was an enormous television screen, beaming out advertising, team news, and messages of encouragement to the home fans in the stadium to get behind their team.

The only criticism that could be made concerned the state of the playing surface. This too reminded me of Subbuteo. In places, its patchiness resembled a cloth pitch upon certain areas of which a steam iron had lingered that moment too long, burning the material.

The two teams took to the field of play. The claret and blue of Burnley, the gold and black of Wolverhampton Wanderers, set against the floodlit green baize of Molineux – footballing tradition embodied. As the passionate roars of both sets of proud supporters drowned out the Tannoy music, I wondered what it might have been like in the fifties and sixties, an era when both sides were at the top of the footballing tree, an era in which both sides won championships, and made it to FA Cup Finals, an era to which only one of the two sides that evening looked like returning.

The opening exchanges of the game illustrated exactly why it was Wolves and not ourselves who looked like rejoining football's elite. With the majority of the crowd urging them on, Wanderers pressured from the first whistle. The off-the-ball work of the front-runners, David Kelly and Steve Bull, was on another plane, as they twisted and turned the Clarets' back-line every which way. Jamie Hoyland clipped Kelly's boots, but survived the subsequent penalty appeal, and menacing-looking crosses hung in the air and flashed across the goal, as Goodman and Dennison ran us ragged down the wings.

On ten minutes, Kelly lobbed a ball into the Burnley box. In the ensuing scramble, Bull appeared to blatantly control the ball with his hand, before poking it past the flapping figure of Wayne Russell. As the Wolves fans celebrated Bully's 199th league goal for the club, it struck me that if he'd scored in such a manner away from home, the goal might well have been ruled out. But Wolves weren't away from home – we were, and we were up against it . . . again. Wolves dominated the remainder of the half, and Russell was kept much busier than he might have liked. The best we could manage was some pretty passing patterns in midfield. Although they may have been marvellous, aesthetically speaking, they lacked the sharpness or speed of thought to cause Wolves any serious problems. Only the magnificent Steve Davis, who left no blade of grass on the field uncovered that evening in his admirably determined quest for success, looked anything like. His pile-driver which went whistling narrowly over the top of the Wolves' crossbar was our only effort of note in the half.

The interval was spent trying to avoid talking about football, eulogising instead about the splendour of our surroundings. 'We're gonna get stuffed second half,' sulked Neil. I tried to remain positive. 'It only takes one mistake and we're in,' I replied. Realistically however, the chances of the Wolves defence making a mistake were slim, to say the least. Slimmer still was any chance of The Nog, who had enjoyed another 45 minutes of on-field anonymity, capitalising on any such errors.

Jimmy changed his battle plan at half-time, introducing Burnley's new signing, Paul Shaw, into the attack, in the place of The Fat Shearer who once again had run the equivalent of five miles in the first half but had failed to make any significant impact. Shaw, a twenty-two year old Arsenal reserve team player, with only five minutes' Premiership experience (as a substitute), had been our only signing on transfer deadline day. It was impossible to judge him, really. He'd been at the club probably less than twenty-four hours and could hardly be expected to fit in right away. He looked reasonably sharp, buzzing around a lot, and holding the ball up well on occasions.

It was his off-the-ball running at the start of the second half that dragged a defender wide, enabling Eyres to get a shot in on Stowell's goal. The keeper took the sting off the effort, but it trickled goalwards, at a toe-curlingly, agonisingly slow pace. Two thousand Clarets held their breath, as the ball rolled towards the goal. Would it go in? Wouldn't it? The ball touched against the foot of the post and softly rebounded into the arms of a grateful Stowell, who cradled the ball in such a protective manner that you might have thought he'd just saved a small child from toppling into a ravine. 'You jammy bastard!' yelled more than one voice from the Upper Tier.

This dreadful piece of bad luck seemed to crack the Clarets, and try as they might, they never created a better chance in the rest of the half. Just under a quarter of an hour later, Wolves sealed the victory. The impressive Neil Emblen was given much too much time and space on the edge of the Burnley box. His goalbound effort caught Russell standing off his line, and although the keeper managed to get his fingertips to the ball, his despairing lunge wasn't enough to divert its goalbound path. The large telly screens played it over and over again, to the delight of the Wolves fans and the horror of the travelling support.

The goal just about wrapped things up. The home fans began a ten minute long Mexican Wave which repeatedly went all around the stadium, except for those rows occupied by Burnley fans, many of whom who were far too moribund and disconsolate to join in the Wolverhampton revelry.

Instead, the Clarets fans begun a defiant and highly impressive half hour of singing and chanting. It was the best we could do. It was all we could do. We were letting them know that even in defeat, even with our dire position, and even with The Nog leading the attack, Burnley fans were as passionate as any supporters in the country. 'Down with the Albion! You're going down with the Albion!' they sang back. That was as maybe, but if we were going down, we were going down making one hell of a racket.

Nine games and twenty-seven points remained. We needed to win six and draw one to reach the mythical fifty-four point target. Of the fixtures remaining, we had six at home and three away. The run-in read: Port Vale (h), Millwall (h), Charlton Athletic (h), Southend United (a), Derby County (h), Port Vale (a), Portsmouth (h), Sunderland (h), and Bolton Wanderers (a).

Of the ten fixtures we had left prior to that evening, the Wolves game was the one we had been expecting to lose. In that respect, although it still hurt as much as any other defeat, it wasn't such a blow. With the next three games at home in the space of eight days, it was essential that we took as many points as we possibly could. If we could put a run together, survival was still possible.

That evening we'd lost the battle, but not the war. Now was the time to re-group, and plan an all-out attack on Port Vale, Millwall and Charlton Athletic, our next three opponents – all of them at home.

Croydon Magistrates' Court sentence Eric Cantona to fourteen days' imprisonment for assaulting a spectator at Selhurst Park. He is released, pending appeal. Paul Ince pleads not guilty and has his case adjourned to a later date.

Scottish ex-international winger, Davie Cooper, dies aged 39.

Chelsea are charged with crowd trouble, following the fracas after their Fourth Round FA Cup exit, at the hands of Millwall earlier in the season.

A quiet transfer deadline day passes. The major action involves Jan Aage Fjortoft moving from Swindon to Middlesbrough, for £1.3 million.

The consortium attempting to buy Gillingham is looking

for none other than The Rolling Stones' Mick Jagger to swell their ranks.

Tuesday 28/03/95
Turf Moor

BURNLEY 4-3 PORT VALE
(Nogan 45, Randall 60, Shaw 64, Sandeman [og] 66)
(Foyle 42, 84, Allon 86)
League position before and after match: 23rd . . . 23rd

Attendance: 10,058

BURNLEY: Russell, Harrison *(Brass 52)*, Winstanley, Davis, Vinnicombe, Hoyland, Randall, Shaw, Thompson, Nogan *(Mullin 88)*, Eyres.
Sub (not used): Beresford.

PORT VALE: Musselwhite, Sandeman, Tankard, Porter, Aspin, Scott, Guppy, Van der Laan, Allon, Foyle, Walker *(Bogie 56)*.
Subs (not used): Naylor, Van Huesden.

Referee: B. Burns

Yellow Cards: Thompson, Winstanley (Burnley)
Porter, Allon (Port Vale)

Red Cards: None

As Mr Burns blew for full-time, the man standing by my side turned to me and laughed. 'Christ,' he said, shaking his head, 'They put you through it, don't they?'
'Put you through it?' I thought. Had I frequented my friendly neighbourhood slaughterhouse and requested the resident butcher 'put me through' his industrial mincer, I entertain serious doubts that my nerves would have emerged any more shredded than they were as a result of watching the last six minutes of this – the mother of all nerve-shredders.
In light of the above then, it is perhaps strange to relate that

215

the first forty minutes of this contest gave no indication that a roller coaster ride of the emotions awaited us in the last half hour. With Port Vale hovering dangerously above the relegation zone, they were in no mood to play risky, adventurous football. Every time we broke forward, the visitors made sure they were back in numbers, with the consequence that the majority of the first period was a sluggish, torpor-inducing affair.

Three minutes of the half remained when Van der Laan threaded a ball through to Martin Foyle. As neither of the two defenders within tackling distance could be bothered to put a challenge in, the number ten took the opportunity to shoot Vale in front. No sooner had I retreated into my cocoon of maudlin self-pity, (my usual reaction to going a goal behind), than three minutes later, I was coaxed back out. Harrison raced up their right flank, cut inside and laid the ball off to Kurt the Shirt, who slid through a crowd of Vale defenders to poke it over the line and equalise. Moments later, the ref blew for half-time. 'That was a bit bloody 'airy,' said Andy, as the majority of those inside Turf Moor breathed a collective sigh of relief and spent the interval counting their blessings that we were back in the game.

Not so Mick, whose inquisitive nature led him to ask the burning question, 'What's Alan Harper up to these days?' It was a good question. Nobody had seen hide or hair of the haystack-haired one since he limped off with a groin strain fifteen minutes into the West Brom game. Surely it was more than coincidence that that particular match saw our run of consecutive defeats come to an end.

A perusal of the programme revealed that the man they called Mooncat was 'now running in straight lines' with 'a possibility of an appearance in the London Marathon'. John tutted.

'That can't be true,' he said.

'What, about Harper doing the marathon?' I asked.

'No, not that,' he replied. 'When have you seen him run in a straight line?'

Whilst we pondered over the whereabouts of Alan Harper, it looked as though Jimmy Mullen and John Rudge, Port Vale's boss, had spent the interval plying both sets of players with copious amounts of valium. It may sound far-fetched, but it seemed a realistic conclusion to draw, as the same dull fare that had been served up in the first forty minutes, spilled over into the opening period of the second half, threatening to rob it of any excitement. It looked as though we were just going to have to tough it out, and hope to sneak a winner.

Then, bang on the hour, Steve Thompson's through ball picked out Adey Randall. Spaceman drew the keeper, and taking the ball round Musselwhite, slotted home to edge Burnley into the lead. Turf Moor roared its approval as Adey wheeled away to celebrate.

The claret and blue faithful barely had time to catch their breath, as four minutes later, Musselwhite, in an extraordinarily good natured display of generosity, didn't so much take a goal kick, as pass the ball to Paul Shaw on the half-way line. The on-loan Arsenal star couldn't believe his luck, and racing towards goal, expertly lifted the ball over the advancing Vale keeper and found the back of the net.

'Three-one to the Burnley!' sang a suitably delighted Longside. Amazingly, there was more to come. Just two minutes after Shaw's splendid effort, the Nog broke down the right hand side and fired in a low cross. Eyres wasn't quick enough to get on the end of it. Fortunately, Vale's ridiculously-named Bradley Sandemann was. 'Go on!' he seemed to say, 'Have this one on me!' and with that, slid the ball over his own line. Four-one! Party time!

Or so we thought.

It was at this point that the Clarets got a little bit too cocky for their own good. Having killed the game off, they should really have shut up shop. Instead, they continued to push up in numbers, leaving themselves more exposed at the rear than a model wearing a Jean Paul Gaultier designer dress.

Within two minutes, Martin Foyle had made the score four-two. The ear-to-ear grin that had been on my face a couple of minutes ago, contracted considerably. I was still fairly confident, though. You don't throw away a three goal lead . . . do you?

With six minutes to full-time, Burnley were again guilty of committing too many to attack and again paid the price, as Joe Allon touched home Martin Foyle's cross to set up a grandstand finish. With just one goal in it, Burnley decided that OK, maybe they'd better start defending after all.

Vale pushed for an equaliser – and pushed bloody hard. Vicious-looking crosses flew over, only to be headed or hooked away, claret-clad bodies flung themselves in the path of rasping shots, and last-ditch tackles kept the visitors at bay, as all the time the Longside whistled, screamed and beseeched Mr Burns to blow for time.

The roar of relief that went up when proceedings were finally brought to a halt could probably have been heard on the outskirts of Manchester. Another three points closer to safety. Another three points that set up what promised to be a gripping last eight games. We were now just four points away from escaping the relegation zone.

Millwall were coming to town on Saturday. I'd be there. So would thousands of others, to see if Burnley could claim three more precious points and haul themselves away from the dreaded drop and closer to safety.

Peter Reid is appointed manager of Sunderland until the end of the season, following Mick Buxton's dismissal.

Eric Cantona's appeal against his jail sentence is successful. He is ordered instead to serve 120 hours' community service. When the press ask him for a quote he replies 'When seagulls follow the trawler, it is because they think sardines will be thrown into the sea.'

Meanwhile, United and Cantona open negotiations to decide whether or not the Frenchman's future lies at Old Trafford, following reports that Inter Milan are ready to offer £5.5 million for the player.

More headaches for Alex Ferguson, as Andrei Kanchelskis is quoted as saying that he does not see himself being at Manchester United at the start of next season.

Happier times off the field for the Reds, who announce a £36.4 million turnover for the first six months of the season.

Andy Cole makes a brief debut for England, nineteen minutes from time, as Terry Venables' team bore the nation with a dull 0-0 draw against Uruguay. The tabloids begin to get on Venables' back, accusing him of being too negative.

Russell Osman is appointed manager of Plymouth Argyle until the season's end.

Reg Burr stands down as chairman of Millwall, as does Bernard Baker at Gillingham.

Saturday 01/04/95
Turf Moor

BURNLEY 1-2 MILLWALL *(Shaw 75) (Oldfield 38, 57)*
League position before and after match: 23rd . . . 23rd

Attendance: 10,454

BURNLEY: Beresford, Parkinson *(Robinson 65)*, Brass, Davis, Winstanley, Randall, Shaw, Thompson, Nogan *(Mullin 72)*, Hoyland, Eyres.
Sub (not used): Russell.

MILLWALL: Keller, Beard, Thatcher, Roberts, Webber, Stevens, Savage *(Chapman 77)*, Oldfield, Dixon, May, Van Blerk.
Subs (not used): Carter, Berry.

Referee: M. Riley

Yellow Cards: Davis (Burnley)
Thatcher, Beard, Van Blerk (Millwall)

Red Cards: None

It's amazing just how quickly your confidence can be shattered.
    Following the Port Vale result on Tuesday night, survival looked a realistic proposition. And whilst confidence may not have exactly flowed, it certainly trickled steadily. But by the time Mick McCarthy's midtable Millwall had successfully completed

their April Fool's Day smash and grab raid, that trickle had slowed to a drip.

The infuriating thing was that we should never have lost. After the match McCarthy, talking about our plight, was quoted as saying:

'If you win twelve corners in the first half of a game, you would expect to get a goal wouldn't you? That's probably why they are in the position they find themselves in.' [26] Absolutely Mick.

With those words, he provided an accurate synopsis of not only that afternoon's action, but much of the season thus far. If you're going through a barren spell of four or five games, you are perhaps entitled to claim 'bad luck' is involved somewhere along the line. But whilst we had certainly had our share of that, forty goals from thirty-nine league games since mid-August told its own story.

That afternoon for example, the Clarets had a tremendous amount of possession throughout the ninety minutes. The Lions' share was virtually nil. Randall, Nogan, Eyres, Shaw, Thompson – all had good opportunities to get their names on the scoresheet, but all either missed or were foiled by the outstanding goalkeeping of Kasey Keller, who enjoyed the game of his life. Millwall had two chances, and bagged them both.

It was a depressingly familiar scenario. All season long, Turf Moor crowds had witnessed good possession and good opportunities provide scant, or no reward. On our own soil, we should (not could, but *should*) have got maximum returns from Stoke, Wolves, Bolton, Swindon and West Brom. The same might also be said of away fixtures – most notably Reading, and West Brom again. Out of the twenty-one points available in those games, we had claimed just four. Mr McCarthy clearly knew what he was on about. Mr Mullen meanwhile confessed to being 'bewildered as to how we lost the game.' [27]

My depression at our inability to get past Millwall that afternoon was further compounded by the news that other teams in the relegation mire (Bristol City, Port Vale, Notts County, Swindon, Southend and Portsmouth) had lost. We'd missed a golden opportunity to make up some ground. The only team that had won was Sunderland, which meant we were seven points adrift of safety, with seven games to go.

The magical fifty-four point target seemed as far away as ever

220

that evening. Of the seven matches which remained, we could afford to lose just one more and that was provided that out of the other six, we won five and drew one. The local press insisted we must win Tuesday night's fixture against Charlton Athletic. And whilst that wasn't strictly true, I felt that after the midweek clash with Charlton and the trip to Southend United on the Saturday, the picture, for better or for worse, would be a lot clearer.

'We are not dead yet,' [28] Jimmy was reported as saying. True enough; but we were very, very ill.

Howard Kendall is sacked as manager of Notts County, after just 78 days in charge. His assistant, Russell Slade, is also axed.

Sheffield Wednesday suffer an incredible 7-1 home defeat at the hands of Nottingham Forest.

Blackburn Rovers go six points clear at the top of the Premiership and have a game in hand, as United are held to a goalless draw at Leeds.

Steve McManaman scores two brilliant individual goals to give Liverpool a 2-1 win over Bolton Wanderers in the Coca-Cola Cup Final.

The consortium hoping to save Gillingham collapses.

Tuesday 04/04/95
Turf Moor

BURNLEY 2-0 CHARLTON ATHLETIC
(*Eyres 25, Shaw 80*)
League position before and after match: 23rd . . . 21st

Attendance: 10,045

BURNLEY: Beresford, Parkinson, Winstanley, Davis,

Vinnicombe, Randall, Shaw, Thompson, Eyres, Hoyland, McMinn (*Robinson 75*).
Subs (not used): Nogan, Russell.

CHARLTON ATHLETIC: Salmon (*Petterson 50*), Brown, Mortimer, Jones, Rufus, Balmer, Robson, Leaburn, Pardew, Grant (*Bennett 75*), Robinson (*Newton 63*).
All subs used.

Referee: K. Lupton

Yellow Cards: Pardew, Rufus (Charlton)

Red cards: None

Alternatively known as the day that spring finally arrived. I knew this, not because I was privy to the sight of new-born lambs gambolling around country meadows, nor because I chanced upon a field of daffodils beginning to blossom, not even because of the multitudinous flocks of birds returning from their winter migrations. No, I knew that spring was here, because this was an evening kick-off and we didn't need the floodlights on until we'd been playing for about a quarter of an hour. This may sound extremely sad, but it is how many football fans finally know that winter has receded for another year, and the end of another season – the footballing one – is also close at hand.

Charlton's 94/95 campaign had really come to a full stop a couple of games prior to that evening's match. Bogged down in mid-table, with no hope of a play-off place and no fear of relegation, they were one of a handful of teams up and down the country whose footballing calendar had been rendered largely meaningless, until the middle of the following August.

That sense of having no real point to the season seemed to have firmly embedded itself in the minds of the visitors that evening. They arrived at Turf Moor, had a look round, and not fancying it much, decided to do the decent thing, by lying down and playing dead – something for which the majority of the 10,045 inside the ground were extremely grateful.

Not that that should detract from the high standard of Burnley's solid, organised performance. Nor should it take the gloss off the two superb goals which sealed the victory and once again stirred hope in the hearts of the Burnley faithful. The first, from Eyres, was a real centre-forward's goal, as he rose to meet Lovely Legs' cross and thundered the ball past Mike Salmon from ten yards out. Paul Shaw's effort also oozed class. The Fat Shearer's flick-on sent the on-loan star clear and he tidily slotted home past Petterson (Charlton's substitute goalie) from the edge of the area. As he did so, I punched the air with delight; not only was I celebrating his goal, but also the extension of his loan period which meant he was ours until the end of the season.

Having scored in each of his last three games, the young forward on loan from Arsenal had added a dimension to our attacking play which had been lacking all season – regular goals. Every time he received the ball, there was a murmur of anticipation in the crowd. Usually he delivered, be it a lay-off, a knock-down or a direct hit.

The three points gave us our highest league position since early January and the gap between ourselves and safety was reduced to four points, which meant that the weekend trip to Southend could be eagerly, if nervously, contemplated, rather than viewed as our possible swansong.

With the exception of our New Year's Eve goal-fest, this was by some margin our easiest victory of the season and I must admit that although my gaze was permanently fixed on the action, there were times when my mind was less than fully focused as regards events on the field of play. I seemed to keep drifting off on various trains of thought, most of which were inconsequential – apart from one.

Before the match, I read an evening paper which had run a story on a local councillor who had questioned why it was that there were no Asians on the books of either Burnley or Blackburn Rovers. I didn't know the answer to that. What I did know was that in the area which myself and my friends occupied on the Longside, I could recall seeing just one Asian face all that season. Why?

The answer might have been that the Asian, or Anglo/Asian community, didn't have any interest in football. However, as East Lancashire was home to a fair proportion of that particular ethnic background, I found it difficult to lend credence to the theory that none of them (in particular those who had been born and raised in England) were impassioned by the national sport.

Perhaps a more plausible reason as to why this section of the community stayed away, was that racism still existed on the terraces. That season I had heard John Gayle referred to as a 'useless coon', an Asian linesman with a shaven head was referred to as 'Ghandi', (oh, the originality of it all!) and Jan Aage Fjortoft was called a 'Norwegian shit-house' as he majestically, almost effortlessly unlocked Burnley's defence. The fact that the Norwegian probably had more grace in just his name than his fascist tormentor had in his entire personality, was one of that season's most blinding ironies.

In saying this, it should be borne in mind that these sickening cries of prejudice were few and far between. The situation on our stretch of the Longside was, I suspected, no better or worse than I imagined it would be at ninety-nine per cent of all other grounds in England. Indeed, in recent years the problem appeared to have been on the decline. But the very fact that this race-baiting still existed was cause for concern. So, if it upset me so much, then why didn't I do something about it?

There were two reasons. Firstly I was, quite simply, afraid. The prospect of being on the wrong end of a right hammering from the thug in question did not appeal. Although I might be more mentally developed than the idiot hurling abuse, I almost always found that he (and it invariably was a he) was built like a tank – and so were all his mates.

Secondly, let's say I did pluck up the necessary courage to confront him. What do you reckon my chances would have been of engaging in intelligent discourse with him and consequently altering his opinion, or even inducing feelings of guilt in him? I reckon slightly less than nil.

I once tried this approach. Burnley were playing Sheffield United in an FA Cup replay. One of their black players, Adrian Littlejohn, had borne the brunt of some terrible racist insults from a certain section of the crowd. In the second half he scored a fantastic solo goal. Celebrating, he ran over to the Longside, raised his arms aloft and stood grinning at some of the morons who had been yelling obscenities at him. It was his (brilliant) answer to the fascists.

His actions prompted a deplorable torrent of racist abuse from a group of 'supporters', standing a few yards away from me. I turned round to one of the offending group, and asked him what his problem was.

His reasoning went along the lines that Littlejohn's actions were tantamount to 'inciting a riot'.

'What?' I replied, 'And you and your mates chanting 'you black bastard' at him for the past hour isn't provoking any kind of trouble at all?'

His response was, 'You should come on here, (ie Turf Moor) more often, mate!'

To this day I have no idea what he meant. Perhaps he was suggesting that increased loyalty to the cause of supporting Burnley Football Club would somehow open my eyes to the apocalyptical state of affairs that would eventually occur, should a multi-racial society be allowed to flourish. He might have been trying to say that. But in all honesty I think he was probably talking complete and utter bigoted bollocks.

Happily, the Charlton game went some way to proving that Turf Moor, or at least the section where I stood, was only rarely frequented by Neo-Nazis. The visitors fielded a number of black players in their side that evening and as far as I could hear, they were not subjected to any racist taunts, only the usual jibes visited upon members of opposition teams (which although at times can be pretty scathing, are rarely as bad as the poisonous xenophobia which is occasionally given breathing space).

And so Burnley ended the night with considerably more hope in their hearts than had been there a couple of hours earlier. The longest trip of the season was coming up at the weekend; at least a thousand Burnley fans would be sacrificing their Saturday to undertake the journey. Another three points would make every mile of the pilgrimage to the East coast worthwhile.

Cambridge United and manager Gary Johnson part company. Tommy Taylor is put in temporary charge.

A Chris Sutton strike gives Blackburn Rovers a 1-0 victory over QPR. More importantly, it puts them eight points clear of second-placed Manchester United, with eight games remaining.

Leeds' Tony Yeboah scores a first half hat-trick as the Yorkshire club add to Ipswich's relegation worries with a 4-0 victory.

Leicester City score their first home victory for almost five months, with a 1-0 win over Norwich City.

Varying fortunes for Arsenal and Chelsea in the first leg of their Cup-Winners' Cup Semi-Final ties. Arsenal have a slender 3-2 lead to take to Sampdoria, whilst Chelsea must pray for a minor miracle in the second leg, as they go down 3-0 away to Real Zaragoza.

Luton Town reveal plans to move to a 20,000, all-seater, indoor stadium.

Saturday 08/04/95
Roots Hall

SOUTHEND UNITED 3-1 BURNLEY
(*Jones 5, Hails 6, Battersby 54*) (*Nogan 82*)
League position before and after match: 21st . . . 22nd

Attendance: 5,027

BURNLEY: Beresford, Parkinson, Winstanley, Davis, Vinnicombe, Randall, Shaw (*Nogan 56*), Brass, Eyres (*Robinson 56*), Hoyland, McMinn.
Sub (not used): Russell.

SOUTHEND UNITED: Royce, Gridelet, Powell, Whelan, Bodley, Dublin, Jones, Sussex (*Roche 83*), Hails, Tilson, Battersby (*Perkins 89*).
Sub (not used): Sansome.

Referee: G. Barber

Yellow Cards: Shaw (Burnley)
                   Bodley (Southend United)

Red Cards: None

The decision to spend the weekend in Southend-on-Sea proved to be a wise one. It could hardly have been more enjoyable. We sampled the wonderful local nightlife, ambled down the longest pier in the world, guzzled ice-cream in the sun and sipped whisky in a sea-front pub, as we watched Everton put the kibosh on Jurgen Klinsmann's FA Cup dream. Generally we had a fantastic time. It was, then, a source of great disappointment, that our main reason for our expedition into deepest Essex was also the nadir of our twenty-four hour East coast sojourner.

Over a thousand Clarets had passed through Southend's turnstiles, as the surprisingly warm and exceedingly welcome early spring sun shone down on the ramshackle ruin that was Roots Hall. Our small group arrived on the North Stand with hats, flags and sanguine expectation. This was to be the turning point of the season, the game that would lift Burnley to the brink of survival and simultaneously drag struggling Southend into the relegation dogfight. This was the day it was all going to come together . . . or so I'd foolishly allowed myself to believe.

Five minutes after kick-off, Keith Dublin's through ball found Davis and Winstanley discussing the price of shinpads, or something (they certainly didn't appear to be interested in marking anybody) as Gary Jones latched on to the pass and blasted past Marlon to give Southend the lead. 'Fantastic, Burnley!' bellowed the chap in the seat in front of me, 'That's bloody fantastic!' Something told me he was being a little sarcastic.

The same bewildered bloke had just about retaken his seat, when forty-three seconds later, our two central defenders were once again paralysed by inertia. Steve Tilson combined with Julian Hails, who lifted the ball over Beresford and tapped it into the gaping goal. This was footballing suicide.

The man who had been so furious with Burnley for going one down, didn't do anything this time. He just sat and gaped in stunned disbelief, along with the rest of the travelling contingent. 'What the hell is going on?' I asked Chris. (I don't know how he was supposed to know, but I needed answers from somewhere.) Meanwhile, four thousand Shrimpers' fans were cheering, jumping up and down and worst of all laughing at us, as Southend's double-whammy effectively ended the game as a contest.

'It is *two*-nil, isn't it?' asked an incredulous Andy, quite understandably unable to take in the fact that Burnley had all but blown it, in one minute of utter madness. 'Er, yeah,' was the best I could muster, as I sat there shell shocked. I looked to the ref for solace. Surely he should have stopped the game. This sort of thing shouldn't be allowed to happen. It was ridiculous! But Mr Barber was standing in the centre circle, about to initiate the game's third kick-off in under ten minutes.

'Come on, defence!' screamed one fan, 'you're fighting for your lives, Burnley!'

'I'll tell you what!' came the instant retort from the back of the stand, 'I'm glad they're not fighting for mine!'

It wasn't just in defence that we were having problems. Midfield was also providing more questions than answers. With Steve Thompson out injured, having suffered a knock in training, (a knock which was to keep him out until the last day of the season), Chris Brass had been asked to fill his boots. Mullen's decision to ask the nineteen-year-old reserve team right-back to play in midfield and man-mark Southend's ex-Republic of Ireland star Ronnie Whelan, had to rank as one of the most ludicrous of the season. Quite simply, the youngster was way off the mark. Time and again, Whelan used his vast skill and experience to humiliate the right back, so much so, that towards the end of the first half, Brass appeared to be hiding from the game.

Randall too, was ineffective. He was missing Steve Thompson. It was no coincidence that Spaceman had enjoyed the best form of his career, following the ex-Leicester star's arrival at Turf Moor. But that afternoon Randall was sluggish and unable to display any of the direction and inspiration that had thrilled Clarets' fans in the past few games. In that respect, he was symbolic of the whole side that sorry afternoon.

Unsurprisingly, the inhabitants of The North Stand were somewhat crestfallen by the time Mr Burns led the two sides off for the interval; some of them couldn't even be bothered to boo. Once again, relegation, surely football's equivalent of The Grim Reaper, was hammering at the door. After that first half, it seemed only a matter of time before he knocked the damned thing down.

Any lingering doubts I might have absurdly harboured about

Burnley staging a comeback were finally and conclusively shattered, eleven minutes into the second period. Tony Battersby was given so much room in our penalty area (he practically had it to himself) that you might have thought he was suffering from some contagious disease, as he was given time and space to control the ball with his back to goal, adjust himself, and make sure his bootlaces were tied, before he walloped an unstoppable effort past Beresford.

This prompted Jimmy, in his infinite wisdom, to take off Shaw, the striker who had scored three times in three and a half outings, and replace him with Noggin, who had netted one goal less in eleven starts. Chants of 'Mullen Out' rang out from the North Stand. At the same time, JM unleashed The Fat Shearer and brought off David Eyres, who had faded from the game to such an extent that when he was subbed, all that remained was his faint, ghostly outline.

Meanwhile, Ronnie Whelan was still running rings around the hapless Chris Brass, who bore the same air of decentred bewilderment more commonly associated with infants on their first day in a new school. It had been a harsh education for the lad, and when he eventually trudged off the field he looked both shattered and dejected. I wasn't sure it was entirely down to the scoreline.

With our two record signings now off the bench and on the pitch, you might have thought that things would start to happen. But they didn't. Instead, the remainder of the half saw the Clarets lumber around the pitch like some freakish deformation of a football team, rather than the genuine article. This was hideously depressing. Rather than being remembered as the game that sparked the Clarets' revival, it seemed destined to go down in the annals as one of the four worst performances of the season.

The afternoon held one bright spot. There were eight miserable minutes remaining when Spaceman lobbed McMinn's partially cleared corner back into Southend's penalty area. As The Nog swivelled on the spot and lashed the ball past Royce, I jumped up and punched the air. Christ, I had to salvage something from the afternoon. I just wished I had been celebrating a goal of a more meaningful nature.

Full-time brought more dismal news. Sunderland and Portsmouth, the two teams on whom Burnley were trying to make up ground, had both scraped home, one-nil. Once again the gap between ourselves and twentieth position was seven points.

Post-match, Mullen was quoted as saying what every football manager says when relegation seems a virtual certainty, namely that survival was still a mathematical possibility – which as every football fan knows is all but the kiss of death. Survival was still possible, but if talk of fifty-four points as the target was to be believed, then that meant we would have to win all of our last five games. To give an indication of how unlikely this was, the record for the most consecutive victories that season was held by Wolves, who had won five times in a row.

For the third time in as many weeks we had let go of the lifeline we had handed ourselves. Victories against Luton, Port Vale and Charlton had the shine taken off them, by defeats at the hands of Wolves, Millwall and now Southend. 'It's not over till The Fat Shearer sings,' said Andy, as we travelled home on the Sunday evening. Maybe, but it was becoming increasingly difficult to see how we could dig ourselves out of this hole.

FA Cup Semi-Final day sees Everton overwhelm Spurs 4-1 to book their place at Wembley on May 20th. Manchester United and Crystal Palace need a replay, after Palace twice surrender the lead.

Tragically, a Crystal Palace fan dies before the match, when he is crushed to death under the wheels of a coach he had been travelling on. The incident occurred in a pub car park after a fight had broken out between rival sets of supporters.

Gary Megson becomes caretaker manager at Norwich City, following John Deehan's departure from the club, after the 3-0 defeat at Newcastle.

The lowest-ever crowd for an FA Cup Semi-Final of just 17,987 (many stay away as a protest against the replay taking place so soon after the supporter's death), sees Manchester United run out 2-0 winners over Crystal Palace. The game is marred by Roy Keane's dismissal, as he loses his head and stamps on a Palace player, despite a pre-match plea from both managers for good behaviour. His dismissal means he is likely to miss the FA Cup Final.

United's misery is further compounded, by news that Andre Kanchelskis is out for the rest of the season with a suspected hernia.

Wimbledon's Hans Segers plans to sue the police for wrongful arrest, false imprisonment and loss of earnings, if the police decide not to charge him, vis-a-vis match fixing.

Saturday 15/04/95
Turf Moor

BURNLEY 3-1 DERBY COUNTY
(Eyres 12, Shaw 19, Davis 70) (Trollope 68)
League position before and after match: 22nd . . . 22nd

Attendance: 11,534

BURNLEY: Beresford, Parkinson, Winstanley, Davis, Vinnicombe, Randall, McMinn *(Robinson 72)*, Shaw, Philliskirk, Hoyland, Eyres.
Subs (not used): Nogan, Russell.

DERBY COUNTY: Hoult, Kavanagh *(Wrack 81)*, Wassall, Trollope, Short, Williams, Harkes, Pembridge, Mills, Gabbiadini, Simpson *(Boden 81)*.
Sub (not used): Sutton.

Referee: A.N. Butler

Yellow Cards: Philliskirk, Eyres (Burnley)
                 Gabbiadini, Harkes (Derby)

Red card: Short (Derby)

It was like being on the end of a bloody yo-yo. It really was. One week we were stopping up, the next we were destined for the drop. And as the Clarets continued to totter along on this most perilous of tightrope walks, my nerves were being eroded at such a rapid rate that I envisaged having none left,come the end of the season.

Not that I was complaining about this marvellous result. In fact, I was delighted. The victory was all the more piquant, as it came hot on the heels of our humiliation at the Baseball Ground just a few weeks previously. I was still smarting from that miserable night in the snow, and the fact that we managed to put the mockers on Derby's play-off hopes was an added bonus which made our revenge that much sweeter.

The spearhead of Burnley's nemesis was Tony Philliskirk. Following a spell of form in the reserves, the blonde bombshell was recalled to the starting line-up for the first time since his appearance at Roker Park in mid-October; and although he may have had his doubters, (myself included), the Phyllis did more than enough to justify his inclusion in the team.

Twelve minutes of Burnley pressure had elapsed, when the Tinman released Philliskirk down the right wing. Making for the bye-line, he cut into the area and lifted a dangerous centre into the Rams' six yard box. It was difficult to tell whether it was Eyres or a Derby defender who bundled the ball over the line, but frankly I couldn't have cared less. I was far too busy celebrating.

The breathtaking audacity with which Burnley had seized the lead over the play-off hopefuls incensed the visiting support. 'You're shit, and you're going down!' came the petulant chant from the Derby fans. The Longside took this on board and considered it for a few seconds, before replying with the infinitely superior, 'We're shit, and we're beating you!' It went remarkably quiet in the Derby end.

The silence of the Rams was deafening, as Burnley took the game to a Derby side who were visibly shocked that the lame dog they had nearly kicked to death at the Baseball Ground a month earlier, had now rounded on them in such a spirited manner.

Nobody was more instrumental in this than our number nine. With the smell of blood in his nostrils and confidence surging through his veins like refined heroin, the Phyllis moved in for the kill. Seven minutes after our opener, Spaceman knocked one over to the back stick. Big Tony was on hand to provide the nod-down made in heaven for the unmarked Paul Shaw, who side-footed home from a matter of yards, for his fourth goal in five starts.

As the balding figure of Shaw adopted a suitably stylish Jesus Christ pose in the back of the Bee Hole End goal, milking the wild applause from the terraces, I felt a vague sense of disbelief. In the same way we shouldn't have lost 3-1 to a mediocre Southend team seven days previously, there is no way we should have been 2-0 up against what was, on paper, a far superior Derby outfit.

Not enjoying the easy ride they had perhaps anticipated, Derby quickly became frustrated. This was best exemplified when Craig Short tried to bring the ball out of defence. As Paul Shaw snapped away at his heels, with the persistence of a particularly tenacious terrier, Short delivered a stunning forearm smash, to our number seven's forehead. Shaw fell to the floor, and with half an hour gone, Derby were down to ten men – which is how it stayed until the interval.

Half-time brought with it fifteen minutes of pure surrealism, entitled 'Bertie Bee's It's A Knockout Madhouse.' They weren't kidding, either. I looked on with what I can only describe as stunned incredulity, as a clutch of ridiculously oversized cloth beasts took to the hallowed turf. Ozzie and Ollie Owl from Sheffield Wednesday danced with each other, Manchester United's Fred the Red (who one observer suggested might have been a disguised Eric Cantona, carrying out his community service) played football with Bertie Bee, and the Bradford Bantam tried to pick a fight with anybody who was interested. Perhaps this is what critics had meant when they spoke of the theatre of the absurd.

The second half saw Derby shift up a gear, but Burnley never really seemed likely to concede the initiative. The defence in particular looked solid, and was superbly marshalled by Steve Davis, who had shorn his locks in favour of the kind of coiffure more readily associated with skinheads. Stylish it might not have been, but it did make him look very, very hard indeed.

'He's having a blinder, is Davis,' I said, turning around to Neil, 'He's not put a foot wrong all match.' sixty seconds later, our skinhead skipper responded to my high praise by putting not one, but both feet wrong, as he somehow managed to slip on the completely dry turf. Marco Gabbiadini took full advantage and sped towards the area. Marlon could only parry his shot, and Paul Trollope thumped home the rebound.

Fortunately we were spared a final twenty minutes of stomach-churning intensity, when ninety seconds after his Buster Keaton tribute, Davis atoned for his error, as his thumping header from the Tinman's free-kick was adjudged to have crossed Derby's goal line, despite Jason Kavanagh's attempted goal-line clearance.

With the two-goal advantage restored, Derby seemed to give up, which was jolly decent of them really. After all, they could have made life difficult for us by getting another, and making us hang on; almost every other bugger we'd played at home recently had done so.

That afternoon's victory meant that we had won five out of our last six home games and had been beaten only once at the Turf since mid-February. Never mind avoiding relegation, this was championship-winning stuff. The problem, of course, was our away form in the corresponding period. Whilst on our travels, we had picked up just one point out of a possible twenty-four since February the eleventh.

Easter Monday would see the Clarets visit Port Vale, who still needed a few points to be sure of avoiding the drop themselves. With the gap between ourselves and twentieth place reduced to four points following that afternoon's win, a victory at Vale Park would set up a cracking last three fixtures. Once again we had handed ourselves a lifeline. Surely we weren't going to throw this one away?

Blackburn Rovers' lead at the top of the Premiership is cut to six points, as Leeds score a dramatic injury-time equaliser against them at Elland Road, and Manchester United record a 4-0 victory over doomed Leicester.

Leeds manager Howard Wilkinson backs Blackburn Rovers to win the Premiership, saying, 'Only the Devon Loch syndrome can stop Blackburn now.'

Monday 17/04/95
Vale Park

PORT VALE 1-0 BURNLEY *(Van der Laan 40)*
League position before and after match: 22nd . . . 22nd

Attendance: 9,663

BURNLEY: Beresford, Parkinson, Winstanley *(Robinson 70)*, Davis, Pender, Randall, Shaw *(Nogan 77)*, Vinnicombe, Philliskirk, Hoyland, Eyres.
Sub (not used): Russell.

PORT VALE: Musselwhite, Sandeman, Tankard, Porter, Aspin, D. Glover, Bogie, Van der Laan, Foyle, Naylor, Guppy *(Kent 75)*.
Subs (not used): L. Glover, Van Heusden.

Referee: R. Harris

Yellow Cards: Musselwhite, Sandeman (Port Vale)

Red Cards: None

As Robin Van der Laan received Steve Guppy's centre in a ridiculous amount of space (roughly the size of Hampshire) and lifted the ball over the diving, despairing Beresford, it seemed that relegation didn't so much threaten, as drag us down a back alley and set about beating us within an inch of our First Division lives.

Other than a bright ten minute spell in the second half, this was a thoroughly dismal affair. In that respect, it was no different from the majority of the Clarets' away days that season, but as the gap between ourselves and safety stretched to five points, many fans felt the game was now well and truly up.

That wasn't necessarily true. Both Portsmouth and Sunderland, neither of whom were yet out of the mire, had still to visit the Turf; but if we lost at home to Portsmouth on Saturday, and Sunderland secured victory over Swindon at Roker Park, then there was absolutely no doubt about it. Burnley would be relegated.

Earlier in the afternoon, there had been an altogether more upbeat feel on the terraces. As the rain teemed down and Burnley struggled for supremacy in the Vale Park mud, the incredible 2,300-strong Claret and Blue Army launched into a round of singing, in an attempt to raise the spirits of the players. The song was one which had been sung up and down many stands and terraces, (with the occasional lyrical variation, dependent on who was in the managerial hot seat at Ewood park at the time), not just that season, but for many seasons before:

'I WENT TO AN ALEHOUSE I USED TO FREQUENT,
I SAW KENNY BASTARD, HIS MONEY WAS SPENT,
HE ASKED ME TO PLAY HIM, I ANSWERED HIM 'NAY!',
SAID, 'RUBBISH LIKE YOURS I CAN BEAT ANY DAY!'

'AND IT'S NO, NAY, NEVER,
NO, NAY, NEVER, NO MORE,
TILL WE PLAY BASTARD ROVERS,
NO, NEVER, NO MORE!'

For any non-Burnley supporters who may be reading, the above ditty (warbled solely by Clarets fans as far as I am aware) is sung to the tune of 'The Wild Rover' and tells of the disdain in which we hold our local rivals, Blackburn Rovers. Although we have not played them in a competitive fixture since Easter 1983, they are quite rightly regarded by Burnley supporters as our natural footballing foes.

There are those Blackburn fans (yes they do have *some*), who argue that since the arrival of Jack Walker and his bottomless pit of a wallet at Ewood Park, the rivalry between the two sets of supporters is no longer valid. Whilst I (painfully) concede the point that Mr Walker's multi-million pound investment in both the ground and the players has enabled them to move in circles that the Clarets have little or no chance of ever inhabiting, I steadfastly refuse to believe that the antipathy between the two clubs will ever, *ever* die.

Football is, if nothing else, a game steeped in tradition. Part of this tradition is local rivalry, or derbies. Think of Manchester United and Manchester City, Newcastle and Sunderland, Liverpool and Everton. Lower down the leagues there's Port Vale and Stoke, Plymouth and Exeter and even the peculiar Anglo-Welsh variety of footballing friction which exists between Chester and Wrexham. To deny this local rivalry is, by logical extension, to deny one of the cornerstones upon which the national game is built.

Blackburn Rovers are perhaps not the best team to have as your arch-enemies – especially when you are in Burnley's position. Unless somebody with the same financial clout as Jack Walker steps into the breach at Turf Moor, it would appear that we are destined to play second fiddle to the team who live just eight miles down the road – which hurts. And yes, if I am to be completely honest, I must admit that in many ways I am jealous.

I would love to have players of the class of Shearer, Flowers and Hendry pulling on the claret and blue every week. I would love the opportunity to follow Burnley into Europe. And I would love to see the likes of Le Tissier, Juninho and Beardsley come to exhibit their wonderful skills at Turf Moor. I would love all these things . . . but I'm not holding my breath.

That's not to say that having such a team as your nearest and not-so-dearest is all doom and gloom. There are still considerable consolations to be had. The jewel in the crown of the 94/95 campaign for instance, was Kenny's millionaires being knocked out of the first round of the UEFA Cup by the part-time footballers of Trelleborgs, a bunch of Swedish bank clerks, carpet-layers and brickies. In the same season, it was also a source of great entertainment to watch them fall by the wayside early on in both the FA and League Cups. The fact that as we played Port Vale that afternoon, they had spent the most obscene amounts of money and had still to pick up any silverware, provided yet further mirth for the claret and blue hordes.

Perhaps where Burnley FC *does* have the edge over their richer rivals, is the incredible passion that the fans (as a set of supporters, rather than as individuals) feel for their club. You want proof?

A local radio phone-in on Saturday evening regularly attracts more calls from Clarets fans than from supporters of any other teams in the region. Why? Presumably because they care more.

The first time Ewood ever hosted European football, (in September of 1994), only 13,000 or so could be bothered to turn up and watch. Later that same week, almost twenty thousand were at Turf Moor to see Burnley play Wolves in a Division One fixture.

Almost 2,500 Clarets fans travelled to Vale Park to watch Burnley on that miserable April afternoon. We were third bottom of the league, on the brink of relegation and had not secured three points away from home since October the previous year. Given that information, the only conclusion you can reasonably draw is that the fans who attended were absolutely fanatical about Burnley Football Club.

I was subsequently informed by a work colleague that at the same time as we stood watching Burnley slip further towards the drop, one local radio station was announcing at regular intervals that there were still plenty of tickets left for Blackburn fans for that evening's *home* game against Manchester City – a game which could have put Rovers eight points clear at the top of the Premiership, with just four games to play (had they not gone on to hilariously lose the match 3-2). Could you imagine such a scenario occurring, if Manchester United, Liverpool or Newcastle were in a similar position? I thought not.

So there you have it. Whilst we may not be as rich, or as talented, or as appealing to the media as Blackburn Rovers are, I'd like to think that Burnley fans have a fanaticism for their club which is not matched by those who watch their football at Ewood Park. And that is why, at least as far as the claret and blue half of East Lancashire is concerned, there will always be a passionate sense of rivalry between the two clubs.

That same passion would be needed in abundance on Saturday for the visit of Portsmouth, a team hovering dangerously just above the relegation zone, and a team over whom victory on Saturday would keep alive the Clarets' rapidly fading hopes of staying in Division One.

Blackburn Rovers spurn a golden opportunity to go eight points clear at the top of the Premiership, as they are outclassed 3-2 at Ewood Park by Manchester City. The point Manchester United pick up against Chelsea closes the gap to five points.

Barry Hearn, majority shareholder at Leyton Orient,

informs joint managers John Sitton and Chris Turner that their contracts will not be renewed after they expire in the summer. Glen Cockerill is appointed manager until the end of the season.

Halifax Town Football Club will cease to be at the end of the season. They are financially crippled.

Paul Futcher leaves Darlington after a disastrous eight weeks in charge. In his ten games as boss, the team didn't win once.

Arsenal progress to the European Cup-Winners' Cup Final, largely thanks to David Seaman, whose three penalty shoot-out saves helped the Gunners to victory.

Their opponents in the Final will be Real Zaragoza. The Spaniards just about hold off a battling Chelsea side who win 3-1 on the night, but go out 4-3 on aggregate.

Blackburn Rovers regain their eight point advantage at the top of the Premiership with a 2-1 home win over Crystal Palace.

Keith Houchen is appointed manager of Hartlepool United, following David McCreery's departure.
Derek Mann becomes the third manager in ten months to part company with Chester City.

Chelsea announce their intention to follow in the footsteps of Manchester United and Tottenham Hotspur, by floating themselves on the Stock Exchange.

Saturday 22/04/95

BURNLEY 1-2 PORTSMOUTH
(Eyres 81) (Durnin 36 [pen.], Symons 61)
League position before and after match: 22nd . . . 22nd

Attendance: 10,666

BURNLEY: Beresford, Parkinson, Winstanley, Davis, Vinnicombe, Randall, McMinn, Shaw *(Robinson 65)*, Philliskirk *(Nogan 65)*, Hoyland, Eyres.
Sub (not used): Russell.

PORTSMOUTH: Knight, Butters, Gittens, McLoughlin, Symons, Russell, Pethick, Burton, Rees, Durnin *(Kristensen 90)*, Hall *(Preki 82)*.
Sub (not used): Poom.

Referee: J. Winter

Yellow Cards: Philliskirk, Vinnicombe, McMinn (Burnley)
Russell, Durnin, Gittens (Portsmouth)

Red card: Hoyland (Burnley)

That was it, then; no more reprieves, no more chances, no more hope. The slender thread which had kept the Damocles sword of relegation suspended menacingly overhead, finally snapped in the howling gale that gusted around Turf Moor that afternoon. It was official. Burnley were down.

It was, perhaps, appropriate that it was Portsmouth who finally sealed our fate and consigned us to Division Two football for the 95/96 season. After all, it was at Fratton Park that our disastrous and ultimately decisive run of eight consecutive league defeats had begun.

Twenty-one league games later, I cast my mind back to that afternoon and remembered how we stood contracting hypothermia on the South Coast terraces, as the Clarets folded in the face of adversity. Looking back, it was as if the Pompey chimes had rung out as a form of warning to Burnley. Four months down the road, those same chimes sounded more like a death knell.

This was the game where all our chickens came home to roost. The points thrown away in our first two home games against Stoke and Bristol, the sloppy goals we had repeatedly conceded from set pieces on our left, the games we should have won against the likes of Wolves and Bolton, our profligacy in front of goal and

240

most tellingly, the months of January and February, during which we failed to pick up a single point from a possible twenty four. Was it any wonder that the following season would see us visiting Millmoor and not Molineux?

Earlier that afternoon, hope had sprung eternal, as I wended my way to Turf Moor. In light of our recent home form – five wins out of the last six – I passed through the Longside turnstiles, feeling not unreasonably optimistic. Why not? We'd seen off better sides than Portsmouth in the past few weeks, and the players were sure to be fired up for this one. With kick-off time fast approaching, I took up my position on the terraces and flicked through the programme. 'Portsmouth won't like this, you know,' said a chap next to me as the teams ran out and the wind and the rain took on such biblical proportions that standing up straight became an achievement of some merit, 'They're Southern softies.'

He was right. The Southern softies didn't like it. The problem was, the Northern softies liked it even less. After an initial spell of pressure, during which Burnley made little headway against a stubborn Portsmouth defence, the Clarets soon became dispirited by the fact that Pompey weren't going to do a Charlton and throw in the towel. This clearly didn't suit some of the players, most noticeably Adrian Randall, who seemed to give up halfway through the first half. Instead of going down fighting, we were going down sulking.

One person who certainly was going down fighting, (almost literally), was Steve Davis and his well 'ard haircut. He proved this nine minutes before half-time, bringing down Alan McLoughlin in our area with such a vicious challenge that had the assault occurred *off* the field, it would almost certainly have earned our skipper a stint behind bars. John Durnin smashed the resultant penalty high into the roof of the net, much to the delight of the away fans, who celebrated with their bloody silly hornpipes and cow bells which had proved such an irritant at Fratton Park. One-nil, Pompey; and it stayed that way till the interval.

Half-time brought with it the appearance of ex-Claret and huge crowd favourite, Martin Dobson. Unfortunately, the only time he stepped onto the pitch that afternoon was to draw the winning ticket in the 'Striker' Match Day Draw. I obviously wasn't the only one who wished that he could peel back the years, pull on a claret and blue shirt and inspire Burnley in their hour of need. 'There's only one Martin Dobson!' sang the Longside, by way of a tribute to the player, who, during his thirteen seasons at Turf Moor in the seventies and eighties, had captained the Clarets and represented England.

However, those in the crowd who had allowed themselves to lapse into dewy-eyed nostalgia had their minds and emotions sharply focused by the Tannoy announcer, who informed us in a suitably funereal tone, that Sunderland were one-up against Swindon. To the majority of football supporters, it was just another half-time scoreline – to Burnley fans, it meant that we had just forty-five minutes in which to save our season.

The first half-hour of the second period was all Burnley. Eyres, Randall and McMinn all had attempts on goal, and had Mr Winter not played silly buggers with our perfectly legitimate penalty appeal, we may well have been level. But then disaster struck. For the first time in the half, Portsmouth managed to get the ball over the half-way line. This would not in itself have been a problem, but for the fact that numbers two to eleven for Burnley were camped inside the visitors' half, as Kit Symons bore down on our goal with only Marlon to stop him. The Pompey number five rounded Beresford with an ease which bordered on contempt; two-nil.

I don't know if the Portsmouth Philharmonic started up with their bizarre collection of musical instruments again. All I could hear following their goal, was the loudest and most sustained 'MULLEN OUT!' chant of the season. It was hardly surprising. The fans had stood by their side through thick, thin and downright transparent over the past few months, and now they'd had enough: enough appalling performances, enough apologies, enough promises that things would get better. Spleens were being vented – and not without a little justification.

Moments later, Jimmy's decision to replace Shaw and Phyllis with Kurt the Shirt and The Fat Shearer further incensed the Longside. 'WE'RE GOING DOWN 'COS OF MULLEN!' they chanted, as a season's-worth of frustration, impatience and bitter disappointment oozed from the terraces and across to the managers' dugout. This was the sound of a season which had finally, perhaps inevitably, come apart at the seams.

David Eyres' strike nine minutes from time meant too little for it to be described as a consolation goal and the dismissal of Jamie Hoyland in the penultimate minute seemed a perfectly terrible ending to a perfectly terrible afternoon.

At quarter to five, Mr Winter blew the whistle on Burnley's hopes of survival. The Tannoy announcer's news that Sunderland had hung on at Swindon and so helped in the process of our relegation, solicited more calls for Jimmy's head from many on the terraces. You might have thought that I would have felt something; dejection, despair, anger maybe. But I can't say that I did. I didn't even feel numb. Sure, I felt the usual sting which always accompanies defeat, but certainly nothing worse than that.

Maybe it didn't hurt, because perhaps subconsciously, I'd resigned myself to our fate weeks ago. Perhaps, in my heart of hearts, I had known we were down, as soon as we slumped to the bottom of the table following our ignominious display at Tranmere, and all that had kept me going since then was my unshakeable and often ridiculous faith in all things claret and blue.

No, the full-blown horror of relegation didn't hit me until later on that evening, when I sat down and viewed, perhaps foolishly, the video of our Play-Off Final victory eleven months previously at Wembley. As I sat and watched, I remembered what a fabulous day that had been; and as the many, wonderful memories of that unforgettable day unfolded before me on my television screen, it struck me that the previous few months had been a glorious opportunity wasted. For the first time since the 1982/83 season, we had had the chance to establish ourselves at the second highest level of football in England . . . and had failed.

I remembered the night we were relegated from the same division, twelve years previously. Fifteen years old, I sat and listened to the radio as Burnley, whose squad boasted such names as Brian Laws, Billy Hamilton, Trevor Steven, Lee Dixon and Martin Dobson (how the hell did we get relegated *that* season?) went down 1-0 at Crystal Palace and dropped into what was, in 1983, the Third Division.

Whilst that relegation hurt, (such vulnerable people as teenagers should never be subjected to the traumatic ordeal that is dropping down a division), I felt that this one, when fully taken in, would have more of an impact. In the decade plus that had elapsed since that night, Burnley FC had come to mean much more to me. I was part of the club and the club was part of me. Relegation, therefore, was personal.

Sunday morning was hideous. The newspapers reported the facts in cold, bold black and white. There we were, eight points adrift from safety, third from bottom of Division One, with a capital 'R' for 'RELEGATED' next to our name and a thick black line separating ourselves, Notts County, Bristol City and Swindon Town from the rest of the division. We were surplus to requirements, we couldn't cut it . . . we were relegated.

Wolves manager Graham Taylor is furious after being spat at by a member of the crowd at Sheffield United. The incident occurs as he makes his way off the pitch following his team's 3-3 draw at Bramhall Lane. United manager Dave Bassett vows the offender will be caught and banned from the ground for life.

Birmingham City triumph 1-0 over Carlisle United, with a sudden-death extra time goal, to win the Auto Windscreens Shield at Wembley.

The Football Association and the Football League hold talks with a view to the former taking over the latter.

Eric Cantona finally ends speculation as to where his future lies, by signing an extension to his contract, which will keep him at Old Trafford until 1999. It is thought the price for securing Cantona's services will amount to £3 million.

The FA fine Wimbledon boss Joe Kinnear £1,500 and ban him from the touchline until October 31st, following comments he has made about certain referees in the course of the season.

Pat Holland is the new manager of Leyton Orient. He names Tommy Cunningham as his assistant.

Saturday 29/04/95
Turf Moor

BURNLEY 1-1 SUNDERLAND *(Eyres 36 [pen.]) (Smith 16)*
League position before and after match: 22nd . . . 21st

Attendance: 15,121

BURNLEY: Beresford, Parkinson, Winstanley, Davis, Vinnicombe, Randall, McMinn *(Mullin 24)*, Shaw *(Nogan 86)*, Philliskirk, Hoyland, Eyres.
Sub (not used): Russell.

SUNDERLAND: Norman, Ord, Ball, Angell, P. Gray *(Russell 69)*, Martin Gray, Michael Gray, Melville, Smith, Scott, Kubicki.
Subs (not used): Preece, Brodie.

Referee: W.A. Flood

Yellow Cards: Parkinson (Burnley)
Martin Gray (Sunderland)

Red Cards: None

That afternoon's match could never be described as a towering monument to all that was good in the beautiful game. Indeed, it was practically a mind-crushingly, mediocre xerox of the earlier fixture up at Roker Park, save for a Sunderland opener so soft that it was positively gooey and a curious penalty decision which led to Burnley's equaliser. Which was a pity, as this was the Clarets' final fixture of the 1994/95 campaign at Turf Moor.

I always find the last home game of the season to be a mildly depressing affair – for a number of reasons. Acquaintances whom I know solely through attending football matches at Turf Moor are lost to me until the middle of the following August, I'm deprived of seeing my claret and blue heroes and villains for a few painfully tedious months, but most of all, I miss standing on Turf Moor's most impassioned section of terracing – the Longside.

This might seem like a strange thing to admit to, but I truly regard it as a sort of second home. I suppose it's the cosy sense of familiarity that does it. The same friends and faces are there, season in, season out. You get used to how the pitch, the players and the rest of the stadium look from your particular perspective. I even stand in the same place for every game – leaning not behind a crush barrier, but against its side, thus allowing me to hop from one step to another to get the best view when play goes into the corner where the Longside and the Cricket Field Stand meet.

Rumour had it that the 94/95 campaign would be the Longside's last full season, as work was due to begin on transforming it into an all-seater stand. Which was, to be quite honest, a bloody shame. Apart from anything else, all-seater stadia (a ridiculous and over-the-top knee-jerk reaction to the Hillsborough tragedy, which has created as many, if not more, problems than it has actually solved) are loathed by thousands of football fans. We'd visited many grounds during the course of the season, and only a few of the stadia which had offered seated accommodation (Oldham, Notts County, Wolves) had proved satisfactory. We'd had a crossbar blocking our view at Luton, (no, we couldn't have moved; we had been allocated specific seats), there had been the extremely uncomfortable experience at Barnsley, and the cheap lumps of plastic bolted onto the terraces at Swindon, to name but three.

If some supporters want to sit down, then fine. But what about the rest of us who want to stand? What about the rest of us, who have to get out of our seats and more often than not crane our necks for a half-decent view, every time our team attacks? What about those of us who enjoy standing at football matches, who enjoy the luxury of being able to take a couple of steps forward or back, in order to get a better view? What about those of us who get a kick out of singing, chanting, jumping up and down and generally getting an atmosphere going?

If some supporters want to sit down, then fine. But why can't we have the choice?

All-seater Armaggedon aside, the vast majority of Burnley supporters would be greatly saddened by the demise of the Longside. For those like myself, who had come to look upon it as an extension of their own home, the news of its impending destruction was not unlike being told someone was going to drive a JCB through your front room and there wasn't a damned thing you could do about it. The terrace was, by some margin, the noisiest, most populated and certainly the most passionate of Turf Moor's four stands. Whether or not the same would be said of the new-look Longside remains to be seen. Personally, I doubt it. I don't see how you can rip the heart and soul out of the ground, re-build it and hope it functions in exactly the same way as it has always done. The Longside – soon to be gone, never to be forgotten.

Regrettably, the fiery fervour that the inhabitants of that famous section of terracing had for victory, wasn't mirrored on the pitch that afternoon. In fact, as Sunderland grabbed the point they needed for survival, in a contest duller than the average sample of ditchwater, the same thing happened that usually happens when the main action isn't up to much. My concentration breaks, I begin daydreaming and before I know where I am, I find myself plundering the treasure trove of memories, made up from almost two decades of watching Burnley.

I don't remember much about my first match. I know my dad took me, we stood on the Bee Hole End and saw a 1-0 victory over QPR in the 1975/76 season, (Burnley's last stint in the top flight), but that's about it. I must have enjoyed it though, because I kept going back; again and again and again. Despite the fact that in my time watching Burnley, the club have been relegated five times, there have been many marvellous memories. Here, in no particular order, are ten of my most treasured reminiscences from twenty years of following the Clarets:

1. The Turf Moor crowd going wild, as Tommy Cassidy knocked himself out heading a dramatic equaliser against Sheffield Wednesday, in the Quarter Finals of the FA Cup in the 82/83 season.
2. Billy Hamilton showing off the 81/82 Division Three Championship trophy, after I'd got soaked to the skin on the Bee Hole End, as we drew 1-1 with Chesterfield.
3. The amazing post-match scenes at White Hart Lane in 1993, when Jimmy Mullen emerged onto the pitch to applaud the fans, after a spirited 3-1 defeat had culminated in a twenty minute chorus of, 'Jimmy Mullen's Claret and Blue Army'.
4. Steve Taylor and Billy Hamilton getting a hat-trick each, as we steam-rollered Charlton 7-1 ten years earlier.

5. Being away in my first year at university and nervously pacing up and down the kitchen for a couple of hours, listening to the radio, as Burnley won 2-1 away at York in injury time, to lift the Fourth Division Championship.

6. 8,000 Clarets' fans at Sheffield United, celebrating two magnificent Adrian Heath goals in the Third Round of the FA Cup in 1992, which gave us a 2-0 first half lead. We went on to draw 2-2 and lose the replay, but at half-time at Bramall Lane, we were in claret and blue heaven.

7. The Play-Off Final victory over Stockport County at Wembley in 1994, and in particular Steve Davis' fantastic solo run, ten minutes from time.

8. The incredibly emotional scenes which followed our 2-1 defeat of Leyton Orient in the last game of the 86/87 campaign, a victory which meant that by the narrowest of margins, Burnley avoided the drop into the wilderness of non-league football.

9. The appearance of Leighton James in the 1988 Sherpa Van Trophy Final against Wolves. With half an hour left, 'Taffy' gave a masterclass in wingplay, as he ran the Wolves' full backs ragged. In the end, it was all for nothing as we lost 2-0, but anything seemed possible whenever James got the ball in that last thirty minutes. Truly dazzling.

10. Beating Liverpool 1-0 in the second leg of the League Cup Semi-Final in 1983. We lost 3-1 on aggregate, but the atmosphere on the terraces and the Clarets' spirit on the pitch was something quite exceptional.

So next time you're on the Turf and the entertainment is less than riveting, if you happen to glance round and see someone who looks as though they're not altogether engrossed with what is happening on the pitch, it may well be me, lost in claret-tinged memories of a wonderful Cup victory, or a last minute winner.

Around 1,000 Norwich supporters hold a post-match protest against the club's chairman Robert Chase. There are a number of arrests.

Relegation-threatened Aston Villa go down 1-0 at Leeds

United. They have now scored just once in their past eight matches, and that was an own goal.

The race for the Premiership intensifies, as Blackburn Rovers fail to extend their lead over Manchester United, when they go down 2-0 at West Ham. Although the gap between the two is still eight points, United now have two games in hand.

Tottenham's Jurgen Klinsmann is named as the Football Writers' Footballer of the Year.

Derby manager Roy McFarland is told his contract will not be renewed at the end of the season.

Middlesbrough play their last ever game at Ayresome Park. They leave on a high note, with a 2-1 victory over Luton Town.

Manchester United keep the pressure on Blackburn Rovers, with a 3-2 victory over Coventry City. The gap is now reduced to five points and United still have one game in hand.

Steve Thompson is confirmed as manager of Southend United, whilst a similar honour is bestowed upon Tommy Taylor at Cambridge United.
Rangers look favourites to sign Paul Gascoigne, who will be leaving Lazio at the end of the season.

Norwich go down 2-1 at Leeds and are relegated to Division One, along with Ipswich Town and Leicester City.

Sunday 07/05/95
Burnden Park

BOLTON WANDERERS 1-1 BURNLEY
(Paatelainen 90) (Philliskirk 60)

League position before and after match: 22nd . . . 22nd

Attendance: 16,853

BURNLEY: Beresford, Parkinson, Winstanley, Davis, Vinnicombe, Randall, Mullin, Nogan, Philliskirk, Thompson, Eyres.
Subs (not used): Joyce, Shaw, Russell.

BOLTON WANDERERS: Davison, Green, Phillips, McAteer, Bergsson, Stubbs, Lee, Patterson, Paatelainen, McGinlay, Thompson.
Subs (not used): Coyle, Dreyer, Shilton.

Referee: W. Burns

Yellow Cards: Davis, Vinnicombe, Eyres (Burnley)

Red Cards: None

And so Burnley's nine month tenure in Division One ended as it had begun.
   Deep into time added on for stoppages, with the Clarets hanging on to a 1-0 lead, Jason McAteer swung a cross into the Burnley area. As Mixu Paatelainen headed goalwards, Marlon acrobatically soared through the air and touched the Finn's effort onto the post. But it was to no avail. The ball dropped behind the goal line, the points were surrendered and the opposition had got a draw – just like Bristol City and Stoke City, way back in August. The grand irony of it all was capped by the inclusion of John Dreyer in the Bolton side that afternoon. Nine months previously at Turf Moor, it had been he who had grabbed Stoke's injury time equaliser.
   With the benefit of hindsight, there was an element of dark humour to it, but as the Bolton number nine wheeled away, his arms raised in celebration, I felt like someone had kicked me in the guts . . . very hard.
   Prior to Paatelainen's party-pooping antics, things had been quite different. With Bolton having secured a place in the play-offs and ourselves doomed to Division Two, you might have

250

thought there was little to play for. Not so; this was, after all, a local derby; and in a game which was blessed with opportunities at both ends, Burnley in particular rose to the occasion, never really looking in danger of being outclassed by the wannabe Premiership outfit.

Two-thirds of the contest had elapsed, when the thousand-plus Clarets who had made the forty minute trip to Burnden Park were transported into the realms of ecstasy, as Phyllis glanced home a Lovely Legs' free-kick. The fact that both Parkinson and Philliskirk had played for Bolton earlier in their careers only served to add a delicious touch of piquancy to the goal.

Having been subjected to an hour's worth of, 'You're shit and you're going down!' from the Trotters' faithful, (a chant which had been sung at us by just about every set of supporters we'd encountered since our visit to Watford), the goal was doubly welcome and was hailed with a communal reading of 'We're shit and we're beating you!' I concede that our riposte may have been far from original, but its ability to silence the Bolton fans could not be overstated.

The goal and the half-hour of stoic resistance which followed it was important for another reason. It marked the beginning of a healing process between the supporters and the team. A lot of damage had been done to the relationship that season, particularly since the turn of the year. The run of eight consecutive league defeats, Jimmy Mullen's seeming inability to cope with management at a higher level, and what many fans perceived as a reluctance on the part of certain members of the squad to give 100% each game, had time and again tried the patience and loyalty of thousands of Clarets.

But as Burnley dug in for those final thirty minutes and defended wholeheartedly against a determined Bolton attack, the reconciliation got under way. 'WE LOVE YOU BURNLEY, WE DO!' came the chants, as Winstanley put in a fantastic last-ditch tackle to deny Alan Thompson, and Marlon performed considerable gymnastics, tipping Mark Patterson's scorching volley round the post. 'FOREVER AND EVER, WE'LL FOLLOW OUR TEAM, THE BURNLEY FC, WHO RULE SUPREME!' These were more than mere chants, they were songs of love and devotion, paeans to our heroes in claret and blue. 'TAKE MY HAND, TAKE MY WHOLE LIFE THROUGH,

FOR I CAN'T HELP FALLING IN LOVE WITH YOU!' roared the Embankment End – and we meant every word of it.

Hell, there was even humour in the Burnley enclosure that afternoon. Whilst we pledged our undying allegiance to the Clarets, as the final moments of the season ebbed away, some of the Bolton fans reminded us that we were on the verge of returning to Division Two. The response was superb: 'DOWN IN FIVE MINUTES! WE'RE GOING DOWN IN FIVE MINUTES!' Then 'four minutes', then 'three', then 'two', then 'one' . . . then Paatelainen scored. But not even that could destroy the spirit of defiance in the Embankment End. We just sang louder.

At a quarter to five, Mr Burns put the whistle to his lips for the last time that afternoon and officially ended our season. And what a season it had been. As the players came over to acknowledge the fantastic support the fans had given during the past few months, I remember thinking that even though we'd been relegated, even though we had the leakiest defence in the division, even though we had the worst disciplinary record in the history of the Football League, it hadn't all been doom and gloom. There had been plenty of good times.

There was that first wonderful victory away at Luton, followed by an exhilarating night in east London four days later, as we overcame Millwall 3-2. You couldn't help but be proud of a couple of resilient performances we'd put in against Liverpool, away in the Coca-Cola Cup, and at home in the FA Cup. What about the superb 4-2 victory over Sheffield United, the nail-biting 4-3 win over Port Vale and the 5-1 obliteration of Southend? You wanted great goals? Think of magnificent strikes from Lovely Legs at Grimsby, Inchy at Chester, and The Fat Shearer at home to Liverpool in the Coca-Cola Cup.

The 94/95 campaign had also provided its share of other memories, not always directly connected with the on-the-field action. Luton's football-ground-cum-front-room and their devotion to the memory of Morecambe and Wise, the celebrity spottings of Neil Kinnock at Charlton and Paul Mariner at Barnsley, John Gayle's supercool goal celebrations, the visits to Anfield and Molineux, the superbly observed minute's silence at both Luton and Sunderland, the weekend in Southend, our attempts to play water polo against Port Vale, Oldham's mad programme seller and pretentious boutique, the zoo-full of bizarre cloth creatures, from Watford's hornet to our very own Bertie Bee, Portsmouth's saucy sailor, Nogan's tantrum at Bristol, our conversion to the Latterday Church Of The Banana en route to Watford, and of course one hazy, crazy, never-to-be-forgotten night in Swindon, featuring an unlikely cast of a soothsayer, a Lord Lucan lookalike, a seven foot fluffy robin and a troupe of majorettes. All in all, the season had been one to remember.

Without the comfort of a World Cup or a European Championship to look forward to, a long, barren, football-free summer lay ahead. Over the course of those three months, the pain of our relegation would, little by little, recede and be replaced with a new optimism; optimism that Burnley would bounce straight back to the First Division, at the first attempt.

If you looked closely enough, there were already signs of some semblance of a new beginning. Details about season tickets for 95/96 were announced, one particular firm of bookies made us 10-1 favourites to win the next Division Two Championship, and a few days before the Bolton game, photographs of an attractive new strip for the following season appeared in the local press. (Unfortunately there was no attractive new footballer modelling it – just a gap-toothed Fat Shearer, now with a suedehead, grinning inanely up at me from the page.)

Also made public was Jimmy's list of players he would be letting go over the summer. Regrettably, the list included (presumably because of financial, rather than footballing reasons) three members of the Youth Team, who just a few days previously had done the club proud by beating Manchester City in the Final of the Lancashire FA Youth Cup. Perhaps more regrettable was the retention of Mooncat, which seemed to confirm that the phrase, 'Bloody hell, Harper!' would once again reverberate around numerous stands and terraces up and down the country in the course of the 95/96 season.

For 268 days, Burnley had played at the highest level of the Football League. It had been the best of times. It had been the worst of times. It ultimately culminated in our return to the footballing hinterland known as Division Two. But if the squad of players who ended the season at the club were still on Burnley's books at the start of the 95/96 campaign, there was no doubt in my mind that the Clarets would be able to launch as strong a push for promotion as any team in the division.

With a lot of hard work, a bit of good luck and the support of the club's incredible fans, whose sheer numbers would make them the best-supported team both home and away in Division Two, Burnley *would* be back.

Arsenal lose 2-1 to Real Zaragoza in the European Cup-Winners' Cup Final. The winner is a spectacular, fifty yard lob, from ex-Spurs player Nayim, whose extra-time goal is the last kick of the game.

After a memorable season in the Premiership with Tottenham, Jurgen Klinsmann activates a get-out clause in his contract, and heads for Bayern Munich.

Wins for Manchester United over Sheffield Wednesday and Southampton make for a thrilling, final day of the season climax to the Premiership. Unfortunately for United, it is all for nothing. Although Blackburn go down 2-1 at Liverpool, the Reds can only manage a draw at West Ham, which means that Blackburn Rovers are Champions, for the first time in 81 years.

Crystal Palace and Alan Smith part company, as the Eagles fill the one remaining relegation slot in the Premiership.

There is also a parting of the ways at Manchester City and Sheffield Wednesday, where managers Brian Horton and Trevor Francis both find themselves out of a job.

Manchester United's season finally collapses around their ears, as a Paul Rideout goal gives Everton victory in the FA Cup Final.

THE UPS AND DOWNS
OF THE 1994/95 SEASON:

PREMIERSHIP:

F. A. Carling Premiership

	P	W	D	L	F	A	Pts
Blackburn	42	27	8	7	80	39	**89**
Man Utd	42	26	10	6	77	28	**88**
Nottm Forest	42	22	11	9	72	43	**77**
Liverpool	42	21	11	10	65	37	**74**
Leeds	42	20	13	9	59	38	**73**
Newcastle	42	20	12	10	67	47	**72**
Tottenham	42	16	14	12	66	58	**62**
QPR	42	17	9	16	61	59	**60**
Wimbledon	42	15	11	16	48	65	**56**
Southampton	42	12	18	12	61	63	**54**
Chelsea	42	13	15	14	50	55	**54**
Arsenal	42	13	12	17	52	49	**51**
Sheff Wed	42	13	12	17	49	57	**51**
West Ham	42	13	11	18	44	48	**50**
Everton	42	11	17	14	44	51	**50**
Coventry	42	12	14	16	44	62	**50**
Man City	42	12	13	17	53	64	**49**
Aston Villa	42	11	15	16	51	56	**48**
Crystal Palace	42	11	12	19	34	49	**45**
Norwich	42	10	13	19	37	54	**43**
Leicester	42	6	11	25	45	80	**29**
Ipswich	42	7	6	29	36	93	**27**

Champions: Blackburn Rovers.
Relegated: Crystal Palace, Norwich City, Leicester City, Ipswich
Town.

DIVISION ONE:

Endsleigh League Division One

	P	W	D	L	F	A	W	D	L	F	A	Pts
			Home				Away					
Middlesbro 46	46	15	4	4	41	19	8	9	6	26	21	82
Reading 46	46	12	7	4	34	21	11	3	9	24	23	79
Bolton 46	46	16	6	1	43	13	5	8	10	24	32	77
Wolves 46	46	15	5	3	39	18	6	8	9	38	43	76
Tranmere.......46	46	17	4	2	51	23	5	6	12	16	35	76
Barnsley 46	46	15	6	2	42	19	5	6	12	21	33	72
Watford 46	46	14	6	3	33	17	5	7	11	19	29	70
Sheff Utd.......46	46	12	9	2	41	21	5	8	10	33	34	68
Derby Co.......46	46	12	6	5	44	23	6	6	11	22	28	66
Grimsby 46	46	12	7	4	36	19	5	7	11	26	37	65
Stoke 46	46	10	7	6	31	21	6	8	9	19	32	63
Millwall 46	46	11	8	4	36	22	5	6	12	24	38	62
Southend 46	46	13	2	8	33	25	5	6	12	21	48	62
Oldham 46	46	12	7	4	34	21	4	6	13	26	39	61
Charlton 46	46	11	6	6	33	25	5	5	13	25	41	59
Luton 46	46	8	6	9	35	30	7	7	9	26	34	58
Port Vale 46	46	11	5	7	30	24	4	8	11	28	40	58
Portsmth 46	46	9	8	6	31	28	6	5	12	22	35	58
W.B.A. 46	46	13	3	7	33	24	3	7	13	18	33	58
Sunderland 46	46	5	12	6	22	22	7	6	10	19	23	54
Swindon 46	46	9	6	8	28	27	3	6	14	26	46	48
Burnley 46	46	8	7	8	36	33	3	6	14	13	41	46
Bristol City 46	46	8	8	7	26	28	3	4	16	16	35	45
Notts Co 46	46	7	8	8	26	28	2	5	16	19	38	40

Champions: Middlesbrough.
Promoted through the play-offs: Bolton Wanderers.
Relegated: Swindon Town, Burnley, Bristol City, Notts County.

256

DIVISION TWO:

			Home				Away				
Endsleigh League Division Two											
	P	W	D	L	F	A	W	D	L	F	A Pts
Birminghm 46	15	6	2	53	18	10	8	5	31	19	**89**
Brentford 46	14	4	5	44	15	11	6	6	37	24	**85**
Crewe 46	14	3	6	46	33	11	5	7	34	35	**83**
Bristol R 46	15	7	1	48	20	7	9	7	22	20	**82**
Huddersfld 46	14	5	4	45	21	8	10	5	34	28	**81**
Wycombe 46	13	7	3	36	19	8	8	7	24	27	**78**
Oxford 46	13	6	4	30	18	8	6	9	36	34	**75**
Hull 46	13	6	4	40	18	8	5	10	30	39	**74**
York 46	13	4	6	37	21	8	5	10	30	30	**72**
Swansea 46	10	8	5	23	13	9	6	8	34	32	**71**
Stockport 46	12	3	8	40	29	7	5	11	23	31	**65**
Blackpool 46	11	4	8	40	36	7	6	10	24	34	**64**
Wrexham 46	10	7	6	38	27	6	8	9	27	37	**63**
Bradford 46	8	6	9	29	32	8	6	9	28	32	**60**
Peterboro 46	7	11	5	26	29	7	7	9	28	40	**60**
Brighton 46	9	10	4	25	15	5	7	11	29	38	**59**
Rotherham 46	12	6	5	36	26	2	8	13	21	35	**56**
Shrewsbry 46	9	9	5	34	27	4	5	14	20	35	**53**
Bournemth 46	9	4	10	30	34	4	7	12	19	35	**50**
Cambridge 46	8	9	6	33	28	3	6	14	19	41	**48**
Plymouth 46	7	6	10	22	36	5	4	14	23	47	**46**
Cardiff 46	5	6	12	25	31	4	5	14	21	43	**38**
Chester 46	5	6	12	23	42	1	5	17	14	42	**29**
Leyton O 46	6	6	11	21	29	0	2	21	9	46	**26**

Champions: Birmingham City.
Promoted through the play-offs: Huddersfield Town.
Relegated: Cambridge United, Plymouth Argyle, Cardiff City,
Chester City, Leyton Orient.

257

DIVISION THREE:

	P	W	D	L	F	A	W	D	L	F	A	Pts
			Home					Away				
Carlisle	42	14	5	2	34	14	13	5	3	33	17	**91**
Wallsall	42	15	3	3	42	18	9	8	4	33	22	**83**
Chesterfld	42	11	7	3	26	10	12	5	4	36	27	**81**
Bury	42	13	7	1	39	13	10	4	7	34	23	**80**
Preston	42	13	3	5	37	17	6	7	8	21	24	**67**
Mansfield	42	10	5	6	45	27	8	6	7	39	32	**65**
Scunthorpe	42	12	2	7	40	30	6	6	9	28	33	**62**
Fulham	42	11	5	5	39	22	5	9	7	21	32	**62**
Doncaster	42	9	5	7	28	20	8	5	8	30	23	**61**
Colchester	42	8	5	8	29	30	8	5	8	27	34	**58**
Barnet	42	8	7	6	37	27	7	4	10	19	36	**56**
Lincoln	42	10	7	4	34	22	5	4	12	20	33	**56**
Torquay	42	10	8	3	35	25	4	5	12	19	32	**55**
Wigan	42	7	6	8	28	30	7	4	10	25	30	**52**
Rochdale	42	8	6	7	25	23	4	8	9	19	44	**50**
Hereford	42	9	6	6	22	19	3	7	11	23	43	**49**
Northmpton	42	8	5	8	25	29	2	9	10	20	38	**44**
Hartlepool	42	9	5	7	33	32	2	5	14	10	37	**43**
Gillingham	42	8	7	6	31	25	2	4	15	15	39	**41**
Darlington	42	7	5	9	25	24	4	3	14	18	33	**41**
Scarboro	42	4	7	10	26	31	4	3	14	23	39	**34**
Exeter ...:.....	42	5	5	11	25	36	3	5	13	11	34	**34**

Champions: Carlisle United.
Promoted in second place: Walsall.
Promoted through the play-offs: Chesterfield.
Bottom of Division Three: Exeter City.

REFERENCES

1. *Lancashire Evening Telegraph*, 22/08/94.
2. *Reds*, (Liverpool Football Club's official programme), P.3, 21/09/94.
3. *Albion News* (West Bromwich Albion Football Club's official programme), Vol. 86 No. 3, P.15, 24/09/94.
4. Horton, Ed. *False Profit*, taken from *When Saturday Comes*, No.93, November 1994, P.26.
5. Macari, Lou. *The Granada Match Live*, Granada Television, 20/10/94.
6. Beglin, Jim. *The Granada Match Live*, Granada Television, 20/10/94.
7. Palmer, Rob. *The Granada Match Live*, Granada Television, 20/10/94.
8. Mullen, Jimmy. *The Granada Match Live*, Granada Television, 20/10/94.
9. Palmer, Rob. *The Granada Match Live*, Granada Television, 20/10/94.
10. Macari, Lou. *The Granada Match Live*, Granada Television, 20/10/94.
11. Hornby, Nick. *Fever Pitch*, P.200, Pub. Gollancz Paperback, 1993.
12. *The Concise Oxford Dictionary of Current English*. Front cover. Pub. Oxford University Press, 1992.
13. *Burnley Express*, 04/01/95.
14. *Lancashire Evening Telegraph*, 23/01/95.
15. *Burnley Express*, 24/01/95.
16. *Clarets News*, (Burnley Football Club's official programme), p.4 and 5, 04/02/95.
17. *Clarets News*, (Burnley Football Club's official programme), p.1 – 47, 04/02/95.

18. *Burnley Express*, 14/02/95.
19. *Burnley Express*, 14/02/95.
20. *Burnley Express*, 14/02/95.
21. *Sunday Express*, 19/02/95.
22. *Lancashire Evening Telegraph*, 17/02/95.
23. *Lancashire Evening Telegraph*, 29/05/95.
24. *Claret News*, (Burnley Football Club's official programme), P.4 and 5, 18/02/95.
25. *Lancashire Evening Telegraph*, 22/03/95.
26. *Lancashire Evening Telegraph*, 03/04/95.
27. *Burnley Express*, 04/04/95.
28. *Lancashire Evening Telegraph*, 03/04/95.